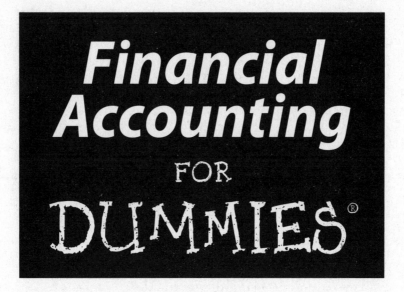

Financial Accounting
FOR DUMMIES®

by Maire Loughran, CPA

WILEY

John Wiley & Sons, Inc.

Financial Accounting For Dummies®

Published by
John Wiley & Sons, Inc.
111 River St.
Hoboken, NJ 07030-5774
www.wiley.com

WILEY

About the Author

Maire Loughran is a certified public accountant and a member of the American Institute of Certified Public Accountants. Her professional experience includes four years of internal auditing for a publicly traded company in the aerospace industry, two years as an auditor in the not-for-profit sector, and even some experience as a U.S. federal agent! Her public accounting experience includes financial reporting and analysis, audits of private corporations, accounting for e-commerce, and forensic accounting.

Maire is a full adjunct professor who teaches graduate and undergraduate auditing, accounting, and taxation classes. Interested in many different business-related fields, she has written *Auditing For Dummies* (a Wiley publication), a training manual for a Microsoft product, and a guide to starting a home-based business, as well as the Arts and Crafts Business Guide for About.com, a part of The New York Times Company.

Dedication

To my much-loved son Joey, who serves his country aboard the USS *Harry S. Truman*: I am prouder of you than mere words can ever describe. And to my late husband Jeff, so long gone from our lives but never absent from our hearts.

Author's Acknowledgments

To the Ursuline nuns and Jesuit priests who provided me with a stellar education, and to my parents, who selflessly footed the bill.

To my agent, Barb Doyen, for all her hard work and support.

And to the wonderful Joan Friedman, for all her fantastic advice, months of editing, and follow-through.

Publisher's Acknowledgments

We're proud of this book; please send us your comments at http://dummies.custhelp.com. For other comments, please contact our Customer Care Department within the U.S. at 877-762-2974, outside the U.S. at 317-572-3993, or fax 317-572-4002.

Some of the people who helped bring this book to market include the following:

Acquisitions, Editorial, and Media Development

Project Editor: Joan Friedman

Acquisitions Editor: Tracy Boggier

Assistant Editor: David Lutton

Technical Reviewers: Linda K. MacFarlane, CPA; Karen Schuele, PhD, CPA

Senior Editorial Manager: Jennifer Ehrlich

Editorial Supervisor: Carmen Krikorian

Editorial Assistant: Rachelle S. Amick

Cover Photos: © iStockphoto.com / ArtmannWitte

Cartoons: Rich Tennant (www.the5thwave.com)

Composition Services

Project Coordinator: Sheree Montgomery

Layout and Graphics: Melanee Habig, Corrie Socolovitch

Proofreaders: Laura L. Bowman, John Greenough

Indexer: Broccoli Information Management

Publishing and Editorial for Consumer Dummies

    Kathleen Nebenhaus, Vice President and Executive Publisher

    David Palmer, Associate Publisher

    Kristin Ferguson-Wagstaffe, Product Development Director

Publishing for Technology Dummies

    Andy Cummings, Vice President and Publisher

Composition Services

    Debbie Stailey, Director of Composition Services

Contents at a Glance

Table of Contents

Part II: Reviewing Some Accounting Basics................... 63

Chapter 5: Booking It: The Process behind Financial Accounting 65

Chapter 6: Focusing on Accounting Methods and Concepts 87

Part IV: Investigating Income and Cash Flow 141

Chapter 10: Searching for Profit or Loss on the Income Statement 143

Chapter 11: Following the Money by Studying Cash Flow 163

Introduction

Accounting is known as the language of business because it communicates financial and economic facts about a business to all sorts of interested parties — both *internal* (employees of the company) and *external* (people not employed by the company in question). External users include investors, creditors, banks, and regulatory agencies such as the Internal Revenue Service and the U.S. Securities and Exchange Commission.

Zeroing in on the external users of accounting information, this book is about financial accounting. *Financial* accounting serves the needs of external users by providing them with understandable, materially correct financial statements. There are three financial statements: the income statement, balance sheet, and statement of cash flows. This book is a step-by-step guide on how to prepare all three.

You also find out the purposes of the financial statements:

- ✔ To report on the financial position of the company — what types of assets the company owns and what types of liabilities it owes.
- ✔ To show how well the company performs over a period of time, which is referred to as an *accounting period.* You measure performance by seeing whether the company made or lost money during the accounting period.

A lot of first-time accounting students tell me that they are afraid they won't do well in their financial accounting class because they haven't done well in math classes they've taken in the past. Forgot about the math — that's why you have a computer and a calculator! Financial accounting is less about adding and subtracting than using logic-based skills. Added to the mix is the importance of gaining a working understanding of the standards set in place by authoritative accounting bodies.

After years spent in the classroom as both a professor and student, I realize that many accounting textbooks are, well, boring. My purpose in writing this book is to breathe some life into the subject of financial accounting and make it more understandable.

About This Book

This book, like all *For Dummies* books, is written so that each chapter stands on its own. I always assume that whatever chapter you're reading is the first one you've tackled in the book. Therefore, you can understand the concepts I explain in each chapter regardless of whether it's your first chapter or your last.

However, certain terms and concepts pertain to more than one subject in this book. To avoid writing the same explanations over and over, whenever I reference a financial accounting term, method, or other type of fact that I fully explain in another chapter, I give you a brief overview and direct you to the spot where you can get more information. For example, I may suggest that you "see Chapter 13" (which, by the way, discusses the statement of cash flows).

Also, in this book I break financial accounting down to its lowest common denominator. I avoid using jargon that only accounting majors with several accounting classes already under their belts will understand. Please keep in mind that the list of financial accounting topics and methods I present in this book isn't all-inclusive. I simply can't cover every possible nuance and twist related to preparing financial accounting data and statements. This book is meant to illuminate the rather dry presentation of topics given in all the financial accounting textbooks from which I've taught, providing a perfect companion to the financial accounting textbook your professor is using.

Furthermore, I briefly discuss the Sarbanes-Oxley Act of 2002 (SOX) and the watchdog over the audits of publicly traded companies, the Public Company Accounting Oversight Board (PCAOB). If you have the time, I recommend reading *Sarbanes-Oxley For Dummies* by Jill Gilbert Welytok, JD, CPA (published by Wiley). This handbook walks you through the new and revised SOX laws.

Conventions Used in This Book

Following are some conventions I use that you'll want to bear in mind while reading this book:

- ✔ I introduce new terms in *italic* with an explanation immediately following. For example, *liquidity* refers to a company's ability or lack thereof to meet current financial obligations. To put it even more simply, does the company have enough cash to pay its bills?

- ✔ Many accounting terms have acronyms (which you'll soon be bandying about with your fellow students after you gain some familiarity or experience with the topic). The first time I introduce an acronym in a chapter, I spell it out and place the acronym in parentheses. For example, I may discuss the American Institute of Certified Public Accountants (AICPA).

- ✔ I use **bold** text to highlight key words in bulleted lists.

✔ All Web addresses are in monofont typeface so that they're set apart from the rest of the text. When this book was printed, some Web addresses may have needed to break across two lines of text. If that happened, rest assured that I haven't put in any extra characters (such as hyphens) to indicate the break. So when using one of these Web addresses, just type in exactly what you see in this book, pretending as though the line break doesn't exist.

What You're Not to Read

I would love it if you read every word of this book, but I realize that people lead busy lives and sometimes just want to get the specific information they need. So if you're under a time crunch, you can safely skip the following without jeopardizing your understanding of the subject at large:

✔ **Material marked with a Technical Stuff icon:** These paragraphs contain extra financial accounting information that, while useful, isn't critical to your understanding of the topic at hand.

✔ **Sidebars:** These gray-shaded boxes contain asides that I think you'll find interesting but that, again, aren't vital to understanding the material your professor discusses in class.

Foolish Assumptions

I assume you don't have more than a rudimentary knowledge of accounting, and I'm guessing you're one of the following people:

✔ A college financial accounting student who just isn't getting it by reading (and rereading) the assigned textbook. (I've seen that deer-in-the-headlights look many times in my classroom.)

✔ A non-accounting student currently enrolled in either business or liberal arts who's considering changing his major to accounting.

✔ A business owner (particularly someone operating a small business with gross receipts of under $1 million) who wants to attempt preparing her own financial statements or just wants to have a better understanding about the financial statements prepared by the in-house or external accountant.

✔ A brand-new accountant working in financial accounting who needs a plain-talk refresher of accounting concepts.

How This Book Is Organized

To help you find the financial accounting facts you need, this book is organized into parts that break down the subject of financial accounting into easily digestible portions that relate to one another.

Part I: Getting a Financial Accounting Initiation

This part introduces you to the world of financial accounting. You receive an initiation into the purpose, constraints, and responsibilities of financial accountants; various financial accounting career options; and the business classes you need to pursue these careers. I also provide an overview of the three financial statements. For the business owner, it provides information about the education, training, certification, and experience of the stranger who comes into your business asking about private accounting facts.

Part II: Reviewing Some Accounting Basics

In this part, I lay the foundation of your financial accounting class. You learn how to enter accounting transactions into a company's books through the use of journal entries. You also find out about the general ledger, which is the place where accountants record the impact of transactions taking place in a business during a particular accounting cycle. Finally, you find out about the two different methods of accounting, cash and accrual — though I concentrate on accrual because this is the method financial accountants use.

Part III: Spending Quality Time with the Balance Sheet

This section contains three chapters, each explaining a different section of the balance sheet. The three sections of the balance sheet are assets, liabilities, and equity, and together they show the financial position of a company. *Assets* are resources a company owns, *liabilities* show claims payable by the company or debts against those assets, and *equity* is the difference between assets and liabilities, which equals the total of each owner's investment in the business.

Part IV: Investigating Income and Cash Flow

This part looks at the income statement and the statement of cash flows. The *income statement* shows a company's revenue and expenses, the ultimate disposition of which shows whether a company made or lost money during the accounting period. The *statement of cash flows* shows the cash received by a company and the cash paid by a company during the accounting period. It tells users of the financial statements how well the company is managing its sources and uses of cash.

Part V: Analyzing the Financial Statements

After all your hard work preparing the financial statements, in this section you learn about key measurements that users of the financial statements perform to gauge the effectiveness and efficiency of the business. I provide the complete picture on *corporate annual reports,* which educate the shareholders about corporate operations for the past year. And you get an overview of corporate governance and explanations about the explanatory notes and other information found in most corporate annual reports.

Part VI: Feeling Brave? Tackling More Advanced Financial Accounting Topics

Here, I delve into other financial accounting topics, like accounting for income taxes and leases, which may receive only cursory mention in your financial accounting class. Learning about these topics makes your financial accounting experience well-rounded, preparing you in case you decide to continue on in your accounting experience by taking an advanced accounting or auditing class.

Part VII: The Part of Tens

I wrap up the book by explaining ten financial statement deceptions to look out for when preparing financial statements. These include ways to inflate income by understating expenses and hiding unfavorable information from the users through the use of accountant geek-speak. I also provide some helpful information about industries that may deviate from generally accepted accounting principles (GAAP) while doing their bookwork and preparing their financial statements.

Icons Used in This Book

Throughout the book, you see the following icons in the left margin:

Text accompanied by this icon contains useful hints that you can apply during your class (or on the job) to make your studies (or work) a bit easier and more successful.

When you see this icon, warm up your brain cells, because it sits next to information you want to commit to memory.

Looking for what not to do in the world of financial accounting? Check out paragraphs next to this icon because they alert you to what can trip you up while taking your class or working in the field.

This icon includes information that enhances the topic under discussion but isn't necessary to understand the topic.

Where to Go from Here

Each chapter stands on its own, so no matter where you start, you won't feel like you're coming in on a movie halfway through. Your motivation for purchasing this book will likely dictate which chapters you want to read first and which you'll read only if you have some spare time in the future.

If you're a financial accounting student, flip to the chapter explaining a topic you're a little fuzzy on after reading your textbook. Business owners can get a good overview of the financial accounting process by starting with Chapters 1 and 3; these two chapters explain the nuts and bolts of financial accounting and its concepts. Otherwise, check out the table of contents or index for a topic that interests you, or jump in anywhere in the book that covers the financial accounting information you're wondering about.

Part I
Getting a Financial Accounting Initiation

The 5th Wave — By Rich Tennant

"This ledger certainly paints a picture of the company. Edvard Munch's 'The Scream' comes to mind."

In this part . . .

1 begin this part of the book by explaining why financial accounting is so important to many different individuals and businesses. You find out about the external users of financial accounting information (investors and creditors) and the internal users (employees of the business). I also briefly introduce four all-important characteristics of financial accounting: relevance, reliability, comparability, and consistency.

In Chapter 2, you discover the many careers paths open to financial accountants. I also explain the relative merits of a financial accountant seeking licensure as a certified public accountant (CPA) or earning a master's degree in business. You find out about the job outlook for financial accountants over the next decade. (Here's a hint: It's great!) Plus, I provide some U.S. Bureau of Labor Statistics information on starting and median salaries for financial accountants.

Rounding out this part, Chapter 3 provides a brief overview of the three financial statements: the balance sheet, income statement, and statement of cash flows. And Chapter 4 introduces the various financial accounting standard-setting and regulatory organizations, such as the Financial Accounting Standards Board (FASB) and the U.S. Securities and Exchange Commission (SEC).

Chapter 1

Seeing the Big Picture of Financial Accounting

In This Chapter

▶ Figuring out why financial accounting matters

▶ Meeting the financial accounting stakeholders

▶ Introducing key financial accounting characteristics

▶ Accepting ethical responsibilities

I assume that you have a very good reason for purchasing this book; most people don't buy a title like *Financial Accounting For Dummies* on a whim in the bookstore. Most likely, you're taking your first financial accounting class and want to be sure you pass it, but perhaps you're a business owner wanting to get a better handle on financial statement preparation. Whatever your motivation, this chapter is your jumping board into the pool of financial accounting.

I explain what financial accounting is and why it's so important to many different individuals and businesses. I spell out the various users of financial accounting data and explain why they need that data. Finally, I briefly introduce four all-important characteristics of financial accounting: relevance, reliability, comparability, and consistency. Whether you're a financial accounting student or a business owner, you need to understand these crucial financial accounting terms from the very beginning.

Knowing the Purposes of Financial Accounting

Broadly speaking, *accounting* is the process of organizing facts and figures and relaying the result of that organization to any interested customers of the information. This process doesn't just relate to numbers spit out by a computer software program; it pertains to any type of reconciliation.

Here's an example from my own life of accounting that doesn't involve numbers or money: A teenager slinks in after curfew, and his parent asks for a complete accounting of why he is late. When the teenager tells the facts, you have information (his car broke down in an area with no cell coverage), the individual producing the information (our mischievous teen), and the interested customer, also known as the user of the information (the worried parent).

The subject of this book, financial accounting, is a subset of accounting. *Financial accounting* involves the process of preparing financial statements for a business. (Not sure what financial statements are? No worries — you find an overview of them in the next section.) Here are the key pieces of the financial accounting process:

- ✔ **Information:** Any accounting transactions taking place within the business during the accounting period. This includes generating revenue from the sales of company goods or services, paying business-related expenses, buying company assets, and incurring debt to run the company.
- ✔ **Business entity:** The company incurring the accounting transactions.
- ✔ **Users:** The persons or businesses that need to see the accounting transactions organized into financial statements to make educated decisions of their own. (More about these users in the "Getting to Know Financial Accounting Users" section of this chapter.)

Preparing financial statements

If you're taking a financial accounting class, your entire course is centered on the proper preparation of financial statements: the income sheet, balance sheet, and statement of cash flows. Financial accountants can't just stick accounting transaction data on the statements wherever they feel like. Many, many rules exist that dictate how financial accountants must organize the information on the statements; these rules are called *generally accepted accounting principles* (GAAP), and I discuss them in Chapter 4. The rules pertain to both how the financial accountant shows the accounting transactions and on which financial statements the information relating to the transactions appears.

Curious about the purpose of each financial statement? (I know the mystery is eating at you!) Here's the scoop on each:

- ✔ **Income statement:** This financial statement shows the results of business operations consisting of revenue, expenses, gains, and losses. The end product is net income or net loss. I talk about the income statement again in Chapter 3, and then I cover it from soup to nuts in Chapter 10.

For now (because I know the excitement is too much for you!), here are the basic facts on the four different income statement components:

- *Revenue:* Gross receipts earned by the company selling its goods or services.

- *Expenses:* The costs to the company to earn the revenue.

- *Gains:* Income from non-operating-related transactions, such as selling a company asset.

- *Losses:* The flip side of gains, such as losing money when selling the company car.

A lot of non-accountants call the income statement a *statement of profit or loss* or simply a *P&L*. These terms are fine to use because they address the spirit of the statement.

✔ **Balance sheet:** This statement has three sections: assets, liabilities, and equity. Standing on their own, these sections contain valuable information about a company. However, a user has to see all three interacting together on the balance sheet to form an opinion approaching reliability about the company.

Part III of this book is all about the balance sheet, but for now here are the basics about each balance sheet component:

- *Assets:* Resources owned by a company, such as cash, equipment, and buildings.

- *Liabilities:* Debt the business incurs for operating and expansion purposes.

- *Equity:* The amount of ownership left in the business after deducting total liabilities from total assets.

✔ **Statement of cash flows:** This statement contains certain components of both the income statement and the balance sheet. The purpose of the statement of cash flows is to show cash sources and uses during a specific period of time — in other words, how a company brings in cash and for what costs the cash goes back out the door.

Showing historic performance

The information reflected on the financial statements allows its users to evaluate whether they want to become financially involved with the company. But the financial statement users cannot make educated decisions based solely on one set of financial statements. Here's why:

> ✔ The income statement is finite in what it reflects. For example, it may report net income for the 12-month period ending December 31, 2012. This means any accounting transactions taking place prior to or after this 12-month window do not show up on the report.
>
> ✔ The statement of cash flows is also finite in nature, showing cash ins and outs only for the reporting period.

While the balance sheet shows results from the first day the company opens to the date on the balance sheet, it doesn't provide a complete picture of the company's operations. All three financial statements are needed to paint that picture.

Savvy financial statement users know that they need to compare several years' worth of financial statements to get a true sense of business performance. Users employ tools such as ratios and measurements involving financial statement data (a topic I cover in Chapter 14) to evaluate the relative merit of one company over another by analyzing each company's historic performance.

Providing results for the annual report

After all the hoopla of preparing the financial statements, *publicly traded companies* (those whose stock and bonds are bought and sold in the open market) employ independent certified public accountants (CPAs) to audit the financial statements for their inclusion in reports to the shareholders. The main thrust of a company's annual report is not only to provide financial reporting but also to promote the company and satisfy any regulatory requirements.

The preparation of an annual report is a fairly detailed subject that your financial accounting professor will review only briefly in class. Your financial accounting textbook probably contains an annual report for an actual company, which you'll use to complete homework assignments. I provide a more expansive look at annual reports in Chapter 16.

Getting to Know Financial Accounting Users

Well, who are these inquisitive financial statement users I've been referring to so far in this chapter? If you've ever purchased stock or invested money in a retirement plan, you number among the users. In this section, I explain why certain groups of people and businesses need access to reliable financial statements.

Identifying the most likely users

Financial statement users fall into three categories:

- ✔ Existing or potential investors in the company's stocks or bonds.

- ✔ Individuals or businesses thinking about extending credit terms to the company. Examples of creditors include banks, automobile financing companies, and the vendors from which a company purchases its inventory or office supplies.

- ✔ Governmental agencies, such as the U.S. Securities and Exchange Commission (SEC), which want to make sure the company is fairly presenting its financial position. (I discuss the history and role of the SEC in Chapter 4.)

And what other governmental agency is particularly interested in whether a company employs any hocus pocus when preparing its financial statements? The Internal Revenue Service, of course, because financial statements are the starting point for reporting taxable income.

Recognizing their needs

All three categories of financial statement users share a common need: They require assurance that the information they are looking at is both materially correct and useful. *Materially correct* means the financial statements don't contain any serious or substantial misstatements. In order to be useful, the information has to be understandable to anyone not privy to the day-to-day activities of the company.

Investors and creditors, though sitting at different ends of the table, have something else in common: They are looking for a financial return in exchange for allowing the business to use their cash. Governmental agencies, on the other hand, don't have a profit motive for reviewing the financial statements; they just want to make sure the company is abiding by all tax codes, regulations, or generally accepted accounting principles.

Providing information for decision-making

The onus is on financial accountants to make sure a company's financial statements are materially correct. Important life decisions may hang in the balance based on an individual investing in one stock versus another. Don't believe me? Talk to any individual close to retirement age who lost his or her whole nest egg in the Enron debacle.

Two of the three groups of financial statement users are making decisions based on those statements: investors and creditors.

Creditors look to the financial statements to make sure a potential debtor has the cash flow and potential future earnings to pay back both principal and interest according to the terms of the loan.

Investors fall into two groups:

✔ **Those looking for growth:** These investors want the value of a stock to increase over time. Here's an example of growth at work: You do some research about a little-known company that is poised to introduce a hot new computer product into the market. You have $1,000 sitting in a checking account that bears no interest. You believe, based on your research, that if you purchase some stock in this company now, you'll be able to sell the stock for $2,000 shortly after the company releases the computer product.

✔ **Those looking for income:** These investors are satisfied with a steady stock that weathers ebbs and flows in the market. The stock neither increases nor decreases in value per share by an enormous amount, but it pays a consistent, reasonable dividend. (Keep in mind that reasonableness varies for each person and his or her investment income goals.)

Remember that there are two ways to make money: the active way (you work to earn money) and the passive way (you invest money to make more money). Passive is better, no? The wise use of investing allows individuals to make housing choices, educate their children, and provide for their retirement. And wise investment decisions can be made only when potential investors have materially correct financial statements for the businesses in which they're considering investing.

Respecting the Key Characteristics of Financial Accounting Information

Now that you understand who uses financial accounting information, I want to discuss the substantive characteristics of that information. If financial accountants don't assure that financial statement information has these characteristics, the statements aren't worth the paper on which they're printed.

The information a company provides must be relevant, reliable, comparable, and consistent. In this section, I define what each characteristic means.

Relevance

Relevance is a hallmark of good evidence; it means the information directly relates to the facts you're trying to evaluate or understand. The inclusion or absence of relevant information has a definite effect on a user's decision-making process.

Relevant information has *predictive value,* which means it helps a user look into the future. By understanding and evaluating the information, the user can form an opinion as to how future company events may play out. For example, comparing financial results from prior years, which are gleaned from the financial statements, can give investors an idea as to the future value of a company's stock. If assets and revenue are decreasing while liabilities are increasing, you have a pretty good indicator that investing in this company may not be such a hot idea.

Relevant information also has *feedback value,* which means that new relevant information either confirms or rebuts the user's prior expectations. For example, you review a company's financial statements for 2012, and your analysis indicates that the company's sales should increase two-fold in the subsequent year. When you later check out the 2013 income statement, the company's gross receipts have, indeed, doubled. Woohoo! With the relevant information in hand, you see that your prediction came true.

Timeliness goes hand in hand with relevance. The best and most accurate information in the world is of no use if it's no longer applicable because so such time has elapsed that facts and circumstances have changed. Look at it this way: If you were in the market to replace your flat-screen TV, and you found out about a killer sale at the local electronics store the day after the sale ended, this information is utterly useless to you. The same thing is true with financial information. That's why the SEC requires publicly traded companies to issue certain reports as soon as 60 days after the end of the financial period. (See Chapter 16 for more about this reporting requirement.)

Reliability

Reliability means you can depend on the information to steer you in the right direction. For example, the information must be free from material misstatements (meaning it doesn't contain any serious or substantial mistakes). It also has to be reasonably free from bias, which means the information is neutral and not slanted to produce a rosier picture of how well the company is doing.

Here's an example of how a company would create biased financial statements. Say that a company has a pending lawsuit that it knows will likely damage its reputation (and, therefore, its future performance). In the financial statements, the company does not include a note that mentions the lawsuit. The company is not being neutral in this situation; it is deliberately painting a rosier picture than actually exists. (See Chapter 15 for my explanation of the purpose of financial statement notes.)

Reliable information must be verifiable and have representational faithfulness. Here's what I mean:

- A hallmark of *verifiability* is that an independent evaluation of the same information leads to the same conclusion as presented by the company. An accounting application of this concept could be an independent third party, such as an auditor, checking that the dollar amount shown on the balance sheet as *accounts receivable* (money owed to the company by customers) is indeed correct.

- *Representational faithfulness* means that if the company says it has gross receipts of $200,000 in the first quarter of 2012, it actually has receipts of $200,000 — not any other amount.

Comparability

Comparability means the quality of the information is such that users can identify differences and similarities among companies they are evaluating — or among different financial periods for the same company. For example, users need to know what particular GAAP the different companies they are examining are using to depreciate their assets. Without this knowledge, the users cannot accurately evaluate the relative worth of one company over the other.

Independent verification of accounts receivable

Many companies sell goods or services to customers *on account,* which means the customer promises to pay in the future. When this happens, the amount of unpaid customer invoices goes into an account called *accounts receivable.* (See Chapters 7 and 10 for detailed info about accounts receivable.) For a business carrying a sizable amount of accounts receivable, an error in this account can have a material effect on the reliability of the income statement and balance sheet.

Independent confirmation of the accounts receivable balance is done by sending requests for confirmation. *Confirmations* are form letters sent to customers listed in the accounts receivable subsidiary ledger (a listing showing all customers with a balance owed). The letters seek to verify the facts and figures contained in the company's books. The confirmation form letter is usually brief, listing the total amount the company shows the customer owes at a certain date.

Some confirmation letters ask for a response; others ask the customer to respond only if the information on the confirmation form is incorrect. An independent party, such as the company's external certified public accountant (CPA), tallies the results of the confirmations and either verifies or refutes the amount the company asserts that its customers owe.

Consider a personal example: Think about the last time you purchased a laptop. To the novice computer buyer, the shiny black cases and colored displays all look pretty much the same. But the price of each model varies — sometimes substantially. Therefore, you have to ferret out the facts about each model to be able to compare models and decide on the best one for your needs. What do you do? You check out the manufacturer's specs for each laptop in your price range, comparing such important facts as the size of the hard drive, processing speed, and (if you want to be truly mobile) the laptop's size and weight. By doing so, you are able to look beyond outward appearance and make a purchasing decision based on comparative worth among your options.

As of this writing, U.S. GAAP are different from accounting principles used by businesses in other countries. Therefore, comparing financial statements of a foreign-based company and a U.S.-based company is difficult.

Consistency

Consistency means the company uses the same accounting treatment for the same type of accounting transactions — both within a certain financial period and among various financial periods. Doing so allows the user to know that the financial accountant is not doing the accounting equivalent of comparing a dog to a cat. Both are animals, both are furry, but as any pet owner knows, you have a basic lack of consistency between the two.

Seeing how depreciation affects the bottom line

Depreciation is the process of systematically reclassifying the cost of an asset from the balance sheet to the income statement over its useful life — a topic I discuss at length in Chapter 12. A few different methods of depreciation are allowed by GAAP, so unless you know which method the company is using, you can't effectively compare one company to another.

Consider an example. For the same asset, here is the amount of depreciation a company can take for the asset's first year of use depending on which commonly used depreciation method it employs:

✔ Straight-line depreciation: $54,000

✔ Double-declining balance depreciation: $120,000

The difference between the two methods is a whopping $66,000 ($120,000 – $54,000)! Now imagine depreciating equipment that costs in the millions of dollars; the effect on the company's bottom line net income of choosing one depreciation method versus another would be even more astonishing.

Luckily for the financial statement users, to aid in comparability, the depreciation method in use by a company must be disclosed in the notes to the financial statements. For much more info about depreciation, jump to Chapter 12. For the scoop on what financial statement notes are, head to Chapter 15.

Keep in mind that a company *is* allowed to switch accounting methods if it has a valid business purpose for the switch; the company isn't stuck using only one method throughout its existence. An example of a good reason for a switch in methods is if using a different accounting method presents a more accurate financial picture. But a change in methods can't be done willy-nilly whenever the business feels like it. I provide the whole scoop on changes in accounting treatment in Chapter 20. Also, the company has to disclose this change in its footnotes to the financial statements; see Chapter 15.

Consistency is crucial when it comes to depreciation. If the company lacks consistency —for example, it uses different depreciation methods when accounting for the same asset in different years — you cannot create truly useful financial statements.

Accepting Financial Accounting Constraints

While preparing financial statements, accountants realize that time is money and there is a limit to the amount of cost that should be incurred for any reporting benefit. The agencies that set the standards for accounting practices (which I introduce in Chapter 4) always perform a cost/benefit analysis before finalizing any reporting requirements. Associated with this financial accounting constraint is the concept of materiality.

Cost/benefit lost in the woods

Years ago, the bookkeeper at one of my client companies spent five hours tracking down the reason why the company bank reconciliation was off by $2.00 to make sure the bank hadn't made a mistake. (Preparing a *bank reconciliation* means you take the balance in the bank account per the bank as of a certain date, add in any deposits that got to the bank too late to hit the statement, and subtract any checks the

company has written that have not yet cleared.) Yikes!

Now, was this an effective and efficient use of that bookkeeper's time and salary expense? No, of course not. Let's say she was paid $10 per hour. It cost the company $50 for her to confirm that the operating account bank balance was indeed off by $2, and it wasn't just an inadvertent mistake on the part of the bank.

Materiality is the importance you place on an area of financial reporting based upon its overall significance. What is material for one business may not be material for another. You have to consider the size of the company, the size of the financial statement transaction, the particular circumstances in which the transaction occurred, and any other factors that can help you judge whether the issue is truly significant to the financial statement users.

For example, an expense totaling $10,000 would be material if the total expense amount is $50,000 but would likely be immaterial if the total expense was $500,000. But the nature of the transaction may make the difference material even if the comparative size is immaterial. For example, $10,000 that is deliberately — not accidentally — excluded from income may be material even if the amount is a small percentage of overall income. That's because the deliberate exclusion may be an attempt by the owner of the company to avoid paying taxes on the income.

Conservatism is very important in financial accounting. It means that when in doubt, the financial accountant should choose the financial accounting treatment that will cause the least effect on revenue or expenses.

Considering Your Ethical Responsibilities

Every professional — and, frankly, every individual — should operate using a code of conduct. This means you should always attempt to act in an ethical manner and do the right thing, regardless of whether doing the right thing is the best choice for you personally.

In this section, I give you the nuts and bolts of the code of conduct that financial accountants must follow. Plus, you find out about the goals toward which financial accountants strive: integrity, objectivity, and independence.

Following the accountant's code of conduct

In a financial accounting class, you learn about different licensing options available to financial accountants — a topic I discuss in Chapter 2. Financial accountants who are serious about their profession normally become *certified public accountants* (CPAs), which means they have to take a certain number of accounting and auditing classes, pass a four-part exam, and comply with any other requirements of their state's licensing board.

Working as a financial accountant doesn't require any special licensing, but a lack of licensing may limit your career options. (However, in the spirit of full disclosure, my sister-in-law never passed the CPA exam but still rose to the vice-presidency level of a large multinational corporation.)

CPAs have to abide by their state's code of conduct and also follow the code of conduct established by the American Institute of Certified Public Accountants (AICPA) — the national professional organization for all CPAs. The AICPA is responsible for establishing accounting, auditing, and attestation standards for private companies in the United States, as well as for enforcing a code of professional conduct for its members. (*Attestation* involves generating reports on subjects that are the responsibility of another person or business.) In Chapter 4, I outline that code of conduct in detail.

But what if you're a financial accountant who isn't a CPA or a member of the AICPA? Do you still have to worry about abiding by a code of conduct? Of course you do! Any profession lacking ethical behavior descends into chaos. Financial accountants must have high professional standards, a strict code of professional ethics, and a commitment to serving the public interest. They achieve these goals through their integrity, objectivity, and independence.

Having integrity

In the world of financial accounting, *integrity* means you act according to a code or standard of values. You demonstrate integrity when you do the right thing, regardless of whether doing so is best for you personally.

Specifically, having integrity means that you serve, to the best of your ability, your employer and/or the client for whom you are preparing financial statements, keeping in mind that doing so may not be the same thing as completely agreeing with the way the employer or client wants you to prepare the financial statements. You can't be worried that your employer or client is going to be mad at you or fire you if you disagree with him.

Maintaining objectivity

Whether you work in public accounting (you have multiple clients) or private accounting (you provide accounting services only for your employer), you must be *objective,* meaning impartial and intellectually honest:

- ✔ Being impartial means you're neutral and unbiased in all decision-making processes. You base your opinion and reporting only on the facts, not on any preconceived notions or prejudices.

- ✔ Being intellectually honest means you interpret rules and policies in a truthful and sincere manner, staying true to both their form and spirit.

If you're objective, you keep an open mind until all facts are revealed, despite what you hear from your client's managers, employees, or anyone else privy to the work you're doing.

Financial accountants must be objective, and the users of the financial statements must perceive that the accountants are objective. You never want to compromise your objectivity or else you risk creating the perception that your work — and the financial statements that result from your work — cannot be trusted.

Achieving independence

Many types of public accounting services, such as auditing, require the financial accountant to be independent in both fact and appearance. Being *independent* while providing services means that you have no special relationship with or financial interest in the client that would cause you to disregard evidence and facts when evaluating your client.

What does it mean to be independent in both fact and appearance? The biggie is that you avoid any real or perceived conflicts of interest: You don't perform services for any client with whom you have either a personal or non-audit-related business relationship. For example, if you have a significant financial interest with a major competitor of your client, your client may question whose best interests you have in mind while performing the accounting services.

Financial accountants providing tax and consulting services do not have to be independent; however, they still have to be objective.

The concepts of independence and objectivity differ somewhat depending on whether you work in public accounting or private accounting. *Public accounting*

is when a financial accountant, most likely a CPA, works for an accounting firm providing services such as auditing or financial statement preparation for clients. *Private accounting* is when you do accounting work for your own employer rather than for a client. Obviously, you can't strive for independence when you're doing accounting work for your own employer. So in private accounting, objectivity is key.

Introducing the Conceptual Framework of Financial Accounting

Every profession needs a roadmap to help the people employed in the field provide the best possible service while doing their jobs. For example, my airline pilot clients have shown me a detailed checklist they must follow each and every time they get in the cockpit, regardless of how many years of experience they have.

For financial accountants, the Financial Accounting Standards Board (FASB) started work on providing a *conceptual framework* — a structure of financial accounting concepts — back in the 1970s. These days, this conceptual framework is organized into Statements of Financial Accounting Concepts (CONs). The CONs cover the financial accounting topics of objectives, characteristics, elements, and financial statement measurement. Not sure what each of these terms means? I discuss this topic in detail in Chapter 6. For now, just remember that this financial accounting conceptual framework exists — or jump to Chapter 6 right now to read all about it!

Chapter 2

Making Mom Proud: Financial Accounting Career Options

In This Chapter

▶ Mapping out your college courses

▶ Finding out the differences between a CPA and an MBA

▶ Considering financial accounting employment opportunities

▶ Examining the future of financial accounting

This chapter gives you the 4-1-1 on the making of a financial accountant. If you're wondering about the types of college courses you need to take in addition to your basic financial accounting course, you've come to the right place! I outline the various business and nonbusiness courses you can expect to take for an undergraduate degree in accounting and explain the additional courses needed for those pursuing a graduate business degree.

Also, I describe the many different career paths a financial accountant can follow, from being self-employed to working for a large accounting firm to working for nonbusiness entities such as charitable organizations.

In this chapter, you find out how much you can expect to earn as a financial accountant fresh out of college. You also get some perspective on the changing nature of business and the effect of that change on financial accounting.

The Making of a Financial Accountant

Personally, I believe that if you have an interest in the word of business, being a financial accountant is a pretty good gig. A plethora of career options is open to you, whether you dream of being self-employed or see yourself working for a larger business, and whether your dream job is part-time or full-time.

Before you consider your employment possibilities, I want to walk through the education and licensing requirements for financial accountants so you know what to expect if you pursue this career path.

Getting educated

Most students interested in financial accounting attend business school, receiving a bachelor's degree with a major in accounting. Usually the degree requires a minimum of 120 credit hours with 54 to 60 hours being core accounting and business courses. Keeping in mind that each college or university has different accounting degree requirements, here is an example of the courses often required for a bachelor's degree in accounting:

✔ **General education core requirements:** These are your English, math, science, social and behavioral science, and arts and humanities classes.

✔ **Business core classes:** These courses apply to all business majors, regardless of specific degree:

- *Financial Accounting:* Focuses on the preparation of financial statements — the topic of this book!

- *Managerial Accounting:* Approaches accounting from the business management angle and focuses on how accounting is used for internal reporting and decision-making.

- *Business Law:* Covers the routine legal problems encountered in the business environment, such as contracts and employment law.

- *Principles of Management:* Introduces the basic processes and concepts of business management, such as planning, leading, controlling, and organizing business processes.

- *Economics:* Introduces supply and demand and marketplace forces and how they affect business and individual decision-making.

- *Finance:* Provides an introduction to the sources of business and financial market information, including the time value of money, the nature and measurement of risk, financial institutions, investments and corporate finance, and financial statement analysis.

- *Marketing:* Introduces the planning and implementation of business activities designed to bring a buyer and seller together.

✔ **Accounting classes:** Here's a typical list and brief descriptions of the required accounting classes. Once again, keep in mind that requirements may vary from school to school:

- *Intermediate Accounting I and II:* More in-depth accounting courses than the Financial Accounting or Managerial Accounting courses.

Accounting theory is taught, along with the development of generally accepted accounting principles (GAAP, which I discuss in Chapter 4).

- *Federal Income Tax I and II:* Cover both business and individual taxation. Topics include gross income, deductions, technical tax research, and types of business entities.

- *Accounting Information Systems:* Looks at how accounting data is managed from the point of view of how a typical company's financial organization is handled.

- *Auditing:* Studies the process involved in auditing a for-profit enterprise, including the planning, internal control review, evidence gathering, and procedures to audit the financial statements. Also covered are professional standards, ethics, and liabilities of certified public accountants (CPAs).

- *Accounting Research/Other Electives:* The fun stuff! These classes include fraud, advanced financial accounting, ethical behavior in business and accounting, corporate governance (see Chapter 15), and accounting independent studies.

Depending on the school you attend, a bachelor's degree with a concentration in accounting can either be a Bachelor of Science, Bachelor of Arts, or Bachelor of Business Administration degree.

Aiming for an MBA or a CPA (or both!)

Many students come to me asking for advice regarding their next educational step after undergraduate graduation. You can get a job in financial accounting with a bachelor's degree. But to stand out from the herd of job seekers, I recommend pursuing a Master of Business Administration (MBA) degree or sitting for the certified public accountant (CPA) exam.

I tell my students that if they are 100 percent positive they will never want to work in public accounting, the MBA is the way to go. (*Public accounting* means you have multiple clients rather than doing accounting work for your own employer.) However, consider this: Depending on the school you attend, you probably have to take at least another 30 graduate business credit hours to obtain your MBA. Depending on your emphasis in the master's program, you may complete (or almost complete) the required courses to sit for the CPA exam by the time you're done. The sidebar "Piggybacking your MBA and CPA classes" in this chapter explains how you may plan your MBA coursework to get yourself prepared for the CPA exam at the same time.

Piggybacking your MBA and CPA classes

Passing the CPA exam is the Holy Grail for financial accountants, so if you plan to work in *public accounting,* which means doing accounting or auditing work for businesses that don't directly employ you, I think it's a good move to earn your MBA and become a CPA. The American Institute of Certified Public Accountants (AICPA) writes and scores the exam and advocates that CPA candidates have 150 college credit hours — 30 more than the commonly required 120 credit hours to earn a bachelor's degree. At present, 40 states include this 150-hour requirement for anyone wishing to be certified as a CPA.

To meet the 150-hour requirement, students can take specified graduate-level classes or earn a master's in accounting or an MBA. Each state's requirements may differ, so you should check on your state's specific requirements. After taking the required courses to sit for the CPA exam, most candidates are halfway through the classes required for an MBA, so they often just finish up that coursework as well.

You have to be very precise as to which courses you take to sit for the CPA exam. So if you're mapping out your MBA courses, keep the CPA exam requirements in mind. Check out the steps to become a CPA by accessing the Uniform CPA Examination Web site at `www.cpa-exam.org/get_started/steps.html`. You can find an exam tutorial and sample tests at `www.cpa-exam.org/lrc/exam_tutorial_parallel.html`.

Identifying other helpful licenses

In addition to the CPA license, you may want to earn other professional certifications that can improve your professional reputation, as well as provide opportunities for advancement:

 ✔ **Forensic Certified Public Accountant:** This CPA specializes in legal disputes or litigation. Examples of civil disputes are contract compliance, economic damages, disagreements related to mergers or acquisitions, hidden assets during bankruptcy or divorce proceedings, and business valuation. The forensic CPA can also get involved in investigating crimes, such as money laundering and murder for hire. And you thought accounting was dull!

  To earn this certification, you must first be a licensed CPA and then pass a five-part exam. However, someone who is already licensed as a

Certified Fraud Examiner (CFE) or who is Certified in Financial Forensics (CFF) is exempt from taking the Forensic CPA examination. (Keep reading to find out about the CFE and CFF designations.) Additional information can be found at shopsite.fcpas.org/index.html. And if you're curious about this accounting specialty, consider picking up *Forensic Accounting For Dummies* by Frimette Kass-Shraibman and Vijay S. Sampath (Wiley).

✔ **Certified Fraud Examiner:** A CFE is a financial accountant who works to find *fraud,* which is the intentional misstatement of facts occurring in businesses. A CFE also provides anti-fraud training and education. Being a CPA is not required to become a CFE, but you must have a bachelor's degree and pass the CFE exam. For more information, visit the Web site for the Association of Certified Fraud Examiners at www.acfe.com/about/about.asp.

✔ **Certified in Financial Forensics:** An accountant with a CFF designation researches and provides testimony regarding financial fraud, which includes intentional misstatements in a company's financial statements (its income statement, balance sheet, and statement of cash flows). You have to be an active CPA and member in good standing of the AICPA to earn this certification. For more information about this certification, go to the AICPA Web site at www.aicpa.org and do a site search for "forensic and valuation membership."

Here are just a couple more certifications, which are tailored toward *private accountants* (those who provide accounting services to their own employers):

✔ **Certified Management Accountant:** Accountants working in financial management for their employers and specializing in financial planning, performance, and decision-making may benefit from this designation. The Institute of Management Accountants sponsors this certification. For more information, visit the Web site at www.imanet.org.

✔ **Certified Internal Auditor:** These accounting professionals provide internal auditing work for their employers, both for-profit entities and governmental agencies. *Internal auditing* involves making sure the company runs efficiently and effectively. Additional information about this certification can be found at the Institute of Internal Auditors' Web site at www.theiia.org.

Do you have what it takes?

Are you wondering whether financial accounting would be a good fit for you? Good accountants tend to have the following characteristics and personality traits, which are vital to enjoying the job:

✔ **The desire to work independently:** You must be able to work independently to succeed as a financial accountant. Even auditors who work in teams divide the tasks up and work independently on different pieces of the accounting puzzle, bringing everything together at the end.

✔ **A love for research, detail, and logic:** Accountants do a tremendous amount of research and use this research to make decisions. Attention to detail is very important. There is also a lot of what I refer to as *circular logic* in accounting: "If this is true, then do that," but "If that is true, do this." Accountants need to be logical thinkers to work their way through tax code and accounting pronouncements.

✔ **Great communication skills:** As a financial accountant, you must explain your decisions and results with other employees, clients, and outside users. Communication skills, both oral and written, are very important. The people with whom you communicate will have different backgrounds, and many of them may have zero knowledge of accounting, so you need to be able to explain your work clearly.

✔ **Decent computer skills:** Reasonable computer software skills and the ability to learn software programs are also a must. The good news is that after you understand one accounting software package, you should have any easy time picking up other accounting software packages. Some employers use *proprietary* software (which is written for their own exclusive use), so specific training is required. Even if they don't use proprietary software, most employers realize that new employees need to be trained to use the company's preferred *boxed* software: the kind purchased off the shelf at a store.

✔ **The willingness to listen and learn:** The ability to *surface learn* is crucial. Here's what I mean: If you are doing the accounting for a surf shop, you do not need to be up to speed on every nuance of running the business — you don't even need to be able to swim! But to do a professional, competent job, you must know basic industry facts. (The average markup on a bikini is 500 percent, while surfboards are marked up only minimally.) Without the basic knowledge of the way a company does its business, you will not know if your facts and figures make sense.

Considering Your Employment Opportunities

As an educated financial accountant with at least a couple years experience under your belt, your career options are pretty darn expansive. Over the years, I've been everything from a bookkeeper to a forensic CPA testifying in court. I've worked full-time, part-time, out of my house, in an office, and on the road. One thing I can say about being a financial accountant is that it's never boring!

Public accounting: Working for yourself or a CPA firm

I've been self-employed for the bulk of my financial accounting career. I started by taking a part-time bookkeeping gig after the birth of my son. Then, after my husband died, I had a small child to support and needed an extremely flexible schedule. That circumstance led me to build an accounting practice of my own. I know from experience that self-employed financial accountants have many career options available to them.

But not everyone seeks the flexibility of self-employment. If you want the challenge of working for many clients (which is the nature of public accounting) but desire the stability of working for an employer, you may prefer to focus on jobs at CPA firms. These firms range in size from the Big Four (KPMG, Ernst & Young, PricewaterhouseCoopers, and Deloitte) to regional CPA firms, such as Grant Thornton and a plethora of others.

Here are a few examples of the work you can do as a public accountant:

✔ **Financial statement preparation:** Many small and mid-sized businesses require help preparing their financial statements. An accountant is contracted to do a *compilation,* which consists of using client source documents (such as bank statements, cleared checks, and invoices) to show revenue, expenses, costs, gains, and losses on the income statement, balance sheet, and statement of cash flows.

Most financial accountants who prepare financial statements also do the year-end tax returns for the same companies, which can be very lucrative. Being a CPA is not a requirement to prepare compilations. However, good people skills and patience are required. (In my experience, compilation work requires quite a bit of client handholding.)

✔ **Forensic accounting:** The word *forensic* means that this type of accounting relates to legal proceedings or testimony. The forensic accountant may be hired by a company that plans to pursue fraud charges against an employee, a lawyer in a divorce case who suspects a spouse is hiding assets, or anyone else involved in litigation. The accountant gathers facts, considers the circumstances, and applies relevant local, state, or federal law to come to an opinion about what a business or individual has done. Then, he may be asked to offer court testimony in the legal proceedings.

In my experience, the forensic accountant follows one simple rule to perform this job: follow the money. From the most complicated engagement (murder for profit) to the most simple (a spouse has a separate bank account with the bank statements going to a personal post office box), if you follow the money you eventually arrive at the truth.

In most states, you don't have to be a CPA to hang out your shingle as a forensic accountant. However, in order to establish your authority, I highly recommend pursuing that certification.

✔ **Assurance services:** You must be a licensed CPA to work in this field, which includes all types of auditing services. For example, all business owners and managers want to know how well their businesses are doing. That's where you come in. Because you're an outsider, you can take a step back and cast a fresh, independent eye on the way a company is doing business. You can give company management a firm foundation upon which to base any needed changes.

A subset of assurance is *attestation* services, meaning the CPA issues written documents expressing her conclusion about the reliability of a written assertion that is the responsibility of another party. The number of topics you may focus on during an attestation engagement is pretty much limitless. For example, you may conduct a *breakeven point analysis,* which requires figuring out how much revenue the client has to bring in to cover expenses.

Public accountants also conduct audits, which means they gather and judge evidence to issue an opinion on the effectiveness of a company's *internal controls:* policies and procedures set in place to provide guidelines on how employees should do their jobs. CPAs also conduct financial statement audits, issuing opinions on whether the financial statements under audit are materially correct.

Private accounting

Not every accountant has multiple business clients. Someone who does accounting work for a single company is called a *private* or *industry accountant.* Quite a few private/industry accounting jobs are available. Depending on the size of the business, the job can be tailored to a specific task or cover the whole extravaganza from start to finish — from recording accounting transactions to preparing financial statements.

Here are a few examples of the types of private accounting jobs available to financial accountants. Being a CPA may not be a requirement but can certainly be helpful — ditto earning an MBA:

✔ **Controller:** A *controller* is the chief accounting officer of a business entity and is responsible for both financial and managerial accounting functions. In a small business, a controller is often just a bookkeeper with a better title.

In a larger corporation, the controller oversees all other accounting departments and is responsible for reporting the results of financial operations to the officers of the corporation and to the board of directors. A CPA license is not necessary for this position, nor is an upper-level degree in accounting, but both are certainly assets for people in this position.

✔ **Departmental accountant:** In this position, you cover the gamut of financial accounting tasks; you could handle accounts payable or receivables, account for company assets, or handle U.S. Securities and Exchange Commission (SEC) reporting. Departmental accountants also take care of cash disbursements and receipts.

This position can be managerial because this person is responsible for such tasks as the monthly closing of the financial statements and consolidation of domestic and international subsidiaries, coordination and support of annual and interim audits, and tax compliance. Departmental accountants interact frequently with senior management and play a critical supporting role in business processes, customer quotes and proposals, and management analyses pertaining to the effectiveness and efficiency of business operations.

✔ **Bookkeeper:** A bookkeeper is a para-professional who works in accounting. No specific education, experience, or licensing is required for this designation. Many bookkeepers learn accounting by doing; they start at a business in the accounts payable or accounts receivable department and then fill the gaps in their accounting knowledge by taking accounting classes after the fact.

Bookkeepers record the daily transactions in the accounting cycle, and they carry out routine tasks and calculations such as bill paying and bank statement reconciliation. In small businesses, the bookkeeper also may double as the receptionist and runner. Depending on their knowledge base, bookkeepers sometimes also prepare the initial financial statements, which are then reviewed and adjusted by an independent CPA hired by the business.

Nonprofit and governmental accounting

Nonbusiness organizations are those lacking a profit motive. Your two biggies are not-for-profit agencies and governmental agencies. Here is a quick look at the accounting work in each:

✔ **Not-for-profit accountants** work for organizations that are run for the public good — not because of any profit motive. In fact, not-for-profits render goods and services to the community regardless of whether the costs they incur to provide the goods or services will ever be recouped from the recipients. For example, patients of a not-for-profit medical office pay only a fraction of the real cost of providing the medical care. These types of organizations include hospitals, schools, religious organizations, and charitable agencies.

✔ **Governmental accountants** work for city, county, state, and federal government agencies. Their job is similar to that of the not-for-profit accountant in that there is no profit motive. The motive comes from providing services to a community, city, state, or nation. Governmental accountants prepare financial statements that are open to the general public. The financial statements must show accountability to citizens while pursuing the goals of efficiency and effectiveness. Some financial statements are also used by external users (see Chapter 1) to decide whether to invest in a municipality's bond issuances (see Chapter 8).

Another good financial accounting gig is working on government audits for your local, state, or federal government. Two big federal employers are the Government Accountability Office (GAO) and the Internal Revenue Service (IRS). Although governmental auditing jobs require that you've completed a minimum number of accounting and auditing classes, a CPA license is not a requirement for any entry-level jobs or most upper-level ones.

GAO auditors generally conduct compliance and operational audits. However, if you want a little more action, the GAO also hires criminal auditors who conduct investigations of alleged or suspected violations of criminal laws, particularly white-collar crimes that involve fraud, waste, abuse, and government corruption.

Fulfilling your social responsibility

One of my part-time jobs while getting my CPA firm up and running was preparing budgets and financial statements and coordinating the work on the United Way grant for a not-for-profit organization that provides medical and dental care for the medically underserved. It was the most fulfilling job I ever had, outside of self-employment. If you are a financial accountant with an altruistic bent, you definitely should consider this specialty. The job was extremely interesting and varied, my fellow employees were supportive, and while I did not provide front-line services, I felt that I was helping to make a difference in the lives of people who genuinely needed aid.

IRS agents examine business and individual tax returns to assure compliance with Internal Revenue Tax Code. One fantastic advantage to working for the IRS is its flexible work options, which include working full-time out of your home.

Crystal Ball Time: Looking into the Future of Financial Accounting

Financial accountant positions are hot and should remain so for quite a while. The U.S. government Bureau of Labor Statistics *2010–2011 Occupational Outlook Handbook* rates accounting and auditing as a high growth field, with growth increasing at a greater rate than the U.S. population. (That's definitely a positive!) Financial accountants and auditors, especially those with CPA certification or MBA degrees, should have the best prospects for the anticipated 22 percent increase in projected accounting employment from 2008 to 2018.

One of the big reasons that financial accountants are now — and are projected to be — in such high demand is that business school enrollments in accounting dropped in prior years. (More people have opted to major in computer and information technology instead.) The supply of newly graduated accountants has not been great enough to meet the demand.

Wondering about the money? As of this writing, the most current year for which there is data (2008) shows the median annual earnings of accountants and auditors to be $59,430. (Keep in mind that this figure includes bookkeepers, who tend to earn less. The top 10 percent of accountants and auditors earned more than $100,000.) As of July 2009, job seekers who were straight out of school with bachelor's degrees were entertaining starting offers at an average of $48,993, and MBA candidates were coming in slightly higher at $49,786.

If the pay sounds good to you, keep reading. Next I explain how changes in the accounting profession and the business world in general will affect the work you do in the future.

Examining the evolution of financial accounting

In addition to the shift in student educational career paths, new business startups are on the rise due to layoffs in the corporate world. Gone are the days when you would be assured of a job with a major corporation from graduation to retirement. The small business has now become the backbone of our economy. Small businesses need financial accountants to help with business startup, financial statement preparation, budgeting, and tax return preparation.

Additionally, accounting scandals in the past decade have brought a change in financial laws and regulations. Enhanced regulation has increased the demand for financial accountants and auditors. For more information about this topic, see Chapter 4 — particularly the sections on the Securities and Exchange Commission (SEC) and the Sarbanes-Oxley Act of 2002 (SOX). And as I discuss earlier in this chapter, financial shenanigans have also opened up new, interesting accounting specialties such as forensic accounting and fraud accounting. (See Chapter 21 for a quick rundown of ten common financial shenanigans.)

Factoring in the changing nature of business

The circumstances under which businesses operate have changed dramatically in the last couple decades. The combination of the introduction of e-commerce in the late 1990s and technological advances that ushered in business-to-business (B2B) and business-to-consumer (B2C) commerce allow businesses to connect electronically with one another and with their customers. The increasing number of e-commerce business startups has boosted the need for financial accountants who can audit *through the computer* (tracing transactions from their original input into a computer system to their eventual resolution). Associated with this need is the demand for accountants who understand how to account for e-business income and expenses.

I have good news for computer geeks who are also interested in accounting! In the past, businesses produced paper trails that auditors, investors, and other interested parties could follow to find clues when examining the financial statements. But these days, those trails are increasingly electronic. Electronic data can be manipulated when a company's internal controls are lacking, and the data is more difficult to track down than a piece of paper in a file cabinet. So financial accountants who are savvy in computer forensics are — and will continue to be — in high demand. An example of computer forensics is knowing how to retrieve password-protected data from a CD or DVD.

Thanks to technological advances, more small businesses are doing business globally. Thus, financial accountants and auditors with knowledge of international accounting and of standards on ethics and auditing used by other countries are in great demand. Since the early 1990s, there has been serious talk about harmonizing U.S. accounting and auditing standards with other countries' standards. That change is inevitable, and all financial accountants should have at least a basic understanding of the subject. For information about international standards, visit the International Auditing and Assurance Standards Board (IAASB) Web site at `www.ifac.org/iaasb`.

As the number of multinational corporations climbs, there is also growing interest in International Financial Reporting Standards (IFRS), which use judgment-based accounting for transactions such as figuring the fair market value of assets and liabilities.

Of course, no one has a crystal ball. But the data indicate that if you're interested in making a career in financial accounting, you should have great employment prospects — especially if you keep your technology skills up to date.

Chapter 3

Introducing the Big Three Financial Statements

This chapter provides a brief overview of the three key financial statements: the balance sheet, income statement, and statement of cash flows. (Later in the book, I go into much more detail about each one.) If you're going to be an accountant, you have to get to know financial statements backward and forward. To get you moving in the right direction, I show you the purpose of each financial statement and which accounts show up on each. I also offer a thumbnail sketch of how accounts on one statement interact with accounts on another.

You find out about the three balance sheet components: assets, liabilities, and equity. I also discuss the various sections on the income statement, including the difference between revenue from operations and other gains and losses. You learn why a statement of cash flows is so crucially important to users of financial statements that are prepared using the accrual method of accounting. And finally, I introduce the three sections of the statement of cash flows — operating, investing, and financing — and explain what types of information you record in each.

You may never love financial statements so much that they become your bedtime or beachside reading material. But if you decide to pursue a career in accounting, you have to enjoy spending time with them at least a little because they're crucial to the work you do.

Gauging the Health of a Business through Its Financials

You may have heard accounting referred to as the "language of business." That's because financial statements are the end result of the accounting process, and these written reports are used by many different people and entities to make their own important investment and business decisions.

As I explain in Chapter 1, *financial accounting* is the process of classifying and recording all events that take place during the normal course of a company's business. The results of these events are arranged on the correct financial statement and reported to the external users of the financial statements. External users include investors, creditors, banks, and regulatory agencies such as the Internal Revenue Service (IRS) and the U.S. Securities and Exchange Commission (SEC).

External users of the financial statements differ from internal users in that the external user is generally less educated than the internal user. When I say *less educated,* I'm not referring to this person's formal education; an external user may very well hold a PhD from an Ivy League school! What I mean is that the external user is less educated about the company's operations. The external user usually has no clue what is going on within the company because this person isn't privy to the day-to-day operations.

In contrast, the internal users of the financial statements are employees, department heads, and other company management — all folks who work at the business.

The facts and figures shown on the financial statements give the people and businesses using them a bird's-eye view of how well the business is performing. For example, looking at the balance sheet, you can see how much debt the business owes and what resources it has to pay that debt. The income statement shows how much money the company is making, both before and after business expenses are deducted. Finally, the statement of cash flows shows how well the company is using its cash. A company can bring in a boat-load of cash, but if it's spending that cash in an unwise manner, it's not a healthy business.

This chapter provides only a brief look at each financial statement. While you prepare each statement using the same accounting facts (see Chapter 5), each one presents those facts in a slightly different way. I provide more detailed information about the three financial statements in other sections of this book: Look to Part III for balance sheet info, Chapter 10 for the lowdown on the income statement, and Chapter 11 for a discussion of counting dollars and cents on the statement of cash flows.

Reporting Assets and Claims: The Balance Sheet

The balance sheet shows the health of a business from the day the business started operations to the specific date of the balance sheet report. Therefore, it reflects the business's financial position. Most accounting textbooks use the clichéd expression that the balance sheet is a "snapshot" of the company's financial position at a point in time. This expression means that when you look at the balance sheet as of December 31, 2012, you know the company's financial position as of that date.

Accounting is based upon a *double-entry system:* For every action, there must be an equal reaction. In accounting lingo, these actions and reactions are called *debits* and *credits* (see Chapter 5). The net effect of these actions and reactions is zero, which results in the balancing of the books.

The proof of this balancing act is shown in the balance sheet when the three balance sheet components perfectly interact with each other. This interaction is called the *fundamental accounting equation* and takes place when

Assets = Liabilities + Equity

The fundamental accounting equation is also called just the *accounting equation* or the *balance sheet equation*.

Not sure what assets, liabilities, and equity are? No worries — you find out about each later in this section. But first, I explain the classification of the balance sheet. And nope, all you James Bond fans, it doesn't have anything to do with having top-secret security clearance.

Realizing why the balance sheet is "classified"

A *classified* balance sheet groups similar accounts together. For example, all current assets (see Chapter 7) such as cash and accounts receivable show up in one grouping, and all current liabilities (see Chapter 8) such as accounts payable and other short-term debt show up in another. This grouping is done for the ease of the balance sheet user so that person doesn't have to go on a scavenger hunt to round up all similar accounts.

Also, people who aren't accounting geeks (poor them!) may not even know which accounts are short-term versus *long-term* (continuing more than one year past the balance sheet date), or equity as opposed to assets. By classifying accounts on the balance sheets, the financial accountant gives them information that is easy to use and more comparable.

Studying the balance sheet components

Three sections appear on the balance sheet: assets, liabilities, and equity. Standing on their own, they contain valuable information about a company. However, a user has to see all three interacting together on the balance sheet to form a reliable opinion about the company.

Assets

Assets are resources a company owns. Examples of assets are cash, accounts receivable, inventory, fixed assets, prepaid expenses, and other assets. I fully discuss each of these assets in other chapters in this book (starting with Chapter 7), but here's a brief description of each to get you started:

✔ **Cash:** Cash includes accounts such as the company's operating checking account, which the business uses to receive customer payments and pay business expenses, and *imprest accounts,* in which the company maintains a fixed amount of cash, such as petty cash.

Petty cash refers to any bills and coins the company keeps handy for insignificant daily expenses. For example, the business runs out of toilet paper in the staff bathroom and sends an employee to the grocery store down the block to buy enough to last until the regular shipment arrives.

✔ **Accounts receivable:** This account shows all money customers owe to a business for completed sales transactions. For example, Business A sells merchandise to Business B with the agreement that B pays for the merchandise within 30 business days. Business A includes the amount of the transaction in its accounts receivable.

✔ **Inventory:** For a *merchandiser* — a retail business that sells to the general public, like your neighborhood grocery store — any goods available for sale are included in its inventory. For a *manufacturing* company — a business that makes the items merchandisers sell — inventory also includes the raw materials used to make those items. See both Chapters 7 and 13 for more information about inventory.

✔ **Fixed assets:** The company's property, plant, and equipment are all fixed assets. This category includes long-lived assets, such as the company-owned car, land, buildings, office equipment, and computers. See Chapters 7 and 12 for more information about fixed assets.

✔ **Prepaid expenses:** *Prepaids* are expenses that the business pays for in advance, such as rent, insurance, office supplies, postage, travel expense, or advances to employees.

✔ **Other assets:** Any other resources owned by the company go into this catch-all category. Security deposits are a good example of other assets. Say the company rents an office building, and as part of the lease it pays a $1,000 security deposit. That $1,000 deposit appears in the "other assets" section of the balance sheet until the property owner reimburses the business at the end of the lease.

Liabilities

Liabilities are claims against the company's assets. Usually, they consist of money the company owes to others. For example, the debt can be owed to an unrelated third party, such as a bank, or to employees for wages earned but not yet paid. Some examples of liabilities are accounts payable, payroll liabilities payable, and notes payable. I fully discuss each of these liabilities in Chapter 8. For now, here's a brief description of each:

✔ **Accounts payable:** This is a current liability reflecting the amount of money the company owes to its vendors. This category is the flip side of accounts receivable because an account receivable on one company's balance sheet appears as an account payable on the other company's balance sheet.

✔ **Payroll liabilities:** Most companies *accrue* payroll and related payroll taxes, which means a company owes its employees money but has not yet paid them. This process is easy to understand if you think about the way you've been paid by an employer in the past. Most companies have a built-in lag time between when employees earn their wages and when the paychecks are cut.

In addition to recording unpaid wages in this account, the company also has to add in any payroll taxes or benefits that will be deducted from the employee's paycheck when the check is finally cut.

✔ **Short-term notes payable:** Notes payable that are due in full less than 12 months after the balance sheet date are short-term — or could be the short-term portion of a long-term note. For example, a business may need a brief influx of cash to pay mandatory expenses such as payroll. A good example of this situation is a *working capital loan,* which a bank makes with the expectation that the loan will be paid back from the collection of the borrower's accounts receivable.

✔ **Long-term notes payable:** If a short-term note has to be paid back within 12 months after the balance sheet date, you've probably guessed that a long-term note is paid back after that 12-month period! A good example of a long-term note is a mortgage. *Mortgages* are used to finance the purchase of real property assets (see Chapter 12).

Equity

Equity shows the owners' total investment in the business, which is their claim to the corporate assets. As such, it shows the difference between assets and liabilities. It's also known as *net assets* or *net worth*. Examples of equity are retained earnings and paid-in capital. I fully discuss both equity accounts in Chapter 9. For now, here's a brief description of each:

✔ **Retained earnings:** This account shows the result of income and dividend transactions. For example, the business opens on March 1, 2012. As of December 31, 2012, it has cleared $50,000 (woohoo!) but has also paid $10,000 in dividends to shareholders. The retained earnings number is $40,000 ($50,000 – $10,000).

Retained earnings accumulate year after year — therefore the "retained" in the account name. So if in 2013 the same business makes $20,000 and pays no dividends, the retained earnings as of December 31, 2013, are $60,000 ($40,000 + $20,000).

✔ **Paid-in capital:** This element of equity reflects stock and additional paid-in capital. Nope, you're not seeing a typo! There is a paid-in capital account called "additional paid-in capital." In brief, here's what the two types of equity are:

- *Stock:* Corporations raise money by selling *stock* — pieces of the corporation — to interested investors. Stock sold to investors usually comes in two different types: common and preferred. Each type of stock has its own characteristics and advantages, which I discuss fully in Chapter 9.

- *Additional paid-in capital:* This equity account reflects the amount of money the investors pay over the stock's par value. *Par value* is the price printed on the face of the stock certificate and quite often is set at a random dollar amount. For example, if the par value of JMS, Inc. stock is $10 per share and you buy 100 shares at $15 per share, additional paid-in capital is $500 ($5 times 100 shares).

There is another stock account: *Treasury stock* is a company's own stock that it buys back from its investors. While treasury stock is a part of equity, it is not a part of paid-in capital. It shows up on the balance sheet as a reduction in equity.

Seeing an example of a classified balance sheet

A classified balance sheet groups together similar accounts so the financial statement user has an easier time reading it. In Chapter 7, I show you a blown-out balance sheet that is structured in accordance with generally accepted accounting principles (GAAP; see Chapter 4). In Figure 3-1, I give you a very abbreviated version of what a classified balance sheet looks like.

Classified Balance Sheet
 December 31, 2012

Assets	
Current assets	14,125
Property, plant & equipment	175,000
Total assets	189,125
Liabilities	
Current liabilities	2,300
Long-term liabilities	90,525
Total liabilities	92,825
Equity	
Paid-in capital	6,000
Retained earnings	90,300
Total equity	96,300
Total liabilities and equity	189,125

Figure 3-1:
An abbreviated classified balance sheet.

Posting Profit or Loss: The Income Statement

Next up in your exciting walkthrough of the three financial statements is (drum roll, please) . . . the *income statement*, which shows income, expenses, gains, and losses. It's also known as a *statement of profit or loss* (or P&L) — mostly among non-accountants, particularly small business owners. As the true financial accountant that you are (or soon will be!), you use the term *income statement* rather than *statement of profit or loss.*

Here, I provide only a brief introduction to the income statement. For the complete scoop on the income statement, the accounts reflecting on it, and how to prepare one, see Chapter 10.

Your generally accepted accounting principles (GAAP) may also refer to this report as *statements of income.* This is because the income statement shows not only income and expenses from continuing operations but also income from myriad other sources, such as the gain or loss that results when a company sells an asset it no longer needs.

Keeping a scorecard for business activity

The income statement shows financial results for the period it represents. It lets the user know how the business is doing in the short-term. And you have to keep in mind that the company's performance is not just a question of whether it made or lost money during the financial period. The issue at hand is more a matter of the relationship among the different accounts on the income statement.

For example, maybe you see that a company's *gross profit,* which is the difference between sales and cost of goods sold, is $500,000. (Not sure what cost of goods sold is? No worries — you find out in the next section of this chapter!) Based on the amount of gross sales or historical trends, you expect gross profit to be $700,000. Well, your scorecard is coming in $200,000 short — not good. And if you're a member of company management or an owner, you need to find out why.

Historical trends, which I discuss in Chapter 14, refer to a company's performance measured in many different ways tracked over a period of time — usually in years rather than in months.

Perhaps you're saying, "But wait — what about the equity section of the balance sheet? Doesn't that provide a scorecard too?" Well, think back to the definition of retained earnings I give earlier in this chapter: *Retained earnings* is the accumulated total of net income or loss from the first day the company is in business all the way to the date on the balance sheet (less dividends and other items that I discuss in Chapter 9). Retained earnings does provide valuable information, but because it's an accumulation of income that you can't definitely tie to any specific financial period, and because it can potentially be reduced by other accounting transactions such as dividends, it does not provide a scorecard like the income statement does.

Studying the income statement components

Your financial accounting textbook homes in on a few income statement components: revenue, cost of goods sold, operating expenses, and other items of gain and loss. In this section, I give you just the basics on each. For a more comprehensive explanation of all the income statement accounts, be sure to read Chapter 10.

First up, let's talk about everyone's favorite topic: revenue!

Revenue

Revenue is the inflow of assets, such as cash or accounts receivable, that the company brings in by selling a product or providing a service to its customers. In other words, it's the amount of money the company brings in doing whatever it's in the business of doing.

The revenue account shows up on the income statement as *sales, gross sales,* or *gross receipts.* All three names mean the same thing: revenue before reporting any deductions from revenue. Deductions from revenue can be *sales discounts,* which reflect any discount a business gives to a good vendor who pays early, or *sales returns and allowances,* which reflect all products customers return to the company after the sale is complete.

Cost of goods sold

The cost of goods sold (COGS) reflects all costs directly tied to any product a company makes or sells, whether the company is a merchandiser or a manufacturing company.

If a company is a *merchandiser* (it buys products from a manufacturer and sells them to the general public), the COGS is figured by calculating how much it cost to buy the items the company holds for resale. Keep in mind that to accurately calculate this amount, you have to understand how to value *ending inventory,* which is the inventory remaining on the retails shop's shelves at the end of the financial period, a topic I discuss in Chapter 13.

Because a manufacturer makes products, its COGS consists of raw material costs plus the labor costs directly related to making any products that the manufacturer offers for sale to the merchandiser. COGS also includes factory overhead, which consists of all other costs incurred while making the products.

A service company, such as a physician or attorney, will not have a COGS because it does not sell a tangible product.

Operating expenses

Operating expenses are expenses a company incurs that relate to central operations and aren't directly tied to COGS. Two key categories of operating expenses show up on the income statement:

- ✓ **Selling expenses:** Any expenses a company incurs to sell its goods or services to customers. Some examples are salaries and commissions paid to sales staff; advertising expense; store supplies; and depreciation (see Chapter 12) of a retail shop's furniture, equipment, and store fixtures. Typical retail shop depreciable items include cash registers, display cases, and clothing racks.

- ✓ **General and administrative (G&A) expenses:** All expenses a company incurs to keep up the normal business operations. Some examples are office supplies, officer and office payroll, nonfactory rent and utilities, and accounting and legal services. If, after getting an A in your financial accounting class, you're so bowled over by the subject that you seek employment as a financial accountant, your payroll is lumped into G&A too.

Other income and expense

You classify all other income the company brings in peripherally as *other revenue* or *other income;* either description is fine. This category includes interest or dividends paid on investments or any gain realized when the company disposes of an asset. For example, the company purchases new computers and sells the old ones; the amount the company makes from the sale of the old ones is included in this category.

Other expenses are expenses the company incurs that aren't associated with normal operations. Here are two types of expenses you typically see:

- ✓ **Interest expense:** The cost of using borrowed funds for business operations, expansion, and cash flow.

- ✓ **Loss on disposal of a fixed asset:** If the company loses money on the sale of an asset, you report the loss in this section of the income statement.

Seeing an example of an income statement

I show you a full-blown income statement prepared in accordance with generally accepted accounting principles (GAAP — see Chapter 4) in Chapter 10. In Figure 3-2, I give you a very abbreviated version of what an income statement looks like.

Income Statement
For the Twelve-Month Period Ending December 31, 2012

Net revenue	45,000
Cost of goods sold	20,000
Gross margin	25,000
Operating expenses	10,000
Operating income	15,000
Other gains and losses	5,000
Net income	20,000

Figure 3-2:
A simple income statement.

Showing the Money: The Statement of Cash Flows

This section offers an overview of the statement of cash flows. You prepare the statement of cash flows using certain components of both the income statement and the balance sheet. The purpose of the statement of cash flows is to show cash sources (money coming into the business) and uses (money going out of the business) during a specific period of time. This information is used by investors and potential creditors to gauge whether the business should have sufficient cash flow to pay dividends or repay loans.

The statement of cash flows is very important for financial accounting because generally accepted accounting principles (see Chapter 4) require you to use the accrual method of accounting. This means that you record revenue when it is earned and realizable (regardless of when money changes hands), and you record expenses when they are incurred (regardless of when they are paid). On the flip side, when using the cash method of accounting, a transaction isn't acknowledged until money changes hands. (A company may use a cash-basis statement for income tax return preparation.)

The statement of cash flows gives the financial statement user a basis for understanding how noncash transactions showing up on the balance sheet and income statement affect the amount of cash the company has at its disposal.

Tracking sources and uses of cash

I tell my students that if I could choose only one of the three key financial statements to evaluate a company's ability to pay dividends and meet fiscal obligations (both of which indicate a healthy business), I would pick the statement of cash flows. That's because even though the income statement shows eventual sources and uses of cash, the statement of cash flows gives you a better idea of exactly how a business is paying its bills.

Not all cash is created equal. As a general rule, a business presents itself in a more positive position if its costs are being covered by cash it brings in from the day-to-day running of the business rather than from borrowed funds. As a potential investor or lender, I want to see that cash the company brings in through operations exceeds any cash brought in by selling assets or borrowing money. This is because selling assets and borrowing money can never be construed as continuing events the way bringing in cash from selling goods or services can be.

Financial accounting, which is done on the accrual basis (see Chapter 6), does not show the cash ins and outs of business operations. The statement of cash flows gives the user of the financial statements a better idea of cash payments and receipts during the year in two ways:

- ✔ By eliminating the effects of accounts receivable and payable
- ✔ By showing cash brought in by means other than the continuing operations of the business and cash paid out for items outside the scope of continuing operations — for example, for the purchase of fixed assets

Studying sections of the cash flow statement

There are three sections on a statement of cash flows: operating, investing, and financing. Each section addresses cash ins and outs that the business experiences under completely different circumstances:

- ✔ **Operating:** This section shows items reflecting on the income statement. The three big differences between the cash and accrual methods (see Chapter 6) will be *accounts receivable,* which is money owed to the company by its customers; *accounts payable,* which is money the company owes to its vendors; and *inventory,* which are goods held by the business for resale to customers.

- ✔ **Investing:** This section usually shows the sale and purchase of long-term assets. The purchase of long-term assets reflects on the balance sheet (see Chapter 7). The sale of long-term assets reflects both on the balance sheet and income statement (see Chapter 10): It reflects on the balance sheet as a reduction of the amount of assets the company owns, and on the income statement as a gain or loss from disposing of the asset.

✔ **Financing:** The financing section shows the cash effects of long-term liability items (paying or securing loans beyond a period of 12 months from the balance sheet date) and equity items (the sale of company stock and payment of dividends).

Seeing a short statement of cash flows

I show you a full-blown statement of cash flows prepared in accordance with generally accepted accounting principles (GAAP — see Chapter 4) in Chapter 11. In Figure 3-3, I give you a very abbreviated version of what a statement of cash flows looks like.

Statement of Cash Flows
For the Twelve-Month Period Ending December 31, 2012

Cash flows from operating activities	5,000
Cash flows from investing activities	(10,000)
Cash flows from financing activities	(200)
Increase (decrease) in cash	(5,200)
Cash balance January 1, 2012	5,672
Cash balance December 31, 2012	472

Figure 3-3: A very basic statement of cash flows.

There are two different ways to prepare a statement of cash flows: the direct method and the indirect method. I show you how to prepare a statement of cash flows using each method in Chapter 11. For now, here's what to remember:

✔ The direct method reports cash receipts and disbursements.

✔ The indirect method starts with net income from the income statement and adjusts for noncash items reflecting on the income statement such as depreciation, which is allocating the cost of long-lived assets over their useful life. (See Chapter 12 for more info about depreciation.)

Chapter 4

Acronym Alert! Setting the Standards for Financial Accounting

*I*f you're not into following rules, financial accounting may not be the best career choice for you. You may want to consider the performing arts instead, or perhaps politics.

But if you're the kind of person who thrives in a structured work environment, you've come to the right profession. The work of an accountant is carefully guided by standards, rules, and regulations that I introduce in this chapter.

After a whirlwind tour through the history of accounting, I present an overview of the financial accounting code of professional conduct, which is set by the American Institute of Certified Public Accountants (AICPA). These standards give you a roadmap to follow when you're trying to figure out how to interact with your clients or employer and how to handle various accounting transactions taking place during day-to-day business operations.

Next, you meet the financial accounting standard-setting bodies and find out why *publicly owned* companies (those whose shares are freely traded on a public stock exchange) abide by different standards than privately owned companies.

Throughout this book, I refer to the acronym GAAP, which stands for *generally accepted accounting principles.* In this chapter, I explain that GAAP define for financial accountants the acceptable practices in the preparation of financial statements in the United States. Finally, I explain how GAAP have been restructured by the Financial Accounting Standards Board (FASB) into a more user-friendly format.

I hope you're hungry, because it's time to get out your spoon and dive into your alphabet soup!

Walking through the Origins of Number Crunching

I'd bet money that your financial accounting textbook takes a walk down memory lane in its first chapter, introducing you to the history of accounting. So I want to touch on a few major points to round out your textbook discussion before I explain current financial accounting standard setting.

If you've already taken an accounting history course, you know that accounting dates back to prehistoric times. If not, here are just a few number-crunching historic facts that place accounting in the context of world history:

✔ Cavemen traded beads and other trinkets to acquire food and other basic necessities. These trades required some equitable method of measuring what trinkets were exchanged for how much food, for example, thus originating the concept of keeping track of — or *accounting* for — items.

✔ Later in history, formal accounting records were kept to make sure subjects were paying the required amount of taxes to the Holy Roman and other empires.

✔ The Industrial Revolution in the eighteenth and nineteenth centuries ushered in the mass production of goods through the use of machinery rather than craftsmen working with their hands. Mass production required a more sophisticated approach to recording the movement of goods, services, and money, ramping up the activities and professionalism of the accounting field. It also resulted in the separation of ownership from management.

✔ Accountants plied their trade in a mostly unmonitored environment until the stock market crash of 1929. After this horrific event, the American Institute of Accountants, which is now the American Institute of Certified Public Accountants, partnered with the New York Stock Exchange to agree upon five principles of accounting.

Advice for the befuddled financial accounting student

Most of my financial accounting students are relative newbies to the wonderful world of accounting and business-related classes. Even at the MBA level, a preponderance of my students know nothing about accounting because they transferred into business after getting their undergraduate degrees in non-business-related disciplines.

If you're an accounting novice, my best advice to you is to forget all your preconceived notions of accounting — especially as they tie into what you feel is logical. Many times, I've seen students banging their heads against the wall because the way GAAP or the AICPA works doesn't make sense to them. Sometimes, financial accountants handle transactions in a certain way simply because *that's the way it's done.* After you go through the alphabet soup of regulatory agencies in this chapter, I hope you come to realize that for this class, at least, you need to have a good overview of the regulatory system and just go with the flow.

✔ Fast-forwarding to the present, these five principles have expanded into hundreds of principles covering every accounting topic imaginable, from how financial statements are prepared to accounting for different types of businesses.

If the financial accounting class you're taking now is your first accounting or business class, you may be wondering why you have to record accounting events in such a nit-picky fashion. You may also wonder who the head nit-pickers are and from whence they get their authority. Well, read on! This chapter answers both questions and gives you a good foundation to tie into the information given in your financial accounting textbook.

Knowing the Role of the American Institute of Certified Public Accountants (AICPA)

Financial accountants absolutely *must* maintain the highest level of ethical behavior and operate using a code of conduct. This means that financial accountants must always attempt to act in an ethical manner and do the right thing — regardless of whether doing the right thing at that particular moment is the best choice for the accountant personally.

Why is the accountant's ethical behavior so crucial? The reports that financial accountants prepare are used by individuals to make important investment decisions that can have a mighty future effect on the users' housing, retirement, and education options. The users of the financial reports must be given accurate, comparable financial statements so they can make educated decisions on how to invest their money.

The American Institute of Certified Public Accountants (AICPA) is the national professional organization for all certified public accountants (CPAs). You don't have to be a CPA or a member of the AICPA to get work as a financial accountant. However, if you think financial accounting is a career path worth exploring, keep in mind that being a CPA is a must for advancement in the field. Also, membership in the AICPA has many rewards, such as automatically informing you about new accounting standards and providing great research and educational resources.

So what exactly does the AICPA do? Through its senior technical committee, which is called the Auditing Standards Board (ASB), the AICPA is responsible for establishing auditing and attestation standards for nonpublic companies in the United States. Before we move on, let me define three key terms in that explanation:

- ✔ The purpose of financial statement *auditing* is to gather enough evidence about a company's documents to be able to issue an opinion on whether the documents are free of material (significant) misstatements.

- ✔ A financial accountant provides an *attestation* service when she issues a report on a subject that is the responsibility of another person or business. For example, a company can hire you to calculate the rate of return on the company's investments (see Chapter 14), making sure your figures match the company's report on the same topic.

- ✔ *Nonpublic* companies are closely held (meaning privately owned). Their stock is not traded on any open-to-the-public stock exchange. For example, if you start a corporation, you aren't required to sell any of your shares of stock unless you want to. In contrast, a *publicly traded* company's shares are available for purchase in stock exchanges such as the American Stock Exchange or over-the-counter markets such as the NASDAQ.

The AICPA also enforces a code of professional conduct for its members, which governs how financial accountants perform their duties. In the next two sections, I provide more information about each key role of the AICPA. First up is an explanation of the audit and attestation standards set by the ASB.

ASB audit and attestation standards

The Auditing Standards Board (ASB) is a senior technical committee of the AICPA. The ASB issues the standards and procedures that financial accountants must follow when conducting attestation and audit services for nonpublic companies. It also sets quality control standards to use when conducting *peer reviews,* which occur when one CPA firm evaluates the operations of another CPA firm.

The ASB has 19 members, most of whom work for public accounting firms (such as KPMG LLP), are university professors, are governmental accountants, or otherwise work in the field of accounting. Members serve one- to three-year terms and are jointly nominated by the director of the AICPA Audit and Attest Standards staff and the ASB chair. The responsibility of approving the nominations falls to the AICPA Board of Directors.

Curious about these mysterious ASB standards? They are called *Statements on Auditing Standards* (SAS), and as of this writing the AICPA Web site lists 120 of them. Here, I explain just a couple so you have some idea of what they cover:

- ✔ **SAS No. 1 Section 410** says the auditor must state whether the financial statements are presented using generally accepted accounting principles (GAAP).

- ✔ **SAS No. 85** defines the responsibilities that management of the company in question has for the preparation of the financial statements and the written representations about the preparation that auditors have to get from management.

A lot of information about the ASB standards and procedures is available free of charge on the AICPA Web site at www.aicpa.org. From the home page, select "Research" and then "Standards." You can access all sorts of good financial accounting info on the topics of audit, attest, compilation, and review standards.

A *compilation* occurs when a financial accountant prepares financial statements for a company using only data given to him by company management. A *review* occurs when the financial accountant gives limited assurance that no material modifications need to be made to financial statements prepared by company management.

AICPA Code of Professional Conduct

The AICPA's Code of Professional Conduct contains six principles of professional conduct by which its members must abide: responsibilities, serving the public interest, integrity, objectivity and independence, taking due care, and the scope and nature of services. You can read all about these six principles at www.aicpa.org/About/code/sec50.htm.

Note: In this section, I use the terms *financial accountant* and *CPA* synonymously. I do so because most financial accountants are CPAs, and vice versa.

Here's a brief explanation of each of the six principles:

- ✔ **Responsibilities:** As an accountant, you hold yourself to high moral and ethical standards so you maintain the public's confidence in your financial reporting. For example, financial accountants have the responsibility to participate in self-governance by performing peer reviews of other CPA/financial accounting firms' work to check for accuracy and consistency among the profession.

- ✔ **Serving the public interest:** A financial accountant's public interest is the company for whom she is preparing the financial statements, as well as the users of the financial statements (such as people and entities thinking about purchasing shares of the company stock).

  The public interest also includes banks and other businesses that are considering granting credit to the company, governmental agencies such as the Internal Revenue Service (which measures the company's compliance with the tax code), investors, and other members of the business and financial community who rely on the objectivity and integrity of CPAs.

- ✔ **Integrity:** This characteristic means you are honest when dealing with others. In the world of financial accounting, integrity means that you serve the company for whom you are preparing the financial statements to the best of your ability, keeping in mind that this may not be the same thing as completely agreeing with the way the company wants its financial statements prepared. You can't be worried that business management is going to be mad at you or fire you if you disagree with them.

- ✔ **Objectivity and independence:** When you are objective, you are neutral and unbiased in all decision-making processes. You base your opinions only on facts and not on any preconceived notions you may have. You interpret rules and policies, such as generally accepted accounting principles (GAAP), in a truthful and sincere manner — staying true to both the form and spirit of the particular principle or regulatory issue.

  Financial accountants who provide auditing and other attestation services must be independent in both fact and appearance. Being *independent* means you have no special relationship to or financial interest with the company that would cause you to disregard evidence and facts when evaluating them. For example, preparing the financial statements for a business owned by a close relative can justifiably cause those viewing your report to doubt its veracity or your objectivity.

- ✔ **Taking due care:** In a nutshell, this principle means you have the education and experience to perform the work at hand. You must be both competent and practice diligence. In addition, due care means you plan and supervise adequately any professional activity for which you are responsible.

> ✔ **Scope and nature of services:** All the above principles lead up to this
> final one. Financial accountants consider all the preceding principles
> when determining whether they can provide specific services in indi-
> vidual circumstances.

If being a member of the AICPA isn't mandatory in order to get a job as a financial accountant, you may wonder why its code of conduct is such a big deal.
Well, if you want to be a financial accountant practicing as a CPA (see Chapter
2), you must be licensed by your state, which recognizes the authority of the
AICPA. State and federal courts consistently hold that all practicing CPAs,
regardless of membership in the AICPA, must follow the professional ethical
standards contained in the AICPA's Code of Professional Conduct.

Following Regulatory Issues

In addition to the AICPA, other organizations give financial accountants official guidance on how to prepare financial statements. Public and nonpublic
corporations have different agencies monitoring them and keeping them on
the right course.

In this section, I discuss the U.S. Securities and Exchange Commission (SEC),
which was created during the Great Depression that followed the stock
market crash of 1929. It was charged with regulating the stock market and
preventing corporate abuses relating to the offering and sale of securities and
corporate reporting. Also in this section, I explain the Sarbanes-Oxley Act of
2002 (SOX), which was enacted in response to corporate abuses that took
place in the 1990s and early 2000s. Finally, you find out about the enforcement arm of SOX, the Public Company Accounting Oversight Board (PCAOB).

The U.S. Securities and Exchange Commission (SEC)

In response to the stock market crash of 1929 and the ensuing Great
Depression, the Securities Exchange Act of 1934 created the SEC. The SEC's
mission is to make sure publicly traded companies tell the truth about their
businesses and treat investors in a fair fashion by putting the needs of the
investor before the needs of the company.

The SEC is run by five commissioners who are appointed to five-year terms
by the president of the United States. Their terms are staggered, and no
more than three commissioners can be from the same political party at the
same time. These commissioners ride herd over the SEC's power to license
and regulate stock exchanges, the companies whose securities are traded on
them, and the brokers and dealers who conduct the trading.

Putting the SEC to work for you!

If you personally dabble in the stock market, you should be quite interested in the workings of the SEC. The SEC enforces the statutory requirement that public companies submit quarterly and annual reports, as well as other periodic reports that are crucial for making sound investment decisions. Additionally, company management is required to submit a narrative outlining their previous year of operations, which explains how well the company performed. Wondering where to find all this great info? The SEC maintains an online database called EDGAR (the Electronic Data Gathering, Analysis, and Retrieval system) from which investors can access this and other information filed with the agency.

You can access EDGAR at the SEC Web site, `www.sec.gov`. From the home page, under Filings and Forms, click on the Quick EDGAR Tutorial link for the lowdown on how to use EDGAR.

The enforcement authority given by Congress allows the SEC to bring civil enforcement actions against individuals or companies alleged to have committed accounting fraud, provided false information, or engaged in insider trading or other violations of the securities law. The SEC also works with criminal law enforcement agencies to prosecute individuals and companies alike for offenses that include criminal violations.

As a financial accountant, your exposure to the regulatory authority of the SEC will be limited unless you work for a company whose shares of stock are publicly traded or you work for a CPA firm conducting financial statement audits for publicly traded companies.

The Sarbanes-Oxley Act of 2002 (SOX)

Beware, fraudulent companies: SOX may sound like a cuddly kitten, but it has claws! The bankruptcies of Enron Corporation and WorldCom, Inc. — and the subsequent billions of dollars of investor losses — prompted the U.S Congress to pass the Sarbanes-Oxley Act of 2002 (SOX) in an effort to renew investor confidence in the regulation of publicly traded companies. (SOX got its name because the legislation was sponsored by U.S. Senator Paul Sarbanes and U.S. Representative Michael G. Oxley.)

Abiding by SOX is mandatory for all publicly traded organizations regardless of size. SOX introduced major changes to the regulation of financial practice and corporate governance.

SOX does not apply to privately held companies; the Auditing Standards Board (ASB) regulates privately held companies.

SOX is organized into 11 titles or sections. You can read all about them at www.sec.gov/about/laws/soa2002.pdf, but here is just a quick rundown:

- **Public Company Accounting Oversight Board (PCAOB):** SOX formed PCAOB, which I discuss in the next section of this chapter. PCAOB is the watchdog of the accounting and auditing professions.

- **Auditor independence:** The legislation establishes standards for external auditor independence in order to limit conflicts of interest.

- **Corporate responsibility:** SOX lays out the responsibility senior executives take for the accuracy and completeness of corporate financial reports.

- **Enhanced financial disclosures:** This part of the legislation requires enhanced reporting for financial transactions so users can make better-informed decisions.

- **Analyst conflicts of interest:** This section addresses the code of conduct for security analysts and requires the analysts to disclose any conflicts of interest.

- **Commission resources and authority:** SOX defines the SEC's authority to censure or bar security professionals from practice.

- **Studies and reports:** The SEC is required to perform studies on topics such as security violations and enforcement actions and report its findings.

- **Corporate and criminal fraud accountability:** This section addresses criminal penalties for "cooking the books" and any other manipulation of financial records.

- **White-collar crime penalty enhancements:** This section beefs up criminal penalties that can be assessed for white-collar crimes, including management's failure to certify corporate financial reports.

- **Corporate tax returns:** This title states that the Chief Executive Officer should sign the company's tax returns.

- **Corporate fraud and accountability:** SOX identifies corporate fraud and altering financial records as criminal offenses.

The Public Company Accounting Oversight Board (PCAOB)

SOX created the watchdog of the public company accounting and auditing profession: the PCAOB. The PCAOB is private, nonprofit corporation charged with bringing a halt to the financial shenanigans on the part of corporate chief financial officers (CFOs) and chief executive officers (CEOs) for publicly traded companies. *Public accountants* — those doing work for companies other than their own employer — support this goal through the preparation of informative, fair, and independent financial statement (audit) reports.

The PCAOB consists of five members, including a chairman appointed by the SEC and two members who must be — or previously have been — certified public accountants (CPAs). The chairman must be one of the two CPA members, but she cannot be an active CPA; in fact, she cannot have been a practicing CPA for at least five years prior to being appointed to the position. Being a member is a full-time, five-year commitment.

The PCAOB sanctions CPA firms for not following its standards. Its authority includes the death knell of revoking the CPA firm's license and barring its partners from working in public accounting. This is pretty serious stuff because it effectively closes the CPA firm's doors and keeps the individual CPAs from plying their trade.

Getting to Know the Financial Accounting Standards Board (FASB)

Resulting from some congressional criticism of the standard-setting work being done by the American Institute of Certified Public Accountants (AICPA), the Financial Accounting Foundation (FAF) was established in the state of Delaware as a nonprofit corporation by accountant Teresa S. Polley in June 1972. (As of this writing, Ms. Polley serves as the organization's president.)

The FAF in turn established the Financial Accounting Standards Board (FASB), which is currently the private-sector body establishing generally accepted accounting principles (GAAP) for all nongovernmental entities. (Governmental entities follow procedures set up by the Governmental Accounting Standards Board or GASB; see Chapter 6 for more information.)

The FASB has five full-time members, who are selected by FAF. All are required to have knowledge of accounting, finance, and business. For more info about the FASB, accounting standards, and FAF, check out the FASB Web site at www.fasb.org/home.

The recognition of the FASB as an authority is contained in the Securities and Exchange Commission (SEC) *Financial Reporting Release No. 1, Section 101* and reaffirmed in its April 2003 Policy Statement and the American Institute of Certified Public Accountants (AICPA) Rule 203, *Rules of Professional Conduct.*

The PCAOB versus the ASB

When the Sarbanes-Oxley Act of 2002 (SOX) was enacted, standard setting for public companies shifted from the Auditing Standards Board (ASB) to the Public Company Accounting Oversight Board (PCAOB). But what's the difference between the ASB and PCAOB standards? Back in April 2003, as an interim measure (because it would have been an insurmountable task to immediately come up with a new set of standards), the PCAOB adopted ASB standards on an interim, transitional basis. While some interim standards have been superseded, PCAOB and ASB standards are still quite similar — at least as of this writing. Check out the PCAOB Web site at `http://pcaobus.org/Standards/Pages/default.aspx` to find out more.

I know your spoon is probably full at this point, but before I explain what GAAP are and why they matter so much, I need you to swallow just one more acronym. The FASB formed the Emerging Issues Task Force (EITF) in 1984 to help identify emerging accounting issues in need of standardization. The EITF is composed of accounting professionals who meet six times a year with non-voting members of the SEC and FASB to mull over current economic, business, and industrial developments.

Understanding generally accepted accounting principles (GAAP)

GAAP define for financial accountants the acceptable practices in the preparation of financial statements in the United States. The preponderance of the information I provide in Parts III, IV, and V of this book directly ties back to GAAP. Specifically, GAAP tell financial accountants exactly how financial data has to show up on the income statement, balance sheet, and statement of cash flows.

For example, GAAP state that assets, liabilities, and equity go on the balance sheet and not on the income statement. GAAP are also pretty darn picky as to how these accounts are arranged on the balance sheet (see Part III). In addition, GAAP give specific rules for separating operating revenue (which is related to the business purpose) from non-operating revenue (non-business-related revenue, such as profit from selling a company asset), which I explain in Chapter 7.

Like most things in life, there are exceptions to the rule that all businesses must follow GAAP. Some businesses can deviate from GAAP, and I cover a few of these instances in Chapter 22. However, your financial accounting class likely won't concern itself much with these exceptions to the GAAP rule.

Are GAAP the same for public and nonpublic companies? For now, yes. The SEC has the statutory authority to set accounting standards for publicly held companies, but historically it has relied on private sector bodies to set those standards.

In the past, establishing and modifying GAAP were collaborative efforts among several different standard-setting bodies: the FASB, the EITF, and the AICPA. At the AICPA, this task fell specifically to the Accounting Standards Executive Committee (AcSEC), which is a senior technical committee composed of 15 CPA members of the AICPA.

But hold onto your hats! How financial accountants view GAAP changed in 2009 with the adoption of FASB Accounting Standards Codification. As of July 1, 2009, the FASB Accounting Standards Codification (ASC) became the single source of authoritative GAAP in the United States. Before you get in a dither, keep in mind that the ASC doesn't change GAAP; the FASB didn't rewrite all the accounting rules as of July 1, 2009. Instead, the ASC organizes GAAP in a more user-friendly fashion and (mercifully) uses a consistent format across the board for all GAAP topics.

Looking online for the FASB's standards

The FASB allows free, limited access to the Accounting Standards Codification. To check it out, go to http://asc.fasb.org/. Look for "New User" on the home page, and click "Order." Then look for "Basic View — Free Access" and click "Select." Follow the order registration instructions.

After you complete the log-in procedure, on the Basic View home page you can browse the topics on the task bar to see how to apply GAAP for accounting topics such as revenue (which I discuss in Chapter 10 of this book), assets, liabilities and equity (which I discuss in Part III), and presentation (see Chapters 15 and 16). Each topic allows you to drill down to more detailed information. For example, if you select "Equity," you can further select "Treasury Stock" (which I explain in Chapter 9) to find out how to account for treasury stock under GAAP.

The ASC professional version annual subscription costs $850. Ask your financial accounting instructor if your school has academic accounting access. If so, you'll have free access to better search functions that allow for a fully functional view of the codification.

Part II
Reviewing Some Accounting Basics

The 5th Wave   By Rich Tennant

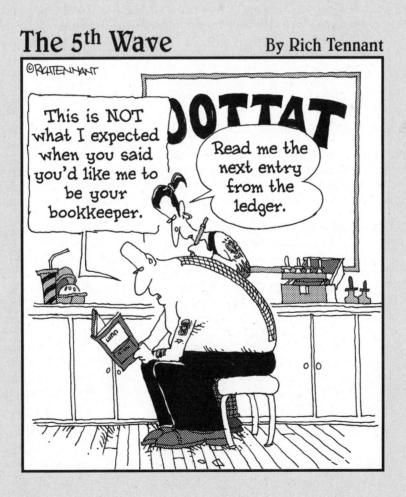

In this part . . .

This part of the book introduces bookkeeping and the basic methodology of financial accounting. In Chapter 5 you get a chance to dig into collecting, sorting through, and entering accounting data into business accounting software. Most bookkeeping duties involve basic data entry done by clerks. However, this work is the foundation for the work financial accountants do, so understanding how bookkeeping works is an integral part of your financial accounting class (and you'll be tested on bookkeeping topics in your course).

In Chapter 6 you get a primer on the difference between the cash and accrual methods of accounting. Your financial accounting class is primarily concerned with the accrual method because it's required under generally accepted accounting principles (GAAP). However, to truly understand the accrual method you have to understand how it differs from the cash method. I also walk you through the Financial Accounting Standards Board's Statements of Financial Accounting Concepts and tie these concepts to material you encounter in Parts III and IV of this book and throughout your financial accounting class.

[Handwritten annotations in margins:]
depends on income in state
10m, 1 state
Bonus depreciation / 179
States won't take
add back amount of bonus for CA.
Fed 50% bonus. teaching you.
Fed 50% bonus dep. on SK amounts
10,000 basis CA 5,000 basis Fed
able to take less of a depreciation expense
IRS... much of... certain... of deduc... AMT dep. NOL Full... still one m... tax.

Chapter 5

Booking It: The Process behind Financial Accounting

● ●

In This Chapter

▶ Defining bookkeeping

▶ Bonding with the fundamental accounting equation

▶ Becoming familiar with journals and the general ledger

▶ Writing journal entries

▶ Balancing the books

● ●

In this chapter, I discuss the nuts and bolts of collecting, sorting through, and entering accounting data into business accounting software. Accountants call the process of recording accounting transactions *booking*.

Some booking tasks involve basic data entry done by clerks. Others, like preparing journal entries, are mostly done by junior accountants or bookkeepers. What are *journal entries?* They're the accountant's way to enter transactions into the accounting system. (For example, the accountant records any bank charges shown on the company's monthly bank statement.) I discuss journal entries in detail later in this chapter.

Will you need to book journal entries during your accounting career? That depends. If you work for a small company in a one- or two-person accounting department, you could very well be the *controller* (the chief accounting officer for the business) and be doing the journal entries yourself. If, instead, you work for a large accounting firm that provides services to many clients, chances are you won't ever book journal entries yourself. However, you'll most certainly review journal entries while providing your services, such as when you audit a company's financial statements. And you may propose journal entries for your client to book if you find errors.

Handwritten margin notes:
- total tax 939
- file a dormant = registered w/ EIN# subject to min. tax for state returns.
- quarterly payments
- Sch. J
- credits are for next year 2015 — catenn ant egrd-in each quarter
- T.I. 155
- 48k tax
- 939 paid in
- How much you paid in PY
- 12/9: Before books close.
- no specific education, experience w licensing related to accounting.

No matter where your accounting career takes you, you need to know what booking involves, and I'm here to help!

Shedding Some Light on Bookkeeping

Most people who are not familiar with accounting think in stereotypes when the word "bookkeeping" comes up. They conjure images of someone who looks like Bob Cratchit from *A Christmas Carol* — a beleaguered clerk bent over a list of accounts doing the boring, mundane task of writing down accounting transactions and making sure all the transactions add up.

In the broadest sense possible, this image does relate to modern financial accounting. Bookkeeping involves recording daily transactions in the accounting cycle, such as entering customer invoices and paying vendor bills. *Bookkeepers* (the name for the employees doing the "keeping") also carry out routine tasks and calculations such as running payroll and doing the *bank statement reconciliation:* making sure the cash reflected in the company's bank account equals the cash reflected by the business checkbook. In small businesses, the bookkeeper may also double as the receptionist and errand runner.

Depending on their knowledge base, bookkeepers sometimes also prepare the company's initial financial statements, which are then reviewed and adjusted by an independent certified public accountant (CPA). So a bookkeeper can be a jack-of-all-trades. But bookkeepers normally do not have four-year degrees in accounting and, therefore, are not usually CPAs themselves.

A bookkeeper is an accounting *paraprofessional.* This means that the person may have no specific education, experience, or licensing related to accounting. Many bookkeepers learn accounting by doing: starting at a business in the accounts payable or accounts receivable department and then filling the gaps in their accounting knowledge by taking some accounting classes after the fact.

Analyzing the Effect of Business Transactions

In this section, I walk you through the basics of bookkeeping, including the rule of debits and credits and why proper debiting and crediting keeps the financial statements in balance. You also learn the five steps for entering transactions into the accounting records.

REMEMBER

Modern financial accounting is a double-entry system: For every entry into the company accounting records, there has to be an opposite and equal entry. In other words, debits must always equal credits. (Financial accounting has quite a bit in common with Newton's third law of motion — the one about every action having an equal and opposite reaction.) Technology gives you a hand here: No accounting software package worth its salt will let you enter a lop-sided transaction into the accounting books.

Working the fundamental accounting equation

REMEMBER

The *fundamental accounting equation* (also known as the *accounting equation* or the *balance sheet equation*) proves that all transactions are equal and opposite. It demands that

Assets = Liabilities + Owners' equity

A truncated version of this equation states

Net assets = Owners' equity

This version of the equation just moves liabilities over to the other side of the equal sign; *net assets* are all assets minus all liabilities. Before we go any further, I need to define our cast of characters in this equation:

- ✔ **Assets** are resources a company owns. Chapter 7 discusses all the typical types of business assets. Some examples are cash, equipment, and cars.

- ✔ **Liabilities** are debts the company owes to others. See Chapter 8 for the complete scoop on liabilities. The biggie liabilities you encounter in your financial accounting class or at work as a financial accountant are accounts payable and notes payable.

- ✔ **Owners' equity** is what's left over in the business at the end of the day — a company's assets minus its debts. Many financial accounting textbooks define owners' equity as the owners' claim to the company's assets. Chapter 8 discusses the different components of owners' equity.

You may read the explanation of owners' equity and think, "That's just another way to say 'net worth'." But you can't use the term *net worth* interchangeably with *owners' equity* in an accounting setting. Generally accepted accounting principles (GAAP), which I explain in Chapter 4, do not allow accountants to restate assets to their actual value, which would be required to calculate a company's net worth.

Here's a simple example of the fundamental accounting equation at work; assume the numbers represent a company's assets, liabilities, and owners' equity in thousands, millions, or perhaps even billions of dollars:

Assets = Liabilities + Owners' equity

100 = 40 + 60

Or

Net assets = Owners' equity

60 = 60

Getting familiar with accounts

As an accountant within a business, you summarize accounting transactions into accounts that you use to create financial reports. Each and every account your company uses is annotated in a list called the *chart of accounts*. The business uses that chart of accounts to record transactions in its *general ledger:* the record of all financial transactions within the company during a particular accounting cycle. You learn all about the general ledger at the close of this chapter.

The chart of accounts is not a financial report. It is merely a list of all accounts you've previously set up to handle the company transactions.

When you're "doing the books," as the saying goes, you record your normal business transactions using accounts you set up in the chart of accounts. Each account in the chart of accounts has a unique account number. Regardless of what accounting software package your company uses, the numbering sequence is pretty much set in stone to ensure consistency among companies and among their financial reports.

The number of accounts you can set up in the chart of accounts is virtually unlimited, so you can customize it to fit your business perfectly. Here's the numbering sequence that's most used for charts of accounts:

Number Sequence	Account Type
1000 to 1999	Assets
2000 to 2999	Liabilities
3000 to 3999	Equity
4000 to 4999	Income
5000 to 5999	Cost of goods sold expenses
6000 to 7999	Operating, general, and administrative expenses
8000 to 9999	Non-business-related items of income and expense

Instead of using a four-digit numbering sequence, some software programs use a three-digit numbering sequence. For example, instead of 1000 to 1999 for assets, some software programs may use 100 to 199.

In the previous section, I define assets, liabilities, and equity. And the income accounts (numbers 4000 to 4999) are pretty easy to understand; they represent any money the business takes in for the products or services it sells. Here's a brief explanation of the accounts in the 5000–9999 numbering sequence:

- **Cost of goods sold (COGS) expenses:** COGS is the cost of the product that a company sells. The company can either make the product that it sells or buy it from someone else and then resell it. I talk much more about COGS in Chapters 10 and 13.

- **Operating, general, and administrative expenses:** These accounts reflect all expenses a business incurs while performing its business purpose that do *not* directly relate to making or wholesaling a product — in other words, any expense that's not a COGS. Some examples are telephone and postage expenses. Find more about these types of expenses in Chapter 10.

- **Nonbusiness-related items of income and expense:** A company may bring money in or spend money that generally accepted accounting principles (GAAP) classify as *nonbusiness-related*. For example, a business treats interest it earns on investments as nonbusiness income. If a company sells an asset at a loss, that's an example of a nonbusiness expense. More about this topic in Chapter 10 as well.

Keep in mind that if a company is in the business of loaning money, interest earned on these loans *is* considered business income. Likewise, a car dealership must report losses on sales of vehicles as business expenses.

Defining debits and credits

Now that you understand the basics of accounts and the chart of accounts, it's time to learn the mechanism of *journal entries,* which you use to enter financial information into the company's accounting software.

Writing journal entries is a major area of concern for first-year accounting students, students who are taking accounting only because it's required for a business degree, and small business owners. The logistics of presenting the journal entry don't cause the concern; instead, the worry is how to figure out which account is debited and which is credited.

REMEMBER

Here's one of the immutable laws of accounting: Assets and expenses are *always* debited to add to them and credited to subtract from them. Liability, revenue, and equity accounts are just the opposite: These accounts are *always* credited to add to them and debited to subtract from them. Always, always, always — there is no exception to this rule.

TECHNICAL STUFF

Many financial accounting textbooks attempt to ease the student into debits and credits through *horizontal analysis,* which uses statement-driven information to record transactions using the terms *adding* and *subtracting* instead of *debits* and *credits.* I find this approach more confusing to my students because it erroneously reinforces the untruth that debiting means "adding to" and crediting means "subtracting from" — which is not always true.

Learning about the transaction methodology

Before you enter an event into a business accounting system, you have to consider the *transaction methodology,* a five-step process for deciding the correctness of whatever entry you're preparing. After you get into the financial accounting rhythm, this becomes an automatic analysis you do by rote. Here are your five considerations:

- **What's going on?** This question addresses the precipitating event for the entry. For example, did the company buy a new piece of business equipment or sell some product to a customer?

- **Which accounts does this event affect?** Is the account an asset, liability, owners' equity, revenue, or expense? Assets would definitely be affected by the purchase of business equipment, and revenue would be affected by a customer sale.

buying adds to this thing

✔ **How are the accounts affected — by a debit or credit?** Looking back to your rules of debits and credits, buying assets adds to the account so it's a debit. Making a sale adds to a revenue account so it's a credit.

✔ **Do all debits for an entry equal all credits for the same entry?** Think about the fundamental accounting equation, which I discuss earlier in this chapter. For every debit there has to be an equal credit.

Really important.

✔ **Does the entry make sense?** Do the actions you take match the facts and circumstances of the business event? For example, although the net effect on the books is the same, you can't credit an expense to record revenue.

In the next section, you learn about the different types of journals available to you to record transactions. I also give you plenty of examples of journal entries so you can see the transaction methodology at work.

Defining Journals

Product Formula

Accounting journals are a lot like the diary you may have kept as a child (or maybe still keep!). They are a day-to-day recording of events. But accounting journals record business transactions taking place within a company's accounting department. Accountants call journals the *books of original entry* because no transactions get into the accounting records without being entered into a journal first.

english—mandetory

A business can have many different types of journals. In this section you learn about the most common ones your financial accounting class discusses, which are tailored to handle cash, accrual, or special transactions. Want to find out more? I discuss cash journals first.

Using journals to record cash transactions

All transactions affecting cash go into the cash receipts or cash disbursements journal. Some accounting software programs or textbooks may refer to the cash disbursements as the *cash payments* journal. No worries — both terms mean the same thing.

Cash receipts journal

Let's talk about the most popular cash journal first: the cash receipts journal. After all, everyone loves to receive cash!

lots of questions

When accountants use the word *cash,* it doesn't just mean paper money and coinage; it includes checks and credit card transactions. In accounting, *cash* is a generic term for any payment method that is assumed to be automatic. When you sign a check and give it to the clerk behind the store counter, part of your implicit understanding is that the funds are immediately available to clear the check. Ditto paying with a credit card, which represents an immediate satisfaction of your debit with the vendor. (Never mind the fact that a three-day lag usually occurs between the time the charge is processed and when the money hits the vendor's checking account.)

Here are examples of some cash events that require posting to the cash receipts journal:

✔ **Customer sales made for paper money and coinage:** Many types of businesses still have booming cash sales involving the exchange of paper money and coins. Some examples are convenience stores, retail shops, and some service providers such as hair salons. I am still amazed by the amount of cash my retail clients take in from customers every day.

✔ **Customers making payments on their accounts:** I talk about *accounts receivable,* which is money customers owe a business, in the "Recording accrual transactions" section later in this chapter. For now, just remember that any payment a customer makes for goods or services previously billed goes in the cash receipts journal.

✔ **Interest or dividend income:** When a bank or investment account pays a business for the use of its money in the form of interest or dividends, the payment is considered a cash receipt.

As a technical matter, many businesses record interest income reflecting on their monthly bank statement in the general journal, which I discuss a little later in this section.

Interest and dividend income is also known as *portfolio income.* Many times it's also considered to be passive income because the recipient doesn't have to work to receive the portfolio income (like you do for your paycheck). One caveat, though: For tax purposes the Internal Revenue Service does not consider interest and dividend income to be passive.

✔ **Asset sales:** Selling a business asset like a car or office furniture can also result in a cash transaction. You may see an example in your textbook where a company is outfitting its executive office space with deluxe new leather chairs so it's selling all the old leather chairs to a furniture liquidator and there is an exchange of some mode of cash between the parties to the sale.

Keep in mind that this list isn't comprehensive; these are just a few of the many instances that can necessitate recording a transaction in the cash receipts journal.

Various types of cash receipts receive different treatment on a company's income statements. For example, cash sales are treated one way, and interest income and dividends are treated another way. I give you the details in Chapter 10.

The cash receipts journal normally has two columns for debits and four columns for credits:

- ✔ **Debit columns:** Because all transactions in the cash receipts journal involve the receipt of cash, one of the debit columns is always for cash. The other is for *sales discounts,* which reflects any discount the business gives to a good vendor who pays early. For example, a customer's invoice is due within 30 days, but if the customer pays early, it gets a 2 percent discount.

- ✔ **Credit columns:** To balance the debits, a cash receipts journal contains four credit columns:

  - • Sales

  - • Accounts receivable

  - • *Sales tax payable,* which is the amount of sales tax the business collects on the transaction (and doesn't apply to every transaction)

  - • *Miscellaneous,* which is a catch-all column where you record all other cash receipts like interest and dividends

Not all sales are subject to sales tax. Your state department of revenue determines what sales transactions are taxable. For example, in many states, fees for accounting or legal services are not subject to sales tax.

In addition to the debit and credit columns, a cash receipts journal also contains at least two other columns that don't have anything to do with debits or credits:

- ✔ The date the transaction occurs
- ✔ The name of the account affected by the transaction

Depending on the company or accounting system, additional columns may be used as well.

Figure 5-1 shows an example of a portion of a cash receipts journal.

Cash Receipts Journal							
				Sales Tax	Accounts	Sales	
		Misc	Sales	Payable	Receivable	Discount	Cash
Date	Account	Credit	Credit	Credit	Credit	Debit	Debit
1	1/15	Interest Income	32.50					32.50
2	1/16	XYZ Corporation				5100.00		5100.00
3	1/23	Customer Sale		100.00	6.00			106.00

Figure 5-1: A partial cash receipts journal.

Cash disbursements journal

On the flip side, any payment the business makes using a form of cash gets recorded in the cash disbursements (or payments) journal. Here are a few examples of transactions you see in a cash disbursements journal:

✔ **Merchandise purchases:** When a *merchandiser,* a company selling goods to the public (see Chapter 10), pays cash for the goods it buys for resale, the transaction goes in the cash disbursement journal.

✔ **Payments the company is making on outstanding accounts:** This includes all cash disbursements a company makes to pay for goods or services it obtained from another business and didn't pay for when the original transaction took place. More on this topic in the "Recording accrual transactions" section later in this chapter.

✔ **Payments for operating expenses:** These transactions include checks or bank transfers a business uses to pay utility or telephone invoices.

The cash disbursements journal normally has two columns for debits and two for credits:

✔ **Credit columns:** Because all transactions in the cash disbursements journal involve the payment of cash, one of your credit columns is for cash. The other is for *purchase discounts,* which are reductions in the amount a company has to pay the vendor for any purchases on account. For example, a business offers customers a certain discount amount if they pay their bills within a certain number of days.

✔ **Debit columns:** To balance these credits, the debit columns in a cash disbursements journal are accounts payable and *miscellaneous* (a catch-all column where you record all other cash payments for transactions, such as the payment of operating expenses).

A cash disbursements journal also contains at least three other columns that don't have anything to do with debiting or crediting:

✔ The date the transaction occurs

✔ The name of the account affected by the transaction

✔ The *pay-to entity* (which means who the payment is made to)

Depending on the company or accounting system used, more columns could be used as well. Figure 5-2 shows an example of a partial cash disbursements journal.

						Accounts	Purchase	
		Ck			Misc	Payable	Discount	Cash
	Date	Num	Pay-To	Account	Debit	Debit	Credit	Credit
1	1/3	125	USPS	Postage Expense	352.63			352.63
2	1/4	126	Vendor A	Merchandise Purchase	412.00			412.00
3	1/5	127	Vendor B	Payment to Vendor		5000.00	100.00	4900.00

Figure 5-2: A partial cash disbursements journal.

Cash Disbursements Journal

Recording accrual transactions

Accrual transactions take place whenever cash doesn't change hands. For example, a customer makes a purchase with a promise to pay within 30 days. Using accruals and recording business transactions using the accrual method are the backbone of financial accounting (see Chapter 6). In my experience teaching financial accounting, students have a big problem with figuring out accruals, understanding how accrual transactions interact with cash transactions, and knowing when it's appropriate to record an accrual transaction.

Don't worry, I walk you through all the accrual transactions you'll see in your financial accounting textbook and give you a complete explanation of each. And, before you finish this section of the book, you can review a sampling of typical accrual transactions.

Following is information about your two accrual workhorse journals, the *sales journal* and *purchases journal*. I discuss other accrual-type journals in the upcoming section "Learning about other journals."

Sales journal

The sales journal records all sales that a business makes to customers *on account,* which means no money changes hands between the company and its customer at the time of the sale. A sales journal affects two different accounts:

accounts receivable and sales. In the sales journal, accounts receivable and sales are always affected by the same dollar amount.

Figure 5-3 presents an example of a sales journal.

				Sales Journal	
			Inv		Accounts Receivable Debit/ Sales Credit
		Date	Num	Name of Customer	3,000.00
	1	6/15	3254	Customer A	521.23
	2	6/17	3255	Customer B	785.25
	3	6/21	3256	Customer C	

Figure 5-3: A partial sales journal.

When you record credit sales in your sales journal, you follow up by posting the transactions to each customer's listing in the accounts receivable ledger. (See the "Bringing It All Together in the Ledger" section of this chapter.)

Use the sales journal only for recording sales on account. Sales returns, which reflect all products the customers return to the company after the sales are done, do not record in the sales journal. Instead, you record them in the general journal, which I discuss later in this section.

Purchases journal

Any time a business buys using credit (*on account*), it records the transaction in its purchases journal. The purchases journal typically has a column for date, number, and amount. It also has the following columns:

✔ **Accounts payable:** Because the company is purchasing on account, the current liability account called "accounts/trade payable" is always affected.

✔ **Terms:** This column shows any discount terms the company may have with the vendor. For example, *2/10, n/30* means the company gets a 2 percent discount if it pays within 10 days; otherwise, the full amount is due in 30 days. (The *n* in this shorthand stands for "net.")

✔ **Name:** The company records the name of the vendor from whom the purchase is made.

✔ **Account:** This column shows to which financial statement account(s) the purchase is taken. In the example shown in Figure 5-4, there are two accounts, accounts payable (A/P) and purchases. Because no other accounts (such as sales tax) are affected, A/P and purchases are for the same dollar amount. If the company collects sales tax too, a column would be added to report this amount as well.

Purchases Journal					
		Inv			Accounts Payable Credit/ Purchase Debit
	Date	Num	Name	Terms	
1	2/4	1993	Vendor 1	2/10, n/30	125.63
2	2/8	2357	Vendor 2		2587.00
3	2/13	185	Vendor 3	2/10, n/30	5000.00

Figure 5-4:
A partial purchases journal.

Learning about other journals

The discussion of journals wouldn't be complete without a brief rundown of other special journals you'll see during your foray into financial accounting, as well as the general journal. I cover both topics in this section.

Special journals

Here are three additional journals you'll encounter:

✔ **Payroll journal:** This journal records all payroll transactions such as gross wages, taxes withheld, and other deductions (such as health insurance paid by the employee) leading to *net pay,* which is the amount shown on the employee's check.

✔ **Purchases return and allowances journal:** This journal shows all subtractions from gross purchases because of products a company returns to the vendor or discounts given to the company by the vendor.

✔ **Sales returns and allowances journal:** This journal shows all subtractions from gross sales because of products customers return or discounts given to the customers.

This list is not all-inclusive; some companies may have other journals, and some smaller companies may not use all of these. However, if you understand the basic methodology of all the journals I discuss in this chapter, you'll be well prepared for your financial accounting class and any work you have to do as a financial accountant.

General journal

The *general journal* is a catchall type of journal where transactions that don't appropriately belong in any other journal show up. Many companies record interest income and dividends in the general journal.

This journal is also used for adjusting and closing journal entries:

- **Adjusting journal entries:** One key reason you would adjust journal entries is to make sure the accounting books are recording using the accrual method. For example, on April 30, employees have earned but not yet been paid $5,000 in gross wages (the next payroll date is May 2). So to make sure that your company's revenue and expenses are matched, you book an adjusting journal entry debiting "wages expense" for $5,000 and crediting "wages payable" for $5,000.

  You also adjust journal entries to *reclassify* transactions when the way a transaction originally records is correct but circumstances change after the fact and the transaction needs to be adjusted. For example, your company buys $1,000 of supplies on April 1, and the transaction is originally booked as supplies inventory. On April 30, an inventory of the supplies is taken (see Chapter 13). Only $800 of the supplies remain, so you have to debit your "supplies expense" account for $200 and credit "supplies inventory" for $200.

- **Closing journal entries:** You use this type of entry to zero out all *temporary accounts,* which reflect all the revenue and expenses for a certain time period. You then transfer the net amounts to the balance sheet. You take this step to set the income statement figures to zero so you know exactly how much revenue and expense are booked during a certain time period. (See Chapter 10 for information about the income statement.) There are four closing journal entries:

  - You debit all revenue accounts and credit income summary for the same amount. *Income summary* is a temporary holding account you use only when closing out a period.

  - You credit all expenses and debit income summary for the same amount.

  - You either debit or credit income summary to reduce it to zero and take the same figure to *retained earnings,* which is the cumulative net income that has not been distributed to the owners of the business.

    Here's an example: If in step one you credit income summary for $5,000 and in step two you debit income summary for $3,000, you now have a credit balance of $2,000 in income summary. So to reduce income summary to zero, you debit it for $2,000 and credit retained earnings for the same amount. And crediting retained earnings is a good thing!

  - Finally, if the owners have paid themselves any dividends during the period, you credit the dividend account reducing it to zero and debit retained earnings.

Honestly, you likely never have to prepare the first three closing entries yourself because all accounting software systems do this task for you automatically. However, you do need to understand what goes on with the debits and credits when the books close. You have to do the fourth closing entry yourself.

You clear out only temporary accounts with closing journal entries. Balance sheet accounts are permanent accounts. Until you cease using the account (for example, you close a bank account), no balance sheet accounts are zeroed out at closing. More about balance sheet accounts in Part III of this book.

Seeing examples of common journal entries

It's time for you to review a few journal entries so the concepts I discuss earlier in the chapter really come to life. First, keep in mind the general format of a journal entry, which is shown in Figure 5-5:

Date	Debited account Credited account	XX,XXX	XX,XXX

Figure 5-5: The standard journal entry format.

- ✔ The date of the entry is offset in the left-hand column.
- ✔ The account debited or credited is in the middle column.
- ✔ The amounts are shown in the right-hand column.

Proper journal entries always list debits first and credits afterwards.

Journal entries can have more than one debit and one credit. And the number of accounts debited and credited don't have to be the same. For example, you can have five accounts debited and one account credited. However, the dollar amount of the debits and credits has to match.

Let's prepare the journal entry for service income, which records cash and accrual income. You provide a service to your client, Mr. Jones, on May 15, 2012, giving him invoice #200 in the amount of $700 for services rendered. Before he leaves your office, he pays you $200 in cash with a promise to pay the remaining balance of $500 next week. The journal entry to record this transaction is shown in Figure 5-6.

has to be that person.

5/15/2012	Cash *Conv.*	200.00	
	Accounts Receivable	500.00	
	Service Revenue		700.00
	To record invoice #200		

Figure 5-6: Recording service income.

service rendered & the income has been earned. so record.

Under the accrual method of accounting (see Chapter 6), both the cash receipts and the promise to pay the remaining balance have to be reported at the time the transaction takes place because the service has been rendered and the income has been earned.

Every journal entry should have a brief explanation. It doesn't have to be a book but should be long enough that you or anyone else reviewing the journal entry can figure out why you made the journal entry. I can't tell you how many times I've been just a little too brief with my journal entry descriptions and had to go back through the transaction to figure out why I made the journal entry. The description for the journal entry in Figure 5-6 ("To record invoice #200") is brief but totally understandable.

Let's do one more journal entry before moving onto the last section in this chapter. Say you borrow $5,000 from your bank on July 1, 2012. Your arrangement calls for you to pay $200 interest on July 31, 2012, and pay the loan back in full plus another $200 in interest on August 30, 2012. Figure 5-7 shows how your journal entries look from soup to nuts.

worried.
nope, didn't expect that.

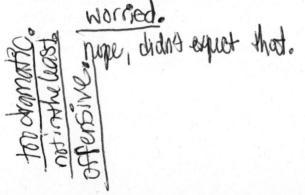

7/1/2012	Cash	5,000.00	
	Notes Payable		5,000.00
	Bank loan received		
7/31/2012	Interest Expense	200.00	
	Cash		200.00
	To record interest paid on note		
8/31/2012	Notes Payable	5,000.00	
	Interest Expense	200.00	
	Cash		5,200.00
	Payment of bank note and interest		

Figure 5-7:
Journalizing
a loan
transaction.

Bringing It All Together in the Ledger

At this point you may be thinking, "Okay, the journals are the books of origi-nal entry, but what happens then? How do entries into these journals turn into financial statements?" That's the topic of this section. The accounts and amounts debited or credited affect the company's ledgers, which I define next.

Realizing what a ledger is

A *ledger* records applicable transactions taking place in a company during a particular accounting cycle. Picture a big book. Every page of the book has a title that corresponds with an account from the chart of accounts. For instance, page 1 may be titled "1001 Cash in Bank." On this page, you'd list the total of the funds you deposited in your company checking account, as well as the total of all the withdrawals for a given period — say for a month.

A business has one big dog ledger: the general ledger. The *general ledger* lists all transactions taking place in all the accounts during the specified accounting period. You may also see subsidiary ledgers that list in detail transactions happening only in specific accounting circumstances. For example, the *payroll subsidiary ledger* lists all payroll transactions. The *accounts receivable subsidiary ledger* lists all customers owing your company money and the amount of their current outstanding balance.

Posting to the ledgers

When you *post to the ledgers,* you simply take accounts and numbers from transactions you enter in the journals and record them in the correct ledger. If a subsidiary ledger is the first point of recording, the transaction eventually flows through the subsidiary ledger to the general ledger. For example, a customer sale on account first posts to the sales journal and then is reported in the accounts receivable subsidiary ledger under the customer's name.

Then, that amount flows from the accounts receivable subsidiary ledger to the accounts receivable listing in the general ledger, combining with all other customers owing the business money to show a grand total of accounts receivable. Following with the same transaction, the combined total of all the transactions in the sales journal also posts to the sales listing in the general ledger.

Until modern accounting software arrived, posting to the ledgers was a laborious process requiring the use of ledger paper with 14 columns. When I first opened the doors of my CPA business, an occasional client would still be manually posting to ledgers via paper entries. Luckily, this practice has become a thing of the past because over-the-counter boxed accounting software has become so cheap and easy to use.

With most accounting software programs, there is no formal procedure to post to the ledgers. Every time you enter a transaction in a journal, it automatically posts to the correct ledger. However, *proprietary* accounting software (which means a business holds exclusive rights to use) may require the user to actively select the posting command.

Viewing an example of a general ledger

While the theory of a general ledger is the same in every instance, general ledgers from one company to another using different types of accounting software will look slightly different. Figure 5-8 shows a very simple partial general ledger for a small services company. It starts with a revenue account, "consulting fees," and ends with an operating expense account, "bank charge."

Walking through the basic accounting cycle

In most businesses, the accounting cycle is based on a calendar month. Using January as an example, during that month's accounting cycle, employees in various accounting departments are hard at work entering daily transactions into journals and ledgers as the accounting events unfold from January 1 through January 31.

Just making sure.

For example, the business receives an invoice from a inventory supply vendor for purchases made on January 12, and the invoice will be paid when the vendor statement arrives showing all purchases the company makes during January. (See Chapter 8 for more information about purchases and payables.) A clerk in the accounts payable department enters this invoice into the purchases journal, increasing inventory and accounts payable. Both actions affect the balance sheet (see Part III of this book). However, by taking an inventory (see Chapter 13), accountants at the company reclassify some of the dollar amount of this purchase to cost of goods sold (COGS) — an income statement account — via a journal entry.

Also, during each accounting cycle the cost of using any long-lived asset such as property, plant, and equipment (see Chapter 7) has to be reclassified from the balance sheet to the income statement. This step is done by preparing a journal entry to book depreciation expense (see Chapter 12). And, of course, the business has to record all types of revenue and any other business and non-business-related expenses in the appropriate journal. *Fine.*

While a company enters accounting transactions in journals contemporaneously during the accounting cycle, preparation of the financial statements takes place after all entries to the journals post to the ledgers and the accounting period ends. How quickly the financial statements are prepared varies by company. However, keep in mind that some journal entries can't be made until after the business bank statement arrives, which varies by bank. In my experience, bank statements usually arrive within ten days of the end of the banking cycle.

purchase rises [Acct Pay] divided all in favor say "I"

COGS

196 ¶ credit section. annoying - she is jealous of me.

The debit, credit, and balance columns in Figure 5-8 should be self-explanatory. Here's what some of the other columns mean:

direct answers make people feel secure

- ✔ **Type:** The original nature of the transaction.
- ✔ **Date:** The day the transaction took place.
- ✔ **No.:** The identifying number from the journal of original entry. For example, 1008 is the company check number used to pay James Fine.
- ✔ **Name:** Whatever name you put in the journal of original entry.
- ✔ **Memo:** Any explanation for the transaction that you put in the original entry.

Figure 5-8: A partial general ledger.

Metropolitan Services, Inc.
General Ledger

Type	Date	No.	Name	Memo	Debit	Credit	Balance
4050 - Consulting Fees							0.00
Deposit	1/1/2012	7		Calderwood Job	0.00	55,000.00	55,000.00
Deposit	3/26/2012	2		John's office colors	0.00	500.00	55,500.00
Deposit	3/31/2012	3		Walk in job	0.00	100.00	55,600.00
Invoice	5/15/2012	1	Bakerfield		0.00	1,725.00	57,325.00
Invoice	5/15/2012	5	Johnson	Monthly storage fee	0.00	75.00	57,400.00
Invoice	5/31/2012	3	Thompson	Original quote #3 hou	0.00	4,207.50	61,607.50
Total 4050 - Consulting Fees						61,607.50	61,607.50
5300 - Labor							0.00
Check	5/31/2012	1008	James Fine	Gross wages	800.00	0.00	800.00
Check	5/31/2012	1008	Phil Lock	Gross wages	200.00	0.00	1,000.00
Total 5300 - Labor					1,000.00	0.00	1,000.00
5400 - Subcontract Labor							0.00
Check	5/31/2012	1010	Bob Smith	Thompson job	1,500.00	0.00	1,500.00
Total 5400 - Subcontract Labor					1,500.00	0.00	1,500.00
5500 - Bank Charge							0.00
Bank fee	3/31/2012	14		March Bank Charges	15.00	0.00	15.00
Total 5500 - Bank Charge					15.00	0.00	15.00

Recognizing the purpose of the trial balance

The *trial balance* is a listing of all the accounts in the general ledger and the balance they hold as of the date of the report. The purpose of the trial balance is to make sure all debits equal credits. Accountants also use it as a front-line tool to review the accuracy of the financial statements.

For example, you run the trial balance, quickly scan it, and see that an expense account carries a balance that seems too high based on your professional judgment and knowledge of the company. You check the general ledger and see that a rent payment to the business landlord for $5,000 was posted to postage expense by mistake. I always first review the trial balance when starting work for a new client because it gives me a good overall view of the business.

Figure 5-9 shows an example of a partial trial balance.

Accounting software should not allow a user to enter a transaction that is out of balance, so technically the trial balance should always be in balance. Should an out-of-balance transaction occur, the software has a serious flaw and should not be used.

Metropolitan Services, Inc.
Trial Balance

Account Name	Account No.	Debit	Credit
Petty Cash	1001	50.00	
Checking Account	1005	2,078.30	
Accounts Receivable	1500	13,194.556	
Merchandise Inventory	1015	27,488.50	
Delivery Van	1600	35,000.00	
Accounts Payable	2600		2,500.00
Sales Tax Payable	2000		265.31
Pending Item Receipts	2500		2.389.25
Business Credit Card	2010		535.00
Social Security Tax	2120		124.00
Medicare Tax	2130		29.00
Federal Income Tax	2140		240.00
State Income Tax	2150		60.00
Note Payable - Computer Equipment	2510		25,000.00
Common Stock	3050		5,000.000
Service Income	4000		14,910.20
Consulting Fees	4050		61,007.50
Other Sales	4060		180.00
Cash Discount Taken	5000		26.85
Purchases	5200	19,835.75	
Labor	5300	1,000.00	
Subcontract Labor	5400	1,500.00	
Bank Charge	5500	15.00	
Insurance Expense	6500	3,150.00	
Officer Wages	6700	1,000.00	
Postage Expense	6900	100.00	
Rent Expense	7200	6,125.00	
Telephone Expense	7600	1,730.00	
Total		112,267.11	112,267.11

Figure 5-9:
A partial
trial
balance.

Chapter 6

Focusing on Accounting Methods and Concepts

. . . .

In This Chapter

▶ Getting clear on the cash and accrual methods of accounting

▶ Walking through other types of accounting besides financial

▶ Learning about FASB's conceptual framework

. . . .

*W*hile most of my students take financial accounting only because it's a core requirement for an undergraduate and graduate business degree, in every seminar I have at least one student who gets fired up about the topic to the point where he considers changing his major to accounting. If you are also thinking that accounting isn't that bad of a gig, this chapter gives you some information about other types of accounting besides financial that you may be interested in. And the good news is that the basic accounting facts you learn in your financial accounting class apply to just about any accounting specialty.

Before I discuss other types of accounting, I explain the difference between the cash and accrual methods of accounting. Your financial accounting class is primarily concerned with the accrual method because it's required under generally accepted accounting principles (GAAP, which I explain in Chapter 4). However, to truly understand the accrual method you have to understand how it differs from the cash method.

In addition, you get an introduction to the Financial Accounting Standards Board's Statements of Financial Accounting Concepts. (If you aren't familiar with the FASB, check out Chapter 4.) I walk you through four of these concepts, tying them into material you encounter in Parts III and IV of this book and throughout your financial accounting class.

Distinguishing between Key Accounting Methods

This book is about financial accounting, which means the company operates on the accrual method of accounting according to GAAP. (If you're fuzzy on the accrual method and GAAP, don't worry — I cover both in the upcoming section called "The accrual basis.")

However, there is another method of accounting besides accrual: the cash method. This section gives you an expanded version of what you'll likely see in your financial accounting textbook.

It's important to go through this information for a few different reasons. First, to really understand a topic, you often have to understand why it differs from the alternatives. Second, if after finishing your financial accounting class you find you have an affinity for the whole debiting and crediting extravaganza, you should know what other accounting specialties are available. Finally, to be a well-rounded financial accountant, you have to have at least a basic understanding of the other method and types of accounting.

The master's level financial accounting course I teach includes one chapter on managerial accounting. If your course does as well, you get a great introduction to the subject later in this chapter in the "Sorting through Standards for Other Types of Accounting" section.

The cash basis

Using the cash basis of accounting couldn't be easier. You record revenue when the company is paid, and you record expenses when they are paid — not when they are incurred. However, the ease of using the cash method is more than offset by the fact that the method fails to match revenue to the expenses the company incurs to earn that revenue. Because of this failure, cash basis financial statements usually do not present as accurate a picture of how the business is performing as accrual method financial statements do.

Consider an example. Let's say ABC Corp. has revenue of $40,000 and expenses totaling $15,000 associating with that revenue in April. $20,000 of the revenue was received in cash, and the rest is on account. ABC Corp. paid cash for the entire $15,000 of expenses.

An "earned and realizable" example

If you're at all confused about how a transaction becomes earned and realizable, here's an example to bring the concept into focus:

A florist customer's wedding is taking place in a couple of days, and the customer has just given the florist a personal check paying in full for the reception table arrangements. Is this income earned? No, the florist has not earned the revenue from the wedding job until all floral arrangements are present and accounted for on the reception tables.

At face value, because the florist has a check in his hot little hands, you may be tempted to say that this revenue is realizable even though the flowers haven't been delivered yet. But wait: A couple days after the wedding, the florist finds out the customer's check has bounced because the customer has closed the account on which the check was drawn. The florist calls the customer's telephone number, but it's disconnected. He subsequently finds out the customer has also moved, leaving no forwarding address.

Is the revenue from this job now earned and realizable? Earned, yes — the florist delivered on his end of the contract. Realizable, no, because the florist has no realistic expectation of ever collecting on this check. Under the accrual method of accounting, this transaction is not recorded as revenue. (And under the cash method of accounting, it's a nonrecognized event because money did not change hands.)

Using the cash method, ABC Corp.'s net income for April is $5,000 ($20,000 cash revenue less $15,000 cash expenses). But that $5,000 of net income grossly under-represents the volume of activity the company had during the month. The figures could be just as wildly inaccurate if the company didn't pay any of its expenses and had cash sales of $30,000 — or for any other scenario involving using cash changing hands as a criteria for recording net income.

Some small businesses use the cash method because they have little activity in the way of accounts receivable or payable. But the vast majority of businesses use the accrual basis, which I explain next.

The accrual basis

Using the accrual method of accounting, you record revenue when it is earned and realizable, and you record expenses when they are incurred regardless of whether they have been paid. Wondering what the criteria are for revenue to be *earned* and *realizable?* The earned criterion is satisfied when the vendor satisfactorily performs on its contract with the customer. *Realizable* means that there is an actual expectation of collecting the money for the job from the customer.

The accrual method takes cash out of the equation, because money changing hands doesn't determine whether you recognize a transaction. As a result, a company using the accrual method will have an *accounts receivable,* which shows how much money customers owe to the business, and an *accounts payable,* which shows all the money a company owes to its vendors.

The statement of cash flows, which I discuss briefly at the end of this chapter and explain in detail in Chapter 11, is the financial accountant's bridge between the cash and accrual methods of accounting. That's because the statement of cash flows shows cash sources and uses — an aspect missing from the accrual method. Therefore, it gives the users of the financial statements a chance to look beyond and through the accrual-based numbers.

Sorting through Standards for Other Types of Accounting

While many certified public accountants (CPAs) work in financial accounting, there are other fields in which accountants can pursue employment. In this section I discuss four accounting fields: managerial, not-for-profit, governmental, and international. (For the scoop on living life as a CPA, be sure to check out Chapter 2.) The basic accounting concepts you learn in your financial accounting class remain the same in these fields, but some important differences exist between these four and financial accounting.

For example, if you work in an accounting field other than financial accounting, you have to follow standards different from (or in addition to) those I discuss in Chapter 4. Other organizations besides the financial accounting standard-setters give official guidance on how to prepare financial statements and reports. For example, instead of following GAAP, governmental entities follow procedures set up by the Governmental Accounting Standards Board (GASB).

But wait, I don't want to get ahead of myself! Read on, because in the next few sections, I give you the lowdown on these four types of accounting and note who provides guidance to accountants in these fields.

Managerial accounting

Managerial accountants provide economic and financial information for the internal users of financial statements, such as a company's department heads, shift leaders, and human resources department. For example, human resources personnel use managerial accounting reports to make sure they have the right mix of employees to keep the business a smooth-running operation. Additionally, managerial accounting reports measure quality, performance, and how close each department or business unit comes to meeting its goals. They also measure managerial effectiveness and efficiency — a topic I touch on in Chapter 1.

In order to be useful, managerial reports are issued frequently — sometimes daily. There's no messing around! Other times, accounting staff prepare and distribute the reports the day after a reporting period ends. For internal reporting to management, the rules are similar to those you follow when playing horseshoes — getting close is many times good enough.

Because these reports are used only internally, no regulatory bodies or other outside agencies mandate how the managerial accountant does her job. Instead, managerial accountants look to the Institute of Management Accountants (IMA) for guidance on carrying out their accounting duties. The managerial accountant code of ethics is contained in the *Standards of Ethical Conduct for Management Accountants.* For more information, check out the IMA Web site at www.imanet.org.

Not-for-profit accounting

As I explain in Chapter 2, not-for-profit businesses are run for the public good — not because of any profit motive. These types of organizations include hospitals, schools, religious organizations, and charitable agencies.

The not-for-profit status of a business is determined at the state level. But state approval has no bearing on whether the business can also be regarded as an exempt organization. The important part of that equation is the fact that net income of an exempt organization is not taxed federally. To qualify for exempt status in the United States, an organization fills out an application package that must be approved by the Internal Revenue Service. After the approval process, which can take months, the organization is then exempt from paying the normal taxes levied on a for-profit business by the federal government.

There are two important components to the not-for-profit accountant's job (in addition to the typical accounting duties): preparing budgets and preparing the financial information for grant applications. Budgets are crucial because the organization needs to be able to predict what amount of money has to be obtained through grants, donations, and fundraising efforts in order to serve the organization's purpose.

Wondering if not-for-profits also have to report using accrual basis accounting and FASB and GAAP standards? As I explain in Chapter 4, the FASB Accounting Standards Codification is the source of authoritative GAAP to be applied by all nongovernmental entities. So the answer is yes, a not-for-profit follows FASB and GAAP standards unless an FASB pronouncement specifically excludes not-for-profits.

One difference in keeping the books for profit-seeking versus not-for-profit organizations is that not-for-profits use *fund accounting,* which groups accounting transactions together into funds or accounts that share a similar purpose. This way, the organization has a better idea of what resources it has available for each specific function. Fund accounting is a topic you will *not* have to worry about for your financial accounting class.

If not-for-profit accounting interests you, check out *Nonprofit Bookkeeping & Accounting For Dummies* by Sharon Farris (Wiley) for much more information about this field.

Governmental accounting

Governmental accountants work for city, county, state, and federal government agencies. Their job is similar to the not-for-profit accountant's job because they deal with budgets and there is no profit motive. Budgeting is important because budgets serve as the primary tool in allocating governmental cash sources to urban, suburban, and rural parts of the communities served.

At the city, county, or state level, the cash comes in from sources such as *ad valorem* (property) taxes; funding from the federal government such as for schools, streets, and roads; interdepartmental governmental transfers; fines and forfeitures; sales and use tax; licenses and permits; and municipal bond issuances. Funds are then appropriated to cover costs. The appropriations are either approved or disapproved during the setting of the budget. Finally, disbursements are made throughout the fiscal year for approved budget items.

Governmental accountants also prepare financial statements that are open to the general public. The financial statements must show accountability to citizens while pursuing the goals of efficiency and effectiveness. The financial statements are also used by external users (see Chapter 1) to decide whether to invest in the municipality's bond issuances; see Chapter 8.

The regulatory authority for governmental accountants is the Governmental Accounting Standards Board (GASB). You can find out more information about GASB at www.gasb.org.

International accounting

International accountants work for multinational businesses performing financial and managerial accounting, tax return preparation, and auditing. (Remember that *auditing* is the process of investigating financial information prepared by someone else to see if it is fairly stated.) They should be familiar with the legal regulations and standards of the countries with which their employer conducts business.

International accountants have to deal with foreign currency translations, such as how many U.S. dollars (USD) equal how many euros (EUR). They also manage two special risks:

- ✓ **Expropriation:** The seizure of company assets by the host government
- ✓ **Blocked funds:** When the host government doesn't allow any company funds to be repatriated to the United States

An important organization for international accountants is the International Accounting Standards Board (IASB), whose Web site is www.iasb.org. The IASB is currently working in tandem with the FASB to provide comparability between the accounting standards — in other words, to bring U.S. and international GAAP together. This process is referred to as *harmonization,* and the purpose is to develop a single set of global accounting standards that will provide high-quality, transparent, and comparable financial statement reporting.

International accounting is a fairly advanced accounting topic that is taught in at least six seminar hours. You shouldn't be tested on this subject in your financial accounting class.

Considering the Conceptual Framework of Financial Accounting

Accounting dates back to the Stone Age as a way of figuring out the supply and demand of commerce. Long before we had stores and cash registers, man had to have some way of making sure there was an equitable trade of good for good or good for service. Also, accounting was put to use as far back as the Holy Roman Empire (and probably even earlier) to make sure that all subjects to the empire were paying their assessed taxes. Note I didn't say their *fair* share of taxes, which is always a lively subject for debate! That's a topic of conversation for any federal income tax classes you may decide to take in the future.

As I note in Chapter 4, there wasn't a lot of standard setting of the accounting biz until after the Great Depression of 1929. And it wasn't until the mid-1970s that the Financial Accounting Standards Board (FASB) began the process of spelling out a framework of financial accounting concepts.

The FASB organizes its conceptual framework in what it calls *Statements of Financial Accounting Concepts* or *Concept Statements.* (Accountants use the abbreviation *CONs* to refer to these statements.) Your financial accounting textbook probably mentions these CONs only in passing. However, because you are probably new to the wonderful world of financial accounting, I think these concepts can give you a firm foundation for your financial accounting class. The information that comes next provides general background on why financial accounting standards work the way they do and what they are attempting to accomplish.

The following four concepts — objectives, characteristics, elements, and financial statement measurement — augment the information your financial accounting textbook provides and give you a handy introduction to the financial accounting information I address in the next two parts of this book.

Here, I provide just the condensed version of the four concepts. But I also cite the chapters you can go to for more detailed information on each. Ready to get started? First let's talk about what financial accounting is attempting to accomplish.

The objective of financial reporting

What is the purpose of financial accounting? It's the process of classifying and recording all accounting events taking place during the normal course of a company's business. These events include earning revenue, paying bills, bringing in gains, and incurring losses.

The results of all these events are arranged on the correct financial statement (the balance sheet, income statement, and/or statement of cash flows) and reported to the external users of the financial statements. External users include investors, creditors, banks, and regulatory agencies such as the IRS and the U.S. Securities and Exchange Commission (SEC; see Chapter 4). Want to know more? I discuss this topic in Chapter 1.

Characteristics of accounting information

Besides organizing accounting events into financial statements, how do financial accountants serve the needs of the external users? Well, just like adding salt instead of sugar to a cookie recipe is going to make your end result seriously out of whack, adding the wrong ingredients to your financial statements is going to give your users the equivalent of an inedible cookie.

What sorts of characteristics must be present so you can make sure the financial statements totally serve the needs of your users? The big three are understandability, relevance, and reliability:

- **Understandability:** The information on the financial statement has to be understandable to people not privy to the internal workings of the business. Of course, having the data be understandable is relative. However, basically this characteristic means the financial information must be laid out in a fashion so that users with a reasonable understanding of the business world (and a willingness to do research on specific topics as needed) can ferret out all important accounting facts about the business.

- **Relevance:** This characteristic means that the financial statements give the users enough info so they can form opinions about the final outcome of events that took place in the past and how any present or future events may shake out. Also, the financial statements should give the users enough info so that they can tell if any opinions they made about future events that have now come to fruition were indeed correct.

- **Reliability:** Financial statements aren't worth the paper they're written on unless their users can rely on the fact that the representations made within the financial statements are verifiable, neutral, and materially correct. For example, if the income statement (see Chapter 10) shows $10 million of sales, these sales actually took place and weren't just the best guess of company management (or what company management wants the users to think occurred).

Elements of the financial statements

The preponderance of tested material in your financial accounting class is about the proper preparation of three financial statements: the income statement, balance sheet, and statement of cash flows. Your instructor needs to make sure that you understand which elements are shown on what financial statement and how (meaning the elements have to appear in their proper places). See Chapter 1 for an introduction to the elements of the financial statements.

Financial statement measurements

Communicating with parties interested in the business via the financial statements requires the measurement of all accounting transactions. *Measurement* refers to the fact that every accounting event has to have a cost or a value in order to be recognized on the financial statements. You may be confused about the difference between cost and value. Well, you're not alone. This issue can be thorny even among seasoned financial accountants.

Depending on their nature, accounting transactions may record in different ways. If a transaction records at *historic cost,* it shows how much the company paid in cash or assumed in debt during the transaction. *Net realizable value (NRV)* can also be used, which is the amount of cash a business anticipates receiving from an asset in the normal course of business — after factoring in any related costs. You find all sorts of good information about historic cost and NRV in Chapter 7.

Part III
Spending Quality Time with the Balance Sheet

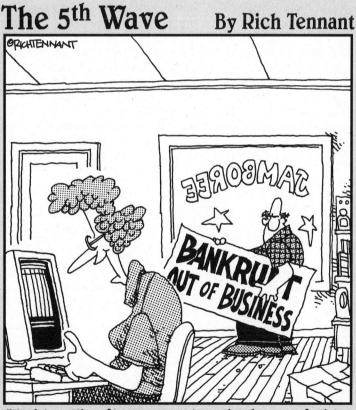

The 5th Wave   By Rich Tennant

"I think I'm finally getting the hang of this accounting system. It's even got a currency conversion function. Want to see how much we lost in rupees?"

In this part . . .

A company's balance sheet contains various asset, liability, and equity accounts. In this part, you learn about all three starting with Chapter 7, which explains common assets a business may have, breaking these assets down between current and noncurrent. You find out about the two categories of intangible assets and how to use amortization to move the cost of intangible assets from the balance sheet to the income statement.

Chapter 8 is all about the claims payable by the company, or debts, which in accountant-speak are *liabilities*. In this chapter, you learn about both current and long-term liabilities. Current liabilities help a business manage its day-to day operations. Businesses use long-term debt obligations, such as mortgages and bonds, to acquire assets. A more advanced financial accounting topic is accounting for bonds, which I cover in enough depth that you'll breeze through this section of your financial accounting class.

Finally, Chapter 9 discusses the equity section of the balance sheet, which shows the combined total of each owner's investment in the business. You learn about corporate equity, represented by stock and additional paid-in capital. I also explain the difference between common, preferred, and treasury stock. And you learn about dividends and how a corporation needs to handle them.

Chapter 7

Assessing the Balance Sheet's Asset Section

*P*art III of this book is all about the financial statement called the *balance sheet,* which reports a company's assets, liabilities (the claims against those assets), and equity. In Chapter 8, I walk you through the liabilities part of the balance sheet, and Chapter 9 is all about the equity part of the equation. This chapter gets the party started by focusing on assets.

Assets are resources a company owns. I like assets almost as much as I like revenue! Businesses have many different types of assets, which are categorized as either current or noncurrent. Current assets (such as checking accounts, accounts receivable, and inventory) are *liquid,* which means they either are cash or can quickly be turned into cash.

Noncurrent assets are not liquid; converting them to cash may take time and/ or result in a loss of cost basis or principal. Examples of noncurrent assets often include *tangible* assets (things you can touch) such as a company's cars, computers, office buildings, or factories. But not every noncurrent asset is tangible. For example, consider a company's patents and trademarks, as well as investments that a business makes in other companies — these are all *intangible* assets. And there's a mysterious asset called *goodwill* that comes into play only during business combinations (a topic I discuss in Chapter 17); it's an intangible asset as well.

Some types of leased equipment are considered assets too, which may seem strange because the company doesn't own them outright. I devote Chapter 19 to accounting for leases.

Current? Noncurrent? Tangible? Intangible? The topic of assets may seem a little overwhelming at first because so many kinds of assets exist. But in this chapter, I give you a straightforward, easy-to-understand tutorial on the ABCs of assets. By the end of it, you'll be more than prepared to tackle the subject in your financial accounting class.

Homing in on Historic Cost

Before I start identifying and explaining typical business assets, I want to explain how the value of most assets normally shows up on the balance sheet. Regardless of their *fair market value,* which is what an unpressured person will pay for the asset in an open marketplace, most assets go on the balance sheet at their original historic cost.

Let me use an example to explain what I mean. Say that a company buys a building for $200,000 in 1999. In 2012, the fair market value of that building is $400,000, but the value of the asset on the balance sheet stays at $200,000. This number is also known as the asset's *book value.* If the asset is subject to depreciation (which I cover in Chapter 12), the historic cost minus the depreciation is known as the asset's *net book value.*

One caveat: You record *marketable securities* — securities that the company purchases to sell in the short term — at their fair market value. I discuss this topic later in the chapter in the "Short-term investments" section.

Learning What Makes an Asset Current

Current assets include cash and any asset that a company anticipates converting to cash within a 12-month period from the date of the balance sheet. On the balance sheet, you should list current assets in order of liquidity. Because cash is the most liquid (it's already cash!), it shows up on the balance sheet first. Other common current assets are short-term investments, accounts receivable, notes receivable, inventory, and prepaid expenses. Here, I cover each type in turn.

Cash

Okay, before we start talking about cash, I want to emphasize that the definition of cash goes beyond paper bills and coinage. Any sort of account that is backed by cash is deemed to be a cash account. For example, when you go to the grocery store and write a check to pay for your groceries, that check is the same as cash. That's because when you sign it, you attest to the fact that there are funds in your checking account allowing this check to immediately clear — that is, funds can be withdrawn upon demand.

Depending on the size of the business, it may organize and manage its revenue and bill paying in one or more types of cash accounts. For example, a retail business probably has a separate operating account and *merchant account* (an account where credit card transactions deposit). A large service business may have a separate operating account and payroll account. Some companies have cash accounts for which they earn interest income.

REMEMBER

You may be wondering why a company complicates its bookkeeping with different bank accounts to pay expenses and accept revenue. In some cases, having different bank accounts creates a safer business environment. For example, having a dedicated payroll account allows payroll disbursing employees to do their job (process payroll paper checks and electronic transfers) while having access to a limited, defined amount of cash.

But when it comes to cash accounts, it's really the Wild West out there in the business world. I've seen small businesses with a bunch of cash accounts — many more than they actually need — and large businesses with only one.

Your financial accounting textbook probably primarily concerns itself with making sure you understand that cash accounts are included in the *current* section of the balance sheet. Don't worry, I provide a full-blown asset section of a balance sheet at the end of this chapter so you can see this fact at work. However, it's also important that you understand the business purpose for different types of cash accounts — so here they are, with brief descriptions:

- ✔ **Operating checking account:** A business usually earmarks a particular checking account, which it calls its *operating* account, to handle business activities such as depositing revenue and paying bills.

- ✔ **Payroll checking account:** Many mid-sized and large companies (and some small ones too!) have a checking account that is used only to pay employees. What the company does is figure up the total dollar amount of checks or transfers going to pay employees and transfer that amount from its operating account to cover the payroll checks.

- ✔ **Merchant account:** If a business allows customers to pay by credit card, it probably has a dedicated merchant account into which the only deposits will be from its *merchant provider:* the company that helps it process customer credit cards. Normally, withdrawals from this account go to the operating account to cover bill-paying withdrawals.

- ✔ **Petty cash account:** Most companies have a cash box to pay for small daily expenses. This account is also known as an *imprest account,* which means it always carries the same balance. By this, I mean that anytime the cash box is checked, it should contain cash or receipts equaling the petty cash fund amount. So if the fund is $300, cash and receipts in the box have to equal $300.

- ✔ **Sweep account:** A sweep account is a way for the company to automatically earn investment income. The way it works is that each evening, any extra cash in the company's operating account is gathered up and transferred (swept) into investment accounts.

Money from many different companies is pooled into a bigger pot, thereby providing the advantage of a higher rate of return. Then as the company needs the money in order to clear checks and withdrawals, the money is swept back into the operating account.

Short-term investments

Short-term investments can be equity (stock) and debt (bond) securities that a company uses to put any idle cash to work making money. (I discuss bonds in Chapter 8 and stocks in Chapter 9.) To be clear: The company is not recording its *own* equity and debt as investments here. Instead, the company is recording stocks and bonds of *other* companies it purchases as investments.

To classify these investments as short-term, the company must be planning to sell them within 12 months of the balance sheet date. Two types of short-term investments your financial accounting textbook covers are trading and available-for-sale. I explain both here and offer examples of how to handle them.

Trading securities

Trading securities are debt and equity securities that a business purchases to sell in the short term to make a profit. You record trading securities on the balance sheet initially at cost. Then, as their value fluctuates, you record them at fair market value with any unrealized gain or loss going to the income statement. *Unrealized* means the gain or loss is on paper only. You won't have realized gain or loss until you actually sell the securities.

For example, let's say your company buys 100 shares of common stock in ABC Corp. for $1,000. To record this transaction, the balance sheet "trading securities" account is increased by $1,000 and cash is decreased for the same amount.

Sadly, at the end of the month after purchase, these 100 shares are now worth only $900. To adjust the current asset section of the balance sheet, you need to reduce "trading securities" by the $100 drop in value. Then you also increase "other losses" on the income statement (see Chapter 10) by $100.

Earlier in the chapter, I explain that historic cost is not used on the balance sheet when you're dealing with marketable securities. In the example I've just offered, you can see that the value of ABC Corp. stock on the balance sheet is reflected at less than historic cost.

Available-for-sale securities

These securities are debit and equity investments that a company opts not to classify as trading securities. The difference is important because unrealized fluctuations in the value of available-for-sale securities do *not* show up on the income statement as gain or loss. Instead, any changes (net of tax) go onto the balance sheet as "accumulated other comprehensive income" (see Chapter 9).

Here's how to handle an available-for-sale transaction: Say that Reeves Corporation buys 2,000 shares of common stock for $5,000, deciding to classify the stock as available-for-sale. At the end of the month, the fair value of the shares is $6,000. Woohoo, an unrealized gain of $1,000!

The company's tax rate is 25 percent, so $250 has to be deducted from the unrealized gain, reducing it to $750 ($1,000 − $250). To record this transaction, you increase the value of the security on the balance sheet by $750 (from $5,000 to $5,750) and increase "accumulated other comprehensive income" by $750.

Beyond the scope of what you'll have to do for your financial accounting course, in real-life financial accounting, the recognition of unrealized gains and losses may have a tax-deferral effect (see Chapter 18).

You won't have to make a judgment call on whether a security is trading or available-for-sale for any homework assignment or test question. This information will be given to you in the narrative for the graded objective (your financial accounting class quizzes, homework assignments, or tests).

Accounts receivable

Accounts receivable (A/R) is the amount of money that customers owe a business for merchandise they purchased from the company or services the company rendered to them. Just about all types of businesses can and probably do have an accounts receivable.

For example, I prepare the financial statements for one of my clients. We review the financial statements together, and I give the client an invoice for $500. A couple weeks later, my client mails me a check for payment in full. In that two-week period between when I drop off the financial statements and receive the payment, that $500 is on my books as an accounts receivable.

Now, it's a sad fact of life that businesses extending credit to their customers almost always have some customers who just won't pay their bills. Under generally accepted accounting principles (GAAP; see Chapter 4), you have to make a valuation adjustment for uncollectible accounts. Figuring the calculation for uncollectible accounts receivable is a popular financial accounting test question. To make sure you are fully prepared, I want to show you how to account for bad debt.

GAAP require that businesses extending credit to their customers estimate uncollectible accounts. Companies use a few different methods to do so, usually based on their past experiences with bad debt.

For example, a company in business for five years has found during this period of time that 2 percent of all credit sales will be uncollectible. If nothing in the current period causes the company to question the correctness of this percentage, it will use the percentage to estimate its uncollectible accounts in the current period.

Say that sales on account are $50,000. Using the 2 percent figure, the estimate for uncollectible accounts is $1,000 ($50,000 × .02). The journal entry (see Chapter 5) to record this amount is made to debit "bad debt expense," an income statement account (see Chapter 10), and to credit "allowance for uncollectible accounts," a balance sheet contra-asset account, for $1,000 each.

A *contra account* carries a balance opposite to the account's normal balance. Because the normal balance for an asset is a debit, the normal balance for a contra-asset account like "allowance for uncollectible accounts" is a credit. "Allowance for uncollectible accounts" is also known as an accounts receivable *valuation account,* which is an offset against the main account. That's because while the A/R account itself is carried at the actual amount that the customers owe, the allowance contra-asset account serves to reduce A/R to the amount estimated to be collected, or what is called *net receivables.*

Until the company is reasonably sure that a customer on account won't cough up the cash, the journal entry is just an estimate not tied to any particular customer.

When you determine that a particular customer's account is uncollectible (maybe the person died and left no estate or a customer closed up shop), your next step is to remove the amount from both "allowance for uncollectible accounts" and the customer accounts receivable balance. After all, there is no longer a mystery — you know the customer won't be paying.

For example, Newbury Supplies owes you $1,000. You send it a past-due notice that the post office returns as undeliverable with no forwarding address. After following up, you have no success at locating Newbury. You must make a journal entry to debit "allowance for uncollectible accounts" for $1,000 and credit "A/R–Newbury Supplies" for $1,000.

Now, what if the owner of Newbury Supplies out of the blue sends you a check for the $1,000 after you have written off the balance due? You need to get the receivable back on the books by debiting A/R and crediting revenue. Then you record the payment by debiting cash and crediting A/R.

Notes receivable

A *note receivable* is a short-term debt that someone owes you, meaning it comes due within 12 months of the balance sheet date. Your financial accounting textbook references the fact that in many cases this current asset arises from a *trade receivable:* money your customer owes to you for the purchase of goods or services you rendered. This situation can arise if the customer has cash flow problems preventing it from paying for its purchases. The customer goes to its vendor and asks for extended terms in the form of a formal written document that replaces the less formal agreement to pay for the goods or services per the terms of the invoice.

A note receivable has three major components:

- ✔ **Principal:** The amount owed to the company by the debtor.
- ✔ **Rate:** The amount of interest the debtor pays on the principal. It's always stated as an annual rate even if the note is for a period shorter than one year.
- ✔ **Time:** The period in which the debtor has to pay back the note.

If you have a test or assignment question asking how to convert an accounts receivable to a note receivable, you can breathe a sigh of relief because it's a simple journal entry (see Chapter 5). You increase (debit) notes receivable and decrease (credit) the customer's accounts receivable.

A note receivable reflects in the current asset part of the balance sheet only for the debt you anticipate will be paid back within 12 months of the balance sheet date. Any portion of the note receivable extending past that 12-month period gets put in the long-term asset section of the balance sheet.

Inventory

For your financial accounting class, you need to have a handle on two different types of inventory. The first is *retail inventory,* which is merchandise available for sale in stores and shops. The second is *product inventory* used by manufacturers, which includes direct materials, work in process, and finished goods.

I devote an entire chapter to inventory — Chapter 13. Here, I give you just brief descriptions and examples of inventory terms.

Retail (or merchandise) inventory

Accounting for retail inventory is easier than accounting for manufacturing inventory because a merchandising company, such as a retail store, has only one class of inventory to keep track of: goods the business purchases from various manufacturers for resale.

Here's an example of how a retailer handles an inventory purchase: The associate in charge of lawn mower inventory at a major home improvement store notices and informs the department manager that the department is running low on a certain type of mower. The manager follows the department store's purchasing process, and the end result is that the department receives a shipment of mowers from its vendor.

This transaction is a purchase (cost), but it's not an expense until the store sells the mowers. So the business records the entire shipment of mowers on the balance sheet as an addition to both inventory (see Chapter 13) and accounts payable (see Chapter 8). I use *accounts payable* instead of *cash* because the department store has payment terms with this vendor, and money has yet to change hands during this transaction.

Manufacturing inventory

Because a manufacturing company doesn't simply buy finished goods for resale to customers, it has a more complicated inventory with three major components:

- ✔ **Direct material inventory:** Also known as *raw materials,* this inventory reflects all materials the company owns that it will use to make a product. For example, for the lawn mower manufacturer this includes the steel to form the body, leather or fabric for the seat, and all the other gizmos and parts that make the mower work. In essence, any materials that you can directly trace back to making the mower are direct material inventory.

- ✔ **Work-in-process inventory:** At any point in time during the manufacturing process, the company probably has items that are in the process of being made but are not yet complete, which is *work-in-process*. With a lawn mower manufacturer, this category includes any mowers that aren't completely put together and ready to give a lawn a haircut at the end of the financial period. The company values its work-in-process inventory based on how far each mower has been processed.

✔ **Finished goods:** These are costs you associate with goods that are completely ready for sale to customers but have not yet been sold. For the lawn mower manufacturer, this category consists of mowers not yet sold to retail home improvement shops.

Companies can use many different methods to place a dollar value on ending inventory. I discuss everything you need to know on this topic for your financial accounting class in Chapter 13.

Prepaid expenses

Rounding out the discussion of current assets are *prepaid expenses,* which are expenses the business pays before they are due. Many companies pay a year's worth of business insurance at once. They may also pay rent and interest expense on loans in advance.

For example, the company pays an invoice for $1,200 that covers 12 months of car insurance for the company vehicle. You originally book this amount as an increase to prepaid expense. Then, as each month goes by, you move the portion of the insurance the company has used off the balance sheet onto the income statement by debiting insurance expense for $100 ($1,200/12 months) and crediting prepaid expense for the same amount.

Okay, you now have enough info to ace any test questions about the current asset section of the balance sheet. It's time to move on to noncurrent assets.

Keeping Track of Noncurrent (Long-Term) Assets

You classify an asset as *noncurrent* or *long-term* if the asset will mature or be used up more than 12 months after the date of the balance sheet. For example, any part of a note receivable that the company expects to receive after the 12-month cutoff date is classified as noncurrent. Natural resources such as coal, oil, and timber are also noncurrent assets. So are mineral deposits, like (two of my favorite subjects) gold and diamonds.

In this section, I focus on the most common types of noncurrent assets you'll encounter both in your financial accounting textbook and in the real world. I start with tangible assets and then discuss intangibles.

Meeting the tangibles: Property, plant, and equipment (PP&E)

In this section, I introduce you to a company's tangible assets. *Tangible* assets, also called *fixed* assets, include "property, plant, and equipment" (PP&E) — a category that includes land, buildings, equipment, furniture, and fixtures.

I devote an entire chapter to PP&E's related account, depreciation. *Depreciation* is the way the cost of using the PP&E is moved from the balance sheet to the income statement (see Chapter 10). To get the complete lowdown on depreciation, check out Chapter 12.

Land

Land, also called *real property,* is the earth on which the company's office buildings or manufacturing facilities sit. After all, you're not George Jetson; these building can't just float in the air! The cost of the land plus any improvements the company has to make to the land to use it for business operations reflect on the balance sheet at historic cost.

Four types of costs relate to the purchase of land:

- ✔ **Contract price:** The purchase price for the land.

- ✔ **Closing costs:** Expenses to exchange the title of the land from buyer to seller. These costs include real estate broker commissions, legal fees, and title insurance.

- ✔ **Survey costs:** Costs for a land surveyor to give you a professional opinion as to where the boundaries of the property lie.

- ✔ **Land improvements:** Expenses the company incurs to get the land ready for use, which include the cost of clearing the land if necessary to build the manufacturing plant or adding sidewalks and fences to an existing property.

Because it's not considered to be "used up" the way that other PP&E is, land is never depreciated.

If a company buys land as an investment, you record it in the investment section of the balance sheet rather than PP&E. Wondering if it would go in the current or long-term section? Well, that classification depends on how long the company plans on owning the land. If it anticipates selling the land within 12 months of the balance sheet date, it's a current asset. Otherwise, record it as long-term.

Building

This category covers the company-owned structures in which the company conducts business operations. It includes office buildings, manufacturing facilities, and retail shops. If the business owns off-site storage facilities or warehouses, these assets go in the building category too. Like land, buildings are also known as *real property* assets.

Unlike land, buildings are depreciable (see Chapter 12). Also, when preparing a balance sheet for your financial accounting class, make sure you list land and buildings separately because doing so is a GAAP requirement.

You may be wondering how to figure out the cost of land versus building. Luckily, you won't have to do this calculation for your financial accounting class. Any homework assignment or test question will provide that info.

In real-life accounting, financial accountants use appraisals to get these values. Or, if the business purchases a piece of raw land and constructs its own building, calculating the cost of each is simple because you have the purchase agreement for the land and all related expenses to erect the building already separated out for you.

Equipment

This category is quite broad, encompassing any equipment a company uses to make the products it sells to customers. For example, a manufacturing company such as a bread baker includes all the mixers, ovens, and packaging machines it uses to turn the yeast and flour into loaves of bread ready to ship to grocery stores.

A merchandising company (which doesn't make any products) includes in this category any office computer equipment it owns, plus forklifts or mechanized ladders to move inventory around. Retail shops also usually categorize their cash registers as equipment.

Furniture and fixtures

Last up in our parade of PP&E are furniture and fixtures, which include desks, chairs, and filing cabinets. Add to these three very common examples any other furniture items you see in an office setting: credenzas, conference tables, area rugs — the list goes on and on.

A merchandiser has fixtures to present wares for sale, such as glass display cases and floor or wall display racks. Mannequins are also considered fixtures and, depending on their quality, can be a very high dollar item on the balance sheet.

If the company leases any of its PP&E, the leased items may not be considered company property and do not show up in the PP&E section of the balance sheet. However, if the lease has aspects of ownership that pass the GAAP sniff test, you do record the leased asset on the balance sheet. This subject is complicated, so to see what leased assets GAAP consider to be owned, check out Chapter 19.

Investigating intangible assets

The big difference between tangible and intangible assets is that *intangible assets* (usually) don't have a physical presence. When you really dig into the subject, you'll probably find intangibles a lot more interesting than steel desks and swivel chairs.

Identifying the two types of intangibles

There are two types of intangible assets. The first type, which is the most common, includes long-lived assets such as leasehold improvements, patents, trademarks, and copyrights:

- ✓ **Leasehold improvements:** When a company leases its business location and updates the rental space with features the company can't take with it at the end of the lease, the assets are called *leasehold improvements*.

  Leasehold improvements are intangible assets, but sometimes they represent tangible improvements to a leased property, such as building out leased office space (by carving out cubicle areas, for example). In this situation, balance sheets prepared per GAAP lump them with PP&E rather than with the nonphysical intangibles such as patents. Confused? Check out Figure 7-1 at the end of this chapter to see what I mean.

- ✓ **Patents:** Patents provide licensing for inventions or other unique processes and designs. Items that can be protected by patents run the gamut from pharmaceuticals to automobile circuitry to unique jewelry designs.

- ✓ **Copyrights:** Securing a copyright means that someone can't use the company's printed work (such as books or articles) or recorded work (such as musical scores or movies) without permission. Any original piece of work is automatically copyrighted.

- ✓ **Trademarks:** These are unique signs, symbols, or names the company can use to create a brand or image. When a company has a trademarked name or symbol, no other company can use it. (There is only one Xerox, for example.)

The second category of intangibles, *goodwill,* occurs only when one business purchases another for a price greater than the fair market value of the net assets acquired during the sale. (*Net assets* are total assets less total liabilities.) For example, ABC Corp. buys XYZ Corp. for $250,000. XYZ's net assets are $175,000. ABC Corp. acquires $75,000 ($250,000 – $175,000) of goodwill in the transaction. You can find out much more about the somewhat complex topic of business combinations and goodwill in Chapter 17.

Writing intangibles off with amortization

Amortization mimics depreciation (see Chapter 12) because you use it to move the cost of intangible assets from the balance sheet to the income statement. Most intangibles are amortized on a straight-line basis using their expected useful life. For example, the U.S. government grants patent protection for a period of 20 years. Unless the patent has become obsolete, 20 years would probably be the expected useful life the business uses for its patent amortization.

What about the balance sheet cost of intangibles? Leasehold improvements are easy: The amount is the actual cost for any improvements the company makes. The useful life for leasehold improvements is usually the term of the underlying lease. Patents, trademarks, and copyrights the business buys are treated similarly: You have the cost of purchase as a basis for the amount you amortize.

However, the cost of developing an intangible asset in-house can be minimal. For example, maybe some employees were just spit-balling in a meeting and came up with a catch phrase that eventually became very valuable because of the success of the product associated with the phrase. In this case, the company may assign the trademark a value of $1 and explain it in the notes to the financial statements (see Chapter 15).

The second category of intangibles, goodwill, is never amortized. Financial accountants test goodwill yearly for *impairment,* which means they see if there is any worthless goodwill needing to be written off (removed) from the balance sheet. This is a complicated accounting topic that you will not cover in your financial accounting class.

Studying the Asset Section of the Balance Sheet

To wrap up this chapter, I show you in Figure 7-1 what the asset section of the balance sheet looks like. Liabilities and equity are each merely a line item in Figure 7-1. Check out Chapter 8 to see the liability section and Chapter 9 to see the equity section of a balance sheet fully developed.

Assets:		
Current assets		
Cash		3,560
Short-term investments		1,600
Accounts receivable	10,000	
less allowance for uncollectible accounts (3,200)		6,800
Notes receivable - current		3,500
Inventory		4,300
Prepaid expenses		500
Total current assets		20,260
Long-term assets		
Notes receivable - long-term		1,000
Property, plant and equipment:		
Land	15,000	
Building	65,000	
Machinery and equipment	23,400	
Furniture and fixtures	2,500	
Capital leases	6,000	
Leasehold improvements	8,000	
less accumulated depreciation and amortization	(67,245)	
Total property, plant and equipment		52,655
Intangible assets (shown net of amortization)		
Patents		830
Trademarks		500
Total intangible assets		1,330
Total assets		75,245
Total liabilities and equity		75,245

Figure 7-1:
The asset section of a balance sheet.

Current assets are always shown first, in order of liquidity, followed by any long-term assets. Your financial accounting textbook probably discusses only one long-term asset: notes receivable (which are those notes due more than 12 months past the balance sheet date).

The company's PP&E lists next with the accumulated adjustment to value shown as a separate line item. Finally, any nonphysical intangibles are shown — usually *net of amortization,* which means that amortization is subtracted before listing the intangibles' values on the balance sheet.

Chapter 8

Digging for Debt in the Liabilities Section

. . . .

In This Chapter

▶ Discovering how a company raises cash

▶ Identifying current liabilities

▶ Learning about long-term debt

▶ Knowing when loss contingencies are reportable

▶ Accounting for bonds

. . . .

Part III of this book is all about the financial statement called the balance sheet, which reports a company's assets and the claims against those assets. In Chapter 7, I walk you through the assets part of the equation. This chapter is all about the claims, or debts, which in accountant-speak are *liabilities*.

Nobody likes debt, but it's often an inevitable part of a company keeping its doors open for business. In this chapter, I cover both current and long-term debt. You find out what types of current liabilities help a business manage its day-to-day operations, and you learn about long-term debt obligations that businesses use to acquire assets. I discuss basic long-term debt such as mortgages and notes payable, and I also discuss bonds, focusing on the facets of this complicated topic that you need to know for your financial accounting homework assignments and tests.

A third type of liability — loss contingencies — also gets some space in this chapter. These liabilities are not always included in financial accounting reports, so I give you the lowdown on when and how to include them.

Seeing How Businesses Account for Liabilities

Liabilities are claims against the company by other businesses or its employees. Examples include:

- ✓ **Accounts payable:** Money a company owes to it vendors for services and products it has purchased.

- ✓ **Unearned revenues:** Money received from clients that pay the business for goods or services they haven't yet received — like deposits.

- ✓ **Salaries payable:** Wages the company owes to employees.

Generally accepted accounting principles (GAAP, which I discuss in Chapter 4) dictate that when you prepare the liability section of the balance sheet, any claims against the company have to be broken out between *current* and *long-term* obligations. The dividing line between the two is the one-year mark: All liabilities that are due within one year of the date of the financial statements are considered current. All others are considered long-term.

Here's a detail that accounting textbooks mention only briefly and you likely won't be tested on until later in your accounting studies: If a company anticipates paying a current liability with a long-term asset (see Chapter 7), or if it expects to refinance a current liability, that liability is treated as if it's long-term.

In Chapter 5, I introduce the fundamental accounting equation, which is this:

Assets = Liabilities + Owners' equity

Based on the order of elements in this equation, liabilities show up on the balance sheet after total assets but before equity accounts. Current liabilities are shown first, followed by long-term. (Current and long-term assets receive similar treatment; see Chapter 7.)

Using the accrual method of accounting (which I explain in Chapter 6), all revenue must be matched with all expenses incurred during the production of that revenue. So if a company incurs costs but money doesn't change hands, a liability shows up on the balance sheet to reflect the amount that eventually has to be paid. For example, the company may make a purchase from a vendor without actually paying for it yet; that item appears in accounts payable, which is a current liability.

Figure 8-1 shows a very simple liability section of the balance sheet, with all asset and equity accounts consolidated to a single line item each (the two shaded lines). Check out Chapter 3 for a more formal presentation of all sections of the balance sheet. Also, please note that I opt to show each account's chart of account number too. (See Chapter 5 for more info about the chart of accounts.) A formal balance sheet usually won't include this detail.

Total Assets		75,245.00
Liabilities & Equity		
Liabilities		
Current Liabilities		
	2010 - Accounts Payable	34,202.62
	2210 - Current maturities of long-term debt	1,365.50
	2215 - Accrued salaries and wages	145.00
	2220 - State tax payable	668.00
	2225 - Advances from customers	500.00
	2230 - Payroll taxes witheld and accrued	2,000.00
	2240 - Accrued expenses	85.00
Total Current Liabilities		38,966.12
Long-term Liabilities		
	2710 - Note payable	20,000.00
Total Long-term Liabilities		20,000.00
Total Liabilities		58,966.12
Total Equity		16,278.88
Total Liabilities & Equity		75,245.00

Figure 8-1:
The liability section of a balance sheet.

Keeping Current Liabilities under Control

In this section, I cover just about every current liability your financial accounting textbook discusses. So by the end of this section you'll be a pro! To make the tie-in to your textbook, I even throw in some journal entries so you can see how the transactions get into the original books of entry (see Chapter 5).

But before you start, I want to make sure you understand why it's so important to break out current from long-term liabilities. GAAP require the division so the user of the financial statements can easily glean the information necessary to compute a company's liquidity and solvency figures such as *working capital,* which is current assets minus current liabilities, or the *current ratio,* which is current assets divided by current liabilities. (A reminder: Users of financial reports may be investors, banks, or anyone else with an interest in the company's financial health; see Chapter 1.)

These financial ratios and tools (which I spell out in Chapter 14) give the user specific criteria for deciding how well the company is performing. For example, a bank thinking about loaning a business money wants to gauge the expectation of being paid back on time. Working capital is very helpful in that arena.

For this reason, it's rarely okay to net current assets with current liabilities under GAAP. To do so would eliminate the ability to use any sort of ratio analysis involving current asset or liability accounts. For example, if you purchase inventory on account, both the inventory and accounts payable accounts increase.

Accounts payable

Accounts payable includes money a company owes it vendors for services and products that it has purchased in the normal course of business and anticipates paying back in the short term. For example, the company purchases inventory from a manufacturer or office supplies from a local supply retail shop. The transaction originally goes in the *purchases journal,* which shows purchases on account, with a debit going to whatever cost or expense account is most applicable and a credit going to accounts payable.

Per GAAP, accounts payable (A/P) is always assumed to be a current liability. However, a transaction originally entered as A/P could eventually be reclassified as a long-term debt. This change might happen if the company couldn't pay the vendor and the vendor agreed to convert the short-term A/P to a long-term *note,* which is a formal document showing an amount owed and a mutually acceptable interest rate and payback period spanning more than a year.

Note that the terms *accounts payable* and *trade payables* are often used synonymously. But technically, *trade payables* generally refer to vendors from which a company buys business supplies and *direct materials:* items it uses to manufacture products for sale (see Chapter 10). Accounts payable include all other short-term vendors. Your financial accounting textbook may include both categories simply as *accounts payable.*

Many vendors selling on credit give a discount to customers who pay their accounts payable early. For example, the terms of the purchase may call for full payment in 30 days but a discount of 2 percent if the customer pays the bill within 10 days. Your financial accounting textbook refers to this type of arrangement as *2/10 net 30.* If the company got a 1 percent discount for paying in 15 days with the total amount due in 45 days, it looks like this: 1/15 net 45.

Figure 8-2 walks you through the debiting and crediting for $1,000 of inventory purchased on account with discount terms of 2/10 net 30 and the subsequent payment. Keep in mind that the words *debit* and *credit* don't show up in journal entries in practice. I show them here just to emphasize which is a debit and which is a credit.

1.   *To record May 21, 2012 purchase*

Debit Inventory   1000

    Credit Accounts Payable   1000

Figure 8-2:
Inventory
purchase
on account
and pay-
ment within
discount
period.

2.   *To record June 1, 2012 payment*

Debit Accounts Payable   1000

    Credit Cash   980
    Credit Purchase Discounts   20

Payroll and taxes

The nature of the beast is that most companies *accrue* payroll and related payroll taxes, which means the company owes them but has not yet paid them. This concept is easy to understand if you think about the way you've been paid by an employer in the past.

Most companies have a built-in lag time between when employees earn their wages and when the paychecks are cut. For example, Penway Manufacturing pays its employees on the 1st and 15th of every month with 15 days of wages in arrears. This means that when the employees get their paychecks on July 15, the paychecks compensate work they did from June 16 through June 30.

To match expenses to revenue when preparing financial statements for the one-month period ending June 30, the gross wages earned but not yet paid as of June 30 have to be added to the balance sheet as a current liability.

Not only that, but you also have to account for any payroll taxes or benefits that will be deducted from the employee's paycheck when the check is finally cut. Here are examples of employee payroll-related accruals:

✔ **Federal Insurance Contributions Act (FICA):** The Social Security portion of this tax provides old age, survivor, and disability benefits. The rate is 6.2 percent on wages up to a certain wage base dollar amount. The Medicare portion provides health benefits and has no base wage limit. Medicare tax is 1.45 percent. Together, the rate is 7.65 percent.

✔ **Federal withholding tax:** The company calculates this tax using the marital status and exemptions the employee lists on the form W-4.

✔ **State and local withholding tax:** The business also deducts any tax for state or local jurisdictions that mandate tax collection.

✔ **Healthcare or other insurance premiums:** An employer may pay only a portion of the health insurance premium for an employee and his family. The additional amount for health and other insurance, such as life insurance, is a deduction as well if the employee authorizes it.

✔ **401(k) and other retirement deductions:** Many employers have plans that allow employees to make benefit deductions on pre-tax dollars. *Pre-tax* means the deduction is made before the employee is assessed federal withholding tax or FICA. So if your gross wage is $500 and you have $100 in pre-tax deductions, you pay tax on $400.

The employer business also has payroll tax expense based on the employees' gross wages. These items are recorded as short-term liabilities as well:

✔ **FICA:** The employer is obligated to match each employee's contribution dollar for dollar.

✔ **State Unemployment Tax Act (SUTA):** This tax percentage varies based on employers' unemployment claim experience, as well as each state's rates. The tax is assessed on the first $7,000 of wages each year.

✔ **Federal Unemployment Tax Act (FUTA):** The employer pays FUTA tax at 6.2 percent of the first $7,000 of wages each year. In times of catastrophic unemployment, FUTA kicks in to pay unemployment claims after SUTA is exhausted.

✔ **Employer benefits:** Additionally, the employer has an expense for the company portion of healthcare, 401(k) match, and any other benefit programs provided to employees.

So that you can better understand this class of current liabilities, here's a payroll and payroll tax accrual question that's similar to what you'll find in your financial accounting textbook:

Penway Manufacturing owes its employees gross wages of $50,000. Employee FICA tax on this amount is $3,825, and employees have opted to have income tax withholdings of $3,680. They also have health insurance for $1,000 and retirement contributions for $2,500 withheld from their paychecks. Total deductions are $11,005. Net payroll is the difference between the gross of $50,000 and the deductions of $11,005, which equals $38,995.

After a company runs payroll, how does it record gross wages, tax, and other deductions made from the employees' checks as short-term liabilities? Additionally, how does it record the related payroll tax expense? Given in this example is the fact that federal unemployment tax totals $80 and state unemployment tax totals $405. The employer has no employer benefit expense.

Wondering how to answer this question via journal entries? I show you how in Figure 8-3.

Wages Expense	50,000.00	
Wages Payable (net)		38,995.00
FICA Tax Witheld (employee) Payable		3,825.00
Income Taxes Witheld Payable		3,680.00
Health Insurance Payable		1,000.00
Retirement Contributions Payable		2,500.00

handwritten: 2321

handwritten: 50000

To record accrued payroll

Payroll Tax Expense	4,310.00	
FICA Tax Witheld (employer match) Payable		3,825.00
Federal Unemployment Taxes Payable		80.00
State Unemployment Taxes Payable		405.00

Figure 8-3: Journal entry to record accrued payroll and taxes.

To record accrued payroll taxes

Unearned revenue

This current liability occurs when a company receives payment for goods or services rendered before it has actually provided the goods or services. Because the business has an obligation to fulfill its end of the contract, the unearned revenue is a current liability until the company completes its end of the transaction.

To record revenue, it has to be earned and realizable. Because the customer has already paid, the *realizable* part is a wrap. However, in this situation, the revenue is not yet earned.

When I teach this topic, I give my class the example of magazine subscriptions. Let's say you pay $120 for an annual subscription of your favorite magazine, consisting of 12 issues. Until the magazine publisher mails the twelfth issue to you, your payment is not 100 percent earned revenue for the publisher.

The way this works on the publisher's end is that it debits cash and credits unearned revenue for your payment of $120. Then each month after it mails you an issue, it records earning that portion by debiting unearned revenue and crediting gross sales for $10 ($120/12).

Other short-term liabilities

Other short-term liabilities include items such as loan payments that are payable within 12 months. Current debt can originate as short-term bank loans, or it can be the portion of a long-term debt that is due within the next 12 months. Another type of current liability you'll see in your financial accounting textbook is *estimated warranty,* which reflects how much money a company may have to pay to repair or replace products sold to customers.

Here's more information on short-term bank loans, current maturities of long-term debt, and estimated warranty expense:

- ✔ **Short-term bank loans:** When a company takes out a loan, it doesn't always have to be for an extensive period (such as a 30-year mortgage). A lot of times, a company anticipates getting paid for a job it has performed and just needs a brief influx of cash to pay mandatory expenses such as payroll.

  A good example of this situation is a *working capital loan,* which a bank makes with the expectation the loan will be paid back from collection of accounts receivable. As long as the loan is due in full less than 12 months after the balance sheet date, you classify borrowed funds as current liabilities.

  Short-term debt is important to examine when determining the financial health of a company because it indicates whether a cash flow issue (see Chapter 11) could arise in the future. If the short-term debt is unreasonably high, the company may not have the excess money to make the loan payments.

  A company can also have a *revolving line of credit,* which is a loan with a pre-set limit on how much the company can withdraw at any one time, reflecting as current debt. This sort of current debt is much more flexible than a loan because the company borrows against it only when necessary.

- ✔ **Current maturities of long-term debt:** Say that a company has a mortgage on its land and building spanning 30 years, and it's in the third year of paying off the loan. To properly reflect this mortgage on the balance sheet, the principal amount the company owes in the next 12 months has to record as a current liability. The rest of the mortgage payable is a long-term liability, a subject I discuss in the next section.

You can use an *amortization schedule,* which shows how much of each mortgage payment goes to principal versus interest, to figure out the current portion of the long-term debt.

✔ **Estimated warranty liability:** Warranties on products may be an assumed part of the purchase price or something the purchaser elects to buy — usually at the time of purchase. A great example is the guarantee of performance relating to the purchase of a computer from an electronics retail shop. For example, the computer comes with a six-month warranty from the manufacturer covering numerous performance and repair issues. Assume that if the computer breaks down within the six-month warranty period, the purchaser can send it back to be fixed, free of charge. The company has to take two steps in this situation to ensure its financial reports are complete:

- Provide a disclosure about the warranty in a footnote to its financial statements (see Chapter 15)

- Calculate and book an estimate of how much it costs the company to fulfill the terms of the warranty

A popular way to estimate warranty expense is to use a percentage of sales. This percentage is normally figured historically. If in the past the company has incurred an actual warranty expense of 4 percent, that same percent should be the current year's estimate until the facts change.

Warranty liability is a frequent midterm or final exam question, so here's an example to consider: How would you book the journal entries (see Chapter 5) related to the following events?

Penway Manufacturing makes computers. In the most recent month of operations, September, it sold $500,000 worth of computers. Historical warranty expense is 4 percent of sales. So the estimated warranty liability is $20,000 ($500,000 multiplied by 4 percent).

Also, during September, Penway has actual expenses of $2,000 for labor and $3,000 (total of $5,000) for materials to fulfill warranty claims. Keep in mind that the $5,000 includes warranty costs not only for September purchases but also for purchases going back six months.

Ready to see how to journalize these transactions? Figure 8-4 gives you the lowdown on the entry to book the estimate and record actual warranty expense.

Warranty Expense	20,000.00	
Estimated Warranty Liability		20,000.00

To record estimated warranty expense for September

Figure 8-4:
Recording
accrued
and actual
warranty
expense.

Estimated Warranty Liability	5,000.00	
Labor Expense		2,000.00
Materials Expense		3,000.00

To record actual warranty cost for September

Planning for Long-Term Obligations

If you own a car you financed, you're probably all too familiar with *long-term debt:* loans that won't be paid off by the end of the next 12-month period. Companies have long-term debt, too. While a company usually uses current debt as a vehicle to meet short-term obligations like payroll, it may incur long-term debt for the financing of company assets.

Financing asset purchases with debt versus equity

Corporations raise money to purchase assets in one of two ways: debt or equity. *Debt* means the company borrows money with an obligation to pay the borrowed funds back. *Equity* means the company sells shares of its own stock to investors.

What makes equity investing appealing is that the company is not under any obligation to buy back the shares of stock from the investors. However, it also means that more voices are heard regarding how the business is run, especially in closely held companies — something that stockholders who also handle the day-to-day operations may not be all that eager to put up with.

Oddly enough, debt can end up making a company money. This situation is called *financial leverage,* and it takes place when the borrowed

money is expected to earn a higher return than the cost of interest payable on the debt.

Additionally, interest expense on debt is a tax deduction while dividends payable to investors is not. Based on many factors combining advanced accounting and finance, the company using debt to finance its asset purchases could also end up in a better position due to the decrease in taxes payable.

Here's an example: Let's say you take out a student loan at 2 percent interest to pay for your college courses. Your Aunt Dottie wants to lend a helping hand and gives you a gift of $2,000 to apply toward your tuition. Because that gift frees up $2,000 of your student loan, you decide to invest these loan dollars in a financial vehicle paying 3 percent. You just made 1 percent using someone else's money. Woohoo!

Managing long-term debt

If the company needs to raise cash and decides to do so by accumulating debt, the most common types are mortgages, notes payable, capitalized leases, and bonds. Following is your financial accounting guide to the first three of these categories of long-term debt. Bonds are a much more complicated subject, and I devote the upcoming "Accounting for Bond Issuances" section to them.

Any type of debt instrument between a lender and a borrower specifies *principal* (the amount borrowed), *rate* (how much interest the company pays to borrow the money), and *time* (the length of the note). So any repayment of the debt is broken out between principal and interest according to the terms of the debt instrument.

Mortgages

Mortgages are used to finance the purchase of real property assets (see Chapter 13). The property *collateralizes* the mortgage, which means the property is held as security on the mortgage. If the company defaults on the mortgage, the lending institution seizes the property and sells it in an attempt to pay off the loan.

Mortgages require a formal closing procedure that's typically done at the offices of a *title company:* an independent middleman that coordinates the rights and obligations during the sale for the buyer, seller, and mortgage company. Much like during the purchase of a personal residence, reams of paperwork (such as the mortgage document and the transfer of the property's title) are passed back and forth among the buyer, seller, and closing agent for approval and signature.

Notes payable

Notes payable are formal written documents that spell out how money is being borrowed. In the earlier section "Other short-term liabilities," I explain that the part of a note payable that's going to be paid off within the 12 months following the financial report release is classified as short-term debt. The remainder of the note is considered a long-term debt.

Capitalized leases

Another type of long-term debt involves *capitalized leases.* A company doesn't always buy its fixed assets (see Chapter 7); sometimes it leases them. Doing so makes sense for any fixed asset that needs to be frequently replaced. For example, leasing computers makes sense for businesses that need to stay current with computer processing technology.

Capital leases have characteristics of ownership, which means the cost of the leased capital asset goes on the balance sheet as a depreciable asset. I offer a full discussion of accounting for leases in Chapter 19.

Anticipating contingent liabilities

A *contingent liability* is a noncurrent liability that exists when a company has an existing circumstance as of the date of the financial statements that may cause a future loss depending on events that have not yet happened (and indeed may never happen). Here are two examples of common contingent liabilities:

- **Pending litigation:** This means the company is actively involved in a lawsuit that is not yet settled.

- **Guarantee of obligations:** This circumstance occurs when a business agrees to step in and satisfy the debt of another company if need be.

You typically record contingent liabilities in the footnotes to the financial statements (see Chapter 15) rather than as an actual part of the financial statements. However, if a loss due to a contingent liability meets two criteria, it should be accrued and reported in the company's financial statements. Here are the two criteria:

- The chance of the loss event happening is *probable,* which means that the future event will likely occur. Consider the guarantee of obligation example: If the debtor business has gone out of business and the owners have disappeared into the night, the lender will probably come after the back-up guarantor to pay off the remaining amount of the loan.

- The amount of the loss can be *reasonably estimated,* which means you can come up with a highly accurate loss dollar amount. Continuing with the guarantee of obligation example, the loss is reasonably estimated because it should be the remaining balance on the loan plus any additional charges tacked on by the lender in accordance with the obligatory note.

If the loss contingency meets these two standards for accrual, the journal entry involves a debit to a relevant loss account (see Chapter 10) and a credit to a liability account. For example, the company could take the debit to "loss on guaranteed debt" and to some sort of noncurrent liability account such as "amount due on guaranteed obligation."

Accounting for Bond Issuances

Well, I saved the best for last! I say that tongue-in-cheek because bonds are a somewhat thorny financial accounting issue. However, if you can get the gist of this section, you'll be a-okay for this topic in your financial accounting class.

Understanding bond basics

Bonds are long-term lending agreements between borrowers and lenders. An example of a bond is when a municipality (such as a city or village) needs to build new roads or a hospital, and it issues bonds to finance the project. Corporations generally issue bonds to raise money for capital expenditures, operations, and acquisitions.

The person who purchases a bond receives interest payments during the bond's term (or for as long as he holds the bond) at the bond's stated interest rate. When the bond *matures* (the term of the bond expires), the company pays the bondholder back the bond's face value.

A bond is either a source of financing or an investment, depending on which side of the transaction you're looking at. The company issuing the bond incurs the long-term liability. The person or company acquiring the bond uses it as an investment; for a business, this investment is an asset (see Chapter 7).

A company can issue bonds to sell at:

- ✔ **Face value** (also known as *par value*): The principal amount printed on the bond
- ✔ A **discount:** Less than face value
- ✔ A **premium:** More than face value

Usually face value is set in denominations of $1,000. In the sections that follow, I explain what it means to the accountant when the company sells at face value, at a premium, or at a discount.

A bond with a face value and market value of $1,000 has a bond price of 100 (no percent sign or dollar sign — just 100). Bonds issued at a premium have a bond price of more than 100. Issued at a discount, the bond price is less than 100. Keep reading to find out how discounts and premiums work.

The rate of interest that investors actually earn is known as the *effective yield* or *market rate*. If the bond sells for a premium, the bond market rate is generally lower than the rate stated on the bond. For example, if the face rate of the bond is 10 percent and the market rate is 9 percent, the bond sells at a premium. That's because the investor receives higher interest income on this bond than can be expected when factoring in the conditions of the current bond market; the investor is willing to pay more than face value for the bond.

On the flip side, if a bond sells at a discount, its market rate is higher than the rate stated on the bond. For example, if the face rate of the bond is 10 percent and the market rate is 11 percent, the bond sells at a discount. In this case, the investor is making less interest income than can be expected when factoring in the conditions of the current bond market. So, to offset that disadvantage, the investor pays less than face value for the bond.

Accounting for bonds sold at face value

The easiest type of bond transaction to account for is when the company sells bonds at face value. The journal entry to record bonds a company issues at face value is to debit cash and credit bonds payable. So if the corporation issues bonds for $100,000 with a five-year term, at 10 percent, the journal entry to record the bonds is to debit cash for $100,000 and credit bonds payable for $100,000.

Addressing interest payments

Let's say the terms of the bond call for interest to be paid *semi-annually,* which means every six months. Suppose the bonds I introduce in the previous section are issued on July 1 and the first interest payment is not due until December 31. The interest expense is principal ($100,000) multiplied by rate (10 percent) multiplied by time (1/2 year). So your journal entry on December 31 is to debit bond interest expense for $5,000 and credit cash for $5,000.

Getting and amortizing a premium

When a bond is issued at a *premium,* its market value is more than its face value. To make the concept come alive for you, let's walk through a common example you will see in your financial accounting textbook. How would you handle journal entries for this situation?

> Penway Manufacturing issues bonds with a face value of $500,000 at 102. The term is ten years, and the rate is 10 percent.

"At 102" means the bonds are issued at 102 percent of face value, which means the bonds are issued at a premium.

The journal entry to record this transaction is to debit cash for $510,000 ($500,000 times 1.02). You have two accounts to credit: "bonds payable" for the face amount of $500,000 and "premium on bonds payable" for $10,000, which is the difference between face and cash received at issuance.

The premium of $10,000 has to be amortized for the time the bonds are outstanding. *Amortization* (writing off the premium over time) means that every year, over the life of the bond, you write off a portion of the premium. The term on these bonds is ten years, so using the *straight-line method* (which means you write off the same amount each period), the amount you have to amortize each year is $1,000 ($10,000 premium divided by the 10-year term).

Finally, to book interest payable on these bonds for each year, you credit "bond interest payable" for $50,000 (figured by multiplying the face of $500,000 times the rate of 10 percent). You also debit "premium on bond payable" for $1,000 (see the calculation in the previous paragraph) and "interest expense" for the $49,000 difference.

GAAP prefer the effective interest amortization method when accounting for bonds issued at a discount or premium. However, using the straight-line method is okay when the results of the straight-line versus effective interest method are materially the same. I use straight-line in this chapter because the straight-line method is often the method used for financial accounting test questions and homework assignments.

Reporting a bond discount

Okay, now let's go through an example of a *bond discount,* which means the bonds are issued at less than face value. Here's the situation:

> Penway Manufacturing issues $500,000 face value bonds at 97. The term is ten years.

Remember that "at 97" means 97 percent of face value. The journal entry to record this transaction is to debit cash for $485,000 ($500,000 times .97) and debit "discount on bonds payable" for $15,000, which is the difference between face of $500,000 and cash received of $485,000. You also have to credit "bonds payable" for the face amount of $500,000. The term on these bonds is ten years, so using the straight-line method, the amount amortized for bond discount each year is $1,500 ($15,000 discount divided by the 10-year term).

Then, to book interest payable on these bonds for each year, you credit "bond interest payable" for $50,000 (figured by multiplying the face of $500,000 times the rate of 10 percent) and credit "discount on bonds payable" for $1,500. You then debit "interest expense" for $51,500.

Retiring and converting bonds

All good things must come to an end. At the end of the ten years, Penway Manufacturing has to *retire the bonds* (pay back the investors). At that point, bonds payable and all the other bond accounts (like bond premium or discount) have to be reduced to zero and the investors paid back for the amount of their investment in the bonds.

If the bonds are retired at full term (maturity), your regular amortization journal entries should have already zeroed out the discount or premium on bonds payable.

Also, if the bonds are retired at full term, the bonds' value on the balance sheet should be equal to the face amount, so it's an easy journal entry just debiting bonds payable and crediting cash. For the Penway Manufacturing bonds, the debit and credit amount is $500,000.

If a bond is *callable* — meaning the issuer pays off the bonds before the maturity date — any unamortized bond premium or discount must be *written off* (reduced to zero) as part of the transaction. This action may trigger a gain or loss on the transaction.

Convertible bonds (debt) can be converted into common shares of stock (equity) at the option of the owner of the bonds. The conversion feature makes convertible bonds more attractive to potential investors because it's possible to reap the benefits of the following circumstances:

- ✔ If the amount of dividends regularly being paid to shareholders is higher than the interest earned on the bonds, the investor gets increased cash by converting to stock.

- ✔ The investor also benefits if the value of the company's common stock increases over the value of the bonds.

Chapter 9

Letting Owners Know Where They Stand: The Equity Section

*P*art III of this book is all about the financial statement called the *balance sheet,* which reports a company's assets, the claims against those assets, and owners' equity. In Chapter 7, I walk you through the assets part of the equation. Chapter 8 is all about the liabilities part of the balance sheet.

This chapter gets into the nitty-gritty of how the owners' interest in the business shows up on the balance sheet. *Equity* is the combined total of each and every owner's investment in the business. Another term for equity is *net assets,* which is the difference between assets (resources a company owns) and liabilities (claims against the company).

Depending on how a business is organized, its owners' equity can appear in a few different types of accounts on the balance sheet. The three types of business entities are sole proprietorships, corporations, and *flow-through entities,* such as partnerships. Because your financial accounting textbook primarily talks about corporations, I give that type of business entity the most attention in this chapter. But I also share all you need to know about sole proprietorships and partnerships so you can handle any question your financial accounting professor may throw at you.

Corporate equity consists of stock and additional paid-in capital. In this chapter I explain the differences among common, preferred, and treasury stock. You also learn about dividends and how your audit clients need to handle them. Plus, I discuss noncash dividend transactions: stock dividends and stock splits.

Wait, I'm not finished! You also receive a tutorial on *retained earnings:* the total profit brought in by the business that has not been paid out as dividends. Finally, you bring all this information together by walking through the equity section of a sample balance sheet for a corporation.

Distinguishing Different Types of Business Entities

Forming a business can be easy as pie or extremely complicated depending on the type of business entity being created. Likewise, the owners' equity section of the balance sheet can range from bare-boned to quite elaborate — again depending on the type of business entity.

Following are the ABCs of the three types of business entities and their unique components of equity. First, I give you a brief overview of sole proprietorships and partnership, which likely receive only a cursory mention in your financial accounting textbook. Then I launch into a discussion of all you need to know about the type of business entity you most often encounter in your financial accounting course: the corporation.

Sole proprietorship

Like the name implies, a *sole proprietorship* has one and only one individual owner. This owner can't collectively own the business with anyone else — even with a spouse or another relative or friend. While there can be only one owner, the sole proprietorship can hire as many employees as it needs.

Forming a sole proprietorship is a snap. Most states don't require a formal filing for a sole proprietorship. Instead, as soon as the company makes its first sale or incurs its first business expense, it is officially in business as a sole proprietorship.

The sole proprietorship has two unique equity accounts: *owner capital* and *owner draw.* The owner capital account shows cash and other contributions (such as equipment) that the owner makes to the business. The owner draw account shows money and other assets the owner takes from the business to convert to personal use.

Figure 9-1 shows the owner's equity section of the sole proprietorship for Penway Manufacturing owned by Mike Penway. Not too complicated, right?

Figure 9-1:
A statement of owner's equity for a sole proprietorship.

Penway Manufacturing
Statement of Owner's Equity
December 31, 2012

Mike Penway, capital January 1, 2012	20,000
Year-to-date net income	15,000
Mike Penway, draw	(5,000)
Mike Penway, capital December 31, 2012	30,000

Partnership

A partnership must have at least two partners holding any percentage of interest in a company. For example, one partner can have 99 percent interest and the other can have 1 percent, or each partner can have 50 percent interest. The division doesn't matter as long as the combined interest adds up to 100 percent. Keep in mind that a partnership is not limited to two partners; there can be as many partners as the partnership wants to have.

In whichever state the partnership wants to operate, the state statutes spell out how to form and operate the partnership. In many states, the partnership has to prepare a written partnership agreement and file paperwork with the Secretary of State. Most states have provisions for both general partnerships and limited partnerships:

✔ With *general partnerships,* all partners are personally liable for any legal action taken against the partnership and for any debts the partnership owes.

✔ Many states also allow for *limited liability partnerships.* If you are a limited partner, your liability for partnership debt is limited to your investment in the partnership. However, as a limited partner, you may not have any say in how the partnership is run.

Partnerships mimic sole proprietorships in that the equity section on the balance sheet has capital and draw accounts. Figure 9-2 shows the partner equity section of the Double-Trouble Partnership, whose partners, Tom and Dottie Double, each own 50 percent of the business.

Double-Trouble Partnership
Statement of Partners' Equity
December 31, 2012

	Tom Double, Capital	Dottie Double, Capital	Total Capital
Partner capital January 1, 2012	10,000	7,000	17,000
Year-to-date net income	12,000	12,000	24,000
Partner draws	(10,000)	(2,000)	(12,000)
Partner capital December 31, 2012	12,000	17,000	29,000

Figure 9-2:
A statement of partners' equity.

The amount of draws and income distributions a partner is allowed to take can be different than that person's partnership interest. So even though you have two equal partners, that doesn't mean they have to take the same draw amount. Hence the differences in beginning and ending partners' capital accounts between partners in Figure 9-2.

Corporate

If a business wants to operate as a corporation, it has to prepare and file articles of incorporation, also known as a *corporate charter,* with the Secretary of State in the state where it wishes to operate. The articles of incorporation cover the basics about the company such as its name and address, the stock it issues (what type and how many shares), and the *registered agent,* who is the person the Secretary of State contacts with any questions about the corporation.

The type of information a state requires for the incorporation is a matter of state statute and can be found online by doing a search for the specific state's name and the word *statute.* (For example, I did a Google search on the phrase "Illinois state statute," and the correct Web site was number one in my search results.) If you scroll through the various statute titles for any given state, you should find one called "business organizations" or something similar. There is more information about incorporation in Chapter 15.

The balance sheet section called "stockholders' equity" represents the claim shareholders of the corporation have to the company's net assets. There are three common components to stockholders' equity: paid-in capital, treasury stock, and retained earnings. Paid-in capital and treasury stock involve transactions dealing with the corporate stock issuances. Retained earnings shows income and dividend transactions. In the sections that follow, I give each of these components their due, starting with paid-in capital and retained earnings and moving on to treasury stock.

Defining Paid-in Capital

Paid-in capital represents money the shareholders in a corporation invest in the business (contributed capital). It consists of purchases for preferred stock, common stock, and additional paid-in capital. (No, you're not seeing double! *Additional* paid-in capital is a subset of paid-in capital.) Here is a definition of each:

- ✔ **Preferred stock:** Preferred stock represents ownership in the corporation and has traits of both debt and equity. What this means is if a corporation sells its assets and closes its doors, preferred shareholders get back the money they invested in the corporation plus any *dividends* owed to them (money paid to the shareholders based on their proportionate stock ownership) before the common stockholders get their piece of the pie. (For more info on dividends, see the upcoming section called "Paying dividends.")

- ✔ **Common stock:** Common stock represents residual ownership in the corporation. *Residual ownership* consists of any remaining net assets after preferred stockholders' claims are paid.

  Common stockholders elect the board of directors that oversees the business. The board of directors elects the corporate officers (president, vice president, secretary, and treasurer) who handle the day-to-day operations of the business. In order to be a real corporation, at least one share of common stock has to be issued. After all, somebody has to be in charge of the corporation!

- ✔ **Additional paid-in capital:** This account represents the excess of what shareholders pay to buy the stock over the par value of the stock. *Par value* is what's printed on the face of the stock certificate. Wondering how par value is determined? Whoever was in charge of originally forming the corporation decided on the amount of par value. Most of the time, par value is an insignificant amount selected at random (although some state statutes may address par value as well).

  For example, the par value for ABC's common stock is $10 per share. You buy 20 shares for $15 a share. The addition to ABC's common stock account is $200 (20 shares at $10 par value). Additional paid-in capital is $100, which is calculated by multiplying those 20 shares by the excess you paid for the stock over its par value (20 shares times $5).

Following the rules for issuing stock

A company's articles of incorporation usually has a section (or article) that sets the limit for the number of shares that can be authorized, issued, and outstanding by the corporation at any point in time. The custodian of the stock, who may be an employee of the company or an unrelated registrar, keeps track of the number of shares outstanding to make sure the company doesn't issue more than is allowed.

Wondering what *authorized, issued,* or *outstanding* means? Here's how these three qualifiers are defined:

✔ *Authorized:* This word refers to the upper limit on the number of shares that the company can issue.

✔ *Issued:* A share is issued when the company sells it to an investor and receives cash or some other benefit in return.

✔ *Outstanding:* After stock is issued, it is classified as outstanding for as long as it's in the hands of the investors. The company can buy back outstanding shares of stock, resulting in treasury stock. I fully explain treasury stock, which is issued but not outstanding, in the "Buying treasury stock" section of this chapter.

GAAP dictate that you properly describe stock transactions on the balance sheet. To follow are the proper balance sheet descriptions for preferred and common stock:

✔ **Preferred:** Preferred stock, 5%, $200 par value, cumulative, 30,000 shares authorized, issued, and outstanding.

Because preferred stock has a debt-like characteristic, the amount of return the corporation has to pay is printed on each share. In this description it is 5 percent. The face value per the corporate charter is $200. The limit for the number of shares the corporation can have outstanding is 30,000. All 30,000 are sold to investors.

✔ **Common:** Common stock, $5 par value, 500,000 shares authorized, 250,000 shares issued at December 31, 2012.

This means the par value of the stock in the corporate articles of incorporation is $5 (remember this is usually an arbitrary number), the total number of shares the corporate can have outstanding is 500,000, and as of December 31, 2012, 250,000 shares have been sold to investors.

Recording Retained Earnings

The *retained earnings* account on the balance sheet shows the company's total net income or loss from the first day it was in business to the date on the balance sheet. (See Chapter 10 for information on how to calculate net income or loss.) While paid-in capital is money contributed by the shareholders, retained earnings is *earned* capital.

Keep in mind that retained earnings are reduced by *dividends:* earnings paid to shareholders based upon the number of shares they own. I discuss dividends in the next section.

For example, your company opens its doors on January 2, 2012. On January 2, retained earnings is 0 because the company didn't previously exist. From January 2 to December 31, 2012, your company has a net income of $20,000 and pays out $5,000 in dividends.

On January 1, 2013, the retained earnings amount is $15,000 ($20,000 – $5,000). Then, to figure retained earnings as of January 1, 2014, you start with $15,000 and add or subtract the amount of income the company made or lost during 2013 (and subtract out any dividends paid).

For a sole proprietorship or partnership, no distinction is usually made between the capital accounts and retained earnings.

Spotting Reductions to Stockholders' Equity

Your financial accounting textbook probably discusses two different accounting transactions (besides the net loss calculation) that reduce stockholders' equity: dividends and treasury stock. Though both transactions reduce equity, they are completely different types of accounts. While you may be scratching your head wondering what treasury stock is all about, you may be somewhat familiar with dividends. Don't worry! I thoroughly explain both in this section.

Corrections of accounting errors made in prior periods and discovered in the current period also reduce equity. However, this topic relates to auditing and is probably given a paragraph at most in your financial accounting textbook. To make sure I cover all the bases, I discuss this topic in Chapter 20.

Paying dividends

Dividends are distributions of company earnings to the shareholders. They can be made in the form of cash (yeah!) or in the form of stock. For me, getting stock dividends isn't quite as exciting as getting a check in the mail. However, stock dividends can be quite profitable in the long run when the investor finally gets around to selling the shares.

Dividends are *not* an expense of doing business. They are a balance sheet transaction only, serving to reduce both cash (in the case of cash dividends) and retained earnings.

Here's an explanation of both cash and stock dividends:

- ✔ **Cash dividends:** Shareholders of record receive money in the form of cash or electronic transfer based upon how many shares of stock they own. For a company to pay cash dividends, two conditions have to be met:

  - The company has positive retained earnings.

  - The company has enough ready cash to pay the dividends.

  For example, you own 1,500 shares of common stock in Penway Manufacturing Corporation. Penway has both a surplus of cash and positive retained earnings so the board of directors decides to pay a cash dividend of $12 per share. Your dividend is $18,000 (1,500 shares times $12).

- ✔ **Stock dividends:** While no money immediately changes hands, issuing stock dividends operates the same way as cash dividends: Each shareholder of record gets a certain number of extra shares of stock based on how many shares she already owns. This type of dividend is expressed as a percentage rather than a dollar amount. For example, if you receive a stock dividend of 5 percent on your Penway shares, you'll receive an additional 75 shares of stock (1,500 × .05).

The reduction to retained earnings for a cash dividend is very straightforward: You reduce retained earnings by the amount of the dividend. But what about when the company issues a stock dividend? No money changes hands, so you may be wondering how this dividend affects retained earnings. Well, read on!

Here's an example of a typical financial accounting class assignment or test question you may encounter testing your knowledge of handling this type of transaction:

Penway declares a 5 percent stock dividend at a time when it has 30,000 shares of $10 par value common stock outstanding. At the date of declaration of the stock dividend, the fair market value (FMV) of the stock was $15. (*Fair market value* is what an unpressured person would pay for the stock in an open marketplace.) How is the company's retained earnings account affected by this dividend?

The stock dividend totals 1,500 shares (5 percent × 30,000 shares). The net effect is to decrease retained earnings by $22,500 (1,500 × FMV of $15 per share) and increase common stock dividends distributable by $15,000 (par value of $10 × 1,500 shares). Additional paid-in capital increases by the difference between the two figures: $7,500.

When Penway issues the stock dividend, common stock increases by $15,000 and the common stock dividends distributable reduces to zero.

Corporations issue stock dividends when they are low in operating cash but still want to throw the investors a bone. The investors stay happy because they feel they are getting more of a return on their investment.

The three important dates in the life of a dividend

The company's board of directors is in charge of deciding how much of a dividend to issue, and when. However, unless it's a closely held corporation, the board can't just wake up one morning and decide that today's the day to distribute some cash! The dividend cycle consists of three events:

1. **Declaring the dividend:** This is the date the board of directors authorizes the dividend. After a dividend is declared, the company has a legal responsibility to pay it.

   The company records this legal responsibility by reducing retained earnings and increasing a short-term liability: dividends payable. The dollar amount reducing retained earnings and increasing the liability is the dividend per share multiplied by all shares outstanding. So if the company has 5,000 shares outstanding and declares a dividend of $2 per share, the amount is $10,000 ($2 × 5,000 shares).

2. **Recording the dividend:** The recording date determines who receives the dividend. All shareholders of record on that date get the moolah. If you sell your shares of stock after the declaration date but before the recording date, you won't be entitled to receive the dividend. No entry for this event is made in the financial records.

3. **Paying the dividend:** Last but certainly not least, the cash dividends are paid out. Stock dividends are issued. Paying cash dividends reduces both cash and dividends payable. For example, if the total dividends paid were $10,000, you debit dividends payable and credit cash for $10,000 each. FYI: If you sell your shares between the date of record and the payment date, *you* receive the dividend rather than the individual to whom you sold the shares.

Buying treasury stock

Before I started studying accounting, I thought treasury stock had something to do with investments offered by the U.S. government. When I took my first financial accounting class, I learned I was dead wrong. *Treasury stock* is a term given to shares of corporate stock previously sold to investors and then bought back by the issuing corporation.

You record treasury stock on the balance sheet as a contra stockholders' equity account. *Contra accounts* carry a balance opposite to the normal account balance. Because equity accounts normally have a credit balance, a contra equity account weighs in with a debit balance.

WARNING!

Under generally accepted accounting principles (GAAP), it is not appropriate to record any sort of gain or loss on treasury stock transactions.

REMEMBER

One reason a corporation may buy back shares of its own stock is to prevent a hostile takeover. The fewer shares trading in the open market, the smaller the chance that a controlling interest in the corporation could be purchased by another company.

Learning about Stock Splits

One other type of stock transaction that does not reduce retained earnings is a stock split. A *stock split* increases the number of shares outstanding by issuing more shares to current stockholders proportionally by the amount they already own. Stock splits are typically done when a company believes the trading price of its stock is too high; the split reduces the price per share.

For example, Penway Manufacturing Corporation stock is trading for $100, and the company thinks this high price affects the average investor's desire to purchase the stock. To get the price of the stock down to $25 per share, the company would issue a 4-for-1 split. Every outstanding share would now be equal to four shares.

The *common stock caption,* which is the descriptive line on the balance sheet, changes to reflect the split on the books. If the caption originally read "Common stock, 1,000 shares at $100 par," it now reads "Common stock, 4,000 shares at $25 par." Note that the total dollar value remains the same — $100,000 — so there is no reduction to retained earnings.

Accounting for Accumulated Other Comprehensive Income

It may seem weird to have an item of income showing up on the balance sheet. After all, isn't that what the income statement is for? Too true — however, revenue, expenses, gains, and losses that under GAAP are part of comprehensive income but not included on the income statement show up in the equity section on the balance sheet.

Your financial accounting textbook will not delve into this subject at any great length. But if you have a basic knowledge of the following two examples, you'll be way ahead of the game for this part of your financial accounting class:

✔ **Unrealized gain or loss from foreign currency translation:** This situation occurs if the corporation has a foreign subsidiary and its financial statements are combined with the U.S. parent company. During the combination, the currency of the company in which the subsidiary operates has to be converted to U.S. dollars. The gain or loss on the conversion reflects in this category.

✔ **Unrealized gain or loss on available-for-sale investments:** These are investments in other companies' stocks or bonds (see Chapter 8). Originally, you record the purchase of the investment at its cost. After that, a company periodically adjusts the value of the investment on its books to match *fair market value,* which is what the stocks or bonds are trading for in the open marketplace.

If fair market value is more than cost, the value of the investment on the balance sheet and accumulated other comprehensive income increases. When fair market value is less than cost, the value of the investment and accumulated other comprehensive income decreases.

Seeing a Sample Equity Section of the Balance Sheet

Figure 9-3 shows you how to prepare the equity section of a balance sheet for a corporation. While assets and liabilities are merely a line item in Figure 9-3, you can go to Chapter 7 to see the asset section fully developed, and Chapter 8 shows the liability section in all its debt-filled glory!

First up is always an accounting of stock. As you can see from the captions, the corporation has issued 100 shares of preferred and 250 shares of common stock. Additional paid-in capital of $4,500 means that investors paid $4,500 over par value for shares purchased. Retained earnings tells us that the corporation has $8,000 of earned capital from the day it opened its doors to December 31, 2012. Plus, the corporation has lost a bit of money on investment sales and foreign currency transactions. Finally, the balance in treasury stock tells you that the company purchased back some of its shares of stock.

Total Assets	**75,245.00**
Total Liabilities	**58,966.12**
Stockholders' Equity	
Capital Stock	
Preferred stock, 5%, $15 par value, cumulative,	
100 shares authorized, issued and outstanding.	1,500.00
Common stock, $75 par value, 500 shares authorized,	
250 shares issued at December 31, 2012	18,750.00
Additional paid-in capital	4,500.00
Retained earnings	8,000.00
Accumulated other comprehensive income (loss):	
Net unrealized loss on available for sale investments	(7,500.00)
Unrealized loss from foreign currency translation	(3,971.12)
Less: Treasury stock	(5,000.00)
Total Stockholders' Equity	**16,278.88**
Total Liabilities & Equity	**75,245.00**

Figure 9-3:
The equity section of a balance sheet.

Part IV

Investigating Income and Cash Flow

"Lucky for us—our Net Income column ended directly over a 'Triple Word Score' square."

In this part . . .

This part gives you a comprehensive overview of how to prepare an income statement and a statement of cash flows. Companies use these two financial statements, combined with the balance sheet (which I discuss in Part III), as the basis to make important operating decisions. Potential investors and creditors also use them to decide whether they should do business with the company.

The income statement shows a company's revenue and expenses, the ultimate disposition of which shows whether a company made or lost money during the accounting period. I discuss how the type of business causes the presentation of the income statement to change slightly, and I discuss each commonly shown section of the income statement. Finally, the income statement in all its glory is laid out on the table — from the entrée (gross revenues) to the dessert (net income after taxes).

The statement of cash flows records accounting transactions from both the balance sheet and the income statement, the purpose of which is to convert the accrual-based bookwork to the cash basis. This step is done so users of the financial statements can see how well the company is managing its sources and uses of cash. You find out about the three sections of the statement of cash flows — operating, investing, and financing — and what types of information you record in each.

Chapter 10

Searching for Profit or Loss on the Income Statement

*T*his chapter gives you a comprehensive overview of how to prepare an *income statement:* the financial document that reflects a company's revenue and expenses. The ultimate purpose of an income statement is to show whether a company made or lost money during the accounting period.

In this chapter, you learn the difference between setting up the income statement in a single-step format and setting it up in a multiple-step format. You also discover how the type of business causes the presentation of the income statement to change slightly.

I introduce each section commonly found on the income statement, and I discuss unusual items that sometimes show up. Finally, the income statement in all its glory is laid out on the table, from the entrée — gross revenues — to the dessert — net income after taxes.

Presenting the Income Statement in One of Two Ways

Before I get into the details of what you find on an income statement, I want you to realize that not every income statement looks exactly the same. That's because you can prepare the basic income statement in one of two ways: single-step and multiple-step. The multiple-step method provides just a bit more information than the single-step method and is the preferred format for the vast majority of *publicly traded companies* (those whose stock is for sale to the general public, like you and me, on one of the stock exchanges such as the NASDAQ).

In this section, I show you an example of each income statement format. Looking at them, you may think that even the multiple-step format isn't all that informative — neither type of statement contains very many numbers. But as I show you later in the chapter in the section "Examining Income Statement Sections," the income statement is actually chock-full of great information.

Recognizing the single-step format

In Figure 10-1, I offer an example of a single-step format income statement. All the main players in the income statement game are present — notably net sales and net income. I offer more details later in the chapter, but for now just know that *net sales* is gross sales less sales returns and allowances, and *net income* is what the company has made at the end of the day after subtracting out all expenses.

ABC, Inc.
Income Statement
For the Year Ending December 31, 2012

Figure 10-1:
A single-
step format
income
statement.

Net sales	$100,000
Cost of goods sold	45,000
Selling, general & administrative expenses	12,000
Interest expense	500
Other income	100
Income before taxes	42,600
Provision for income taxes	6,400
Net income	$ 36,200
Basic earnings per share of common stock	$ 3.25

Completing the statement is the calculation for *basic earnings per share of common stock,* which shows net income allocated to investors based on the number of shares of common stock outstanding. This bottom line number is very important to the users of financial statements (see Chapter 1) because it tells them how well their investment in the stock of the company is faring.

Breaking it out with the multiple-step format

Using the same facts and circumstances as in Figure 10-1, Figure 10-2 shows the multiple-step format for an income statement. The big differences between the single- and multiple-step formats are the following:

ABC, Inc.
Income Statement
For the Year Ending December 31, 2012

Net sales	$100,000
Cost of goods sold	45,000
Gross profit	$ 55,000
Selling, general & administrative expenses	12,000
Income from operations	$ 43,000
Other income (expense):	
Interest expense	(500)
Other income	100
Income before taxes	42,600
Provision for income taxes	6,400
Net income	$ 36,200
Basic earnings per share of common stock	$ 3.25

Figure 10-2: A multiple-step format income statement.

✔ The multiple-step format has line items for gross profit and income from operations. This information is very helpful when doing ratio analysis (see Chapter 14).

✔ The multiple-step format uses parentheses to indicate certain items that are subtracted rather than added. The single-step format assumes the readers can figure out this information on their own.

✔ Finally, the multiple-step format has a separate section showing other income and (expense), while on the single-step format other income and other expense merely show up as line items.

I know, I know, these differences must seem insignificant. But they're worth noting from the start of our discussion because in your career you'll run across both types of income statements.

Defining Different Types of Businesses

You can break every business into one of three types: service, manufacturing, and merchandising. It's important to realize which type you are working with when reviewing or creating any financial statement — including the income statement. That's because not every type of account (which I introduce in Chapter 5) shows up on the financial statements for every company.

Providing a service

When the true value of what a business provides derives from any type of personal service rather than a tangible product, that business is a *service* type. Accountants, attorneys, physicians, and hair stylists are examples of people who run service businesses.

Here's an example: As a certified public accountant (CPA), I create reports that are on paper and bound in client folders for my clients. Each client folder is a tangible product, but the client isn't paying me for the relatively small cost of the paper and ink; it's paying me for the intellectual product I provide on the paper.

One major tipoff that a company is a service type is if it doesn't have any appreciable inventory. Most service type companies make purchases only for the job at hand so they won't carry an inventory; the purchases are expensed to each job. If the company does retain some purchases, the amount is inconsequential, especially when compared to a *merchandising* company (which sells products another company makes) or a *manufacturing* company (which makes the products it sells). I discuss these two types of companies next.

Merchandising to the public

A *merchandiser* is a retail business like Target or Sears or your local grocery store. The business purchases goods from a manufacturer (see the next section) and in turn sells them to the end user — a consumer like you or me.

Unlike a service business, the merchandiser has an inventory. The inventory consists of goods available for sale, which are ready to be stocked on the shelves of the store. So your local grocery store's inventory includes milk, produce, canned goods, baked goods, and so on. I show you how to account for merchandise inventory in Chapter 13.

Manufacturing a product

The finished goods sold by merchandisers have to come from somewhere, and that somewhere is the manufacturer. Because the manufacturer makes products from scratch, accounting for this type of inventory is much more complicated than accounting for products held by a merchandiser.

Manufacturers have three types of inventory:

- ✔ **Direct materials:** This is the inventory the company purchases to make the products. For example, to make a dress, it purchases fabric, thread, and buttons.

- ✔ **Work in process:** This inventory category includes all materials that have been partially but not completely made into sellable products. A work-in-process item could be a dress whose sleeves have not yet been sewn to the body of the dress.

- ✔ **Finished goods:** Finished goods are all products that are completely assembled but not yet sold to a customer. So our dresses are ready to leave the manufacturing plant as soon as a buyer puts in an order.

You learn how to account for manufacturing inventory in Chapter 13.

Examining Income Statement Sections

As you see in Figures 10-1 and 10-2, income statements are broken out into different sections. The main reason that items of revenue and expense are separated and reported in distinct sections is so the business owner can better use the income statement to make decisions and to isolate problems with the way the business is being run. (This will make more sense after you review all the income statement parts in this section — I promise.)

Before you get into the meat of the matter — all the different types of revenues and expenses — you have to know how to prepare a heading for a financial statement. The first line of the heading is always the name of the company. The second line identifies the type of report — in this case, "Income Statement." The third line in an income statement indicates the period covered by the statement; for example, "For the year ending December 31, 20XX." (Note that the date on the report is *not* the date when the report itself was prepared.)

Two types of revenue

In this section, I explain two revenue accounts that appear on an income statement: gross sales and other income.

Gross sales

The first account on the income statement is always *gross sales,* which is the amount of income the company brings in doing whatever it's in the business of doing. Some accountants refer to gross sales as *gross receipts.* Both names mean the same thing: revenue before reporting any deductions from revenue. (I discuss these deductions later in this chapter in the section "Contra revenue accounts.")

Gross sales start with an implicit or written contract between a company and its customer (and end with reporting the gross sales after they are earned and realizable, which I discuss in a moment). The contract states that an agreed-upon good or service is to be provided for a set amount of money.

Here's an example of an implicit contract: I walk into a department store and buy a pair of pants. It is implicitly understood that when I take that garment to the checkout, I will exchange cash or a claim for cash (a credit card transaction) for the amount on the pants' price sticker.

An example of a written agreement is a contract for sale. Say that a department store signs a contract stating it wants to buy 500 pairs of pants from the manufacturer. This contract states all the expenses and obligations on the side of both the seller and the purchaser.

A company's gross sales revenue includes only transactions that relate to the purpose of the business. In the department store example, revenue includes the gross amount of merchandise sold to customers. If that same company sells one of its company cars, you record the gain or loss on that transaction in the line called "other income or loss," not gross sales. That's because the company isn't in the used car sales business. Income or loss unrelated to the business purpose isn't part of gross sales. Find out more about this subject in the upcoming "Other income" section.

Financial accounting uses the accrual method of accounting (see Chapter 6) so a company can't record gross receipts unless that money is earned and realizable. Here's what these terms mean:

> ✔ For revenue to be *earned,* the job, whether it involves goods or services, has to be complete based upon the terms of the contract between the company and the customer.

✔ For revenue to be *realizable* means there is an expectation that the company performing the service or providing the goods will be paid. When might revenue *not* be realizable? If, after the job is complete (but before the company is paid), a customer closes its doors and disappears or goes into bankruptcy, the revenue is no longer realizable.

Based on the above information, you can understand that cash doesn't have to change hands for gross receipts to be earned and realizable. To address this fact, a company has an "accounts receivable" account holding the dollar amount of revenue that has not been paid. I discuss accounts receivable in Chapter 7.

Other income

You classify all other income the company brings in peripherally as *other revenue* or *other income*. (Either name is fine.) Your financial accounting textbook highlights three kinds of other income:

✔ **Interest:** Revenue a company earns from money on deposit

✔ **Dividends:** Revenue a company earns on investments it owns, such as stock in other businesses

✔ **Gain on disposal of an asset:** Revenue a company earns when it sells one of its assets, such as a car or desk, and makes money on the deal

Note that while the gross sales account is your first income statement account, other income does not appear until later in the statement. That's because, frankly, it's not quite as significant as some of the other financial facts about the business. But the biggie reason in financial accounting is because that's what generally accepted accounting principles (GAAP) dictate. (I explain why following GAAP is important in Chapter 4.)

Contra revenue accounts

In Chapter 5, I give you the lowdown on the rules of debits and credits. One of the immutable rules of accounting is that revenue accounts normally carry a credit balance. However, in the wonderful world of accounting, you have what are called *contra accounts,* which means the account carries a balance contrary to the normal balance. So a contra revenue account carries a debit balance instead of a credit balance.

The two contra revenue accounts you cover in your financial accounting class are "sales discounts" and "sales returns and allowances," which I discuss here.

Sales discounts

Sales discounts reflect any discount a business gives to a good vendor who pays early. For example, a customer's invoice is due within 30 days of receipt of the good or service. If the customer pays early (what is considered *early* is spelled out in the terms of the contract), it gets a 2 percent discount. So if the invoice is for $100, the customer has to pay only $98. This doesn't seem like such a big deal, but consider the difference between the invoice amount and payment amount if the invoice is for $10,000 or $100,000.

Sales returns and allowances

Sales returns reflect all products that customers return to the company after the sale is complete. For example, after I buy a pair of pants, perhaps I decide that I no longer want them. Back to the department store I go to return the garment and get a full refund for the purchase price plus sales tax.

Sales allowances reflect a discount in price given to a customer wanting to purchase damaged merchandise. A perfect example is that some stores sell scratch-and-dent appliances.

Gross sales less sales discounts and sales returns and allowances equals *net sales.* Figure 10-3 shows an example of how this calculation looks if a company has gross sales of $300,000, sales discounts of $25,500, and sales returns of $1,000.

Sales		
Sales		$300,000
Less: Sales discounts	$25,500	
Sales returns and allowances	1,000	(26,500)
Net sales		$273,500

Figure 10-3:
Net sales.

The examples of income statements in your financial accounting textbook may show all three accounts (gross sales, sales discounts, and sale returns and allowances) with a net sales total like I show in Figure 10-3 and Figure 10-7 at the end of this chapter. Or your textbook may show just the consolidated line item "net sales," which I show in Figures 10-1 and 10-2. Either mode of presentation is fine as long as you understand the accounting behind how gross sales turns into net sales.

Also, keep in mind that net sales is not an account in the chart of accounts. It's merely a total reflecting the ending figures in the revenue and contra revenue accounts.

Cost of goods sold

The *cost of goods sold* (COGS) on the income statement reflects all costs directly tied to any product a company sells, be it a merchandiser or a manufacturing company. A service company will not have a COGS line because it does not sell a tangible product.

Because merchandisers sell products they purchase from manufacturers, their COGS is fairly easy to compute. That's because merchandisers have only one type of inventory to keep track of: goods they purchase for resale. As I note earlier in the chapter, a manufacturer has several different types of inventory, so figuring its COGS is a little trickier.

In this section, I talk about the easier COGS (merchandising) first and then tackle the more difficult COGS of the manufacturing company.

Merchandising COGS

Figuring COGS for a merchandising company starts with *beginning inventory,* which is the merchandise the company has available for sale at the beginning of the month (in other words, the leftover inventory from the prior month). I discuss inventory in depth in Chapter 13.

Next, you have to figure the cost of purchases. To do so, you add together two items:

- ✓ **Purchases:** Any new merchandise the company buys during the current month
- ✓ **Freight-in:** The shipping expense the business incurs in order to get the merchandise purchases from the manufacturer to its location

For example, if purchases for the month of April are $125,000 and freight-in is $10,500, your cost of purchases is $135,500.

Your next step is to figure *net purchases,* which means cost of purchases less contra purchases. Once again, contra accounts raise their ugly heads! Two contra purchase accounts exist:

- ✓ **Purchase discounts:** This contra account reflects any discount a company receives because it pays a merchandise invoice early. It's the flip side of the contra revenue account "sales discount" — looking at the same event from the eyes of the customer rather than the seller.
- ✓ **Purchase returns and allowances:** This contra account consists of items a merchandiser orders that it returns to the supplier. Items may be returned if an order arrives too late to use, arrives damaged, or doesn't contain what the company actually ordered. This account is the flip side of "sales returns and allowances" — looking at the same event from the side of the customer instead of the seller.

Because purchases are an expense and normally carry a debit balance, a contra purchase expense will carry a credit balance.

Cost of purchases less the two contra purchase accounts equals *net purchases.* For example, start with our cost of purchases of $135,500. Figure purchase discounts being $5,000 and purchase returns and allowances equaling $7,000. Your net purchases amount is $123,500.

Adding net purchases to beginning inventory gives you *cost of goods available for sale.* So if beginning inventory is $5,000, costs of goods available for sale is $128,500 ($123,500 + $5,000).

Okay, just one more calculation! Subtract *ending inventory,* which is the merchandise the company still has available for sale on the last day of the accounting period, from cost of goods available for sale. (Because the ending inventory was not sold, we are subtracting its costs from the goods available for sale.) Then you have your cost of goods sold! Continuing our example, if ending inventory is $10,000, your cost of goods sold is $118,500 ($128,500 – $10,000).

Manufacturing COGS

Earlier in the chapter, I explain that manufacturers have three types of inventory: direct materials, work in process, and finished goods. To figure a manufacturing company's COGS, you first have to calculate the cost of goods manufactured. What appears to be a simple single line item in the cost of goods sold for a manufacturing company is really a calculation in which many different variables are added and subtracted.

Check out Figure 10-4 to see how the manufacturing company's COGS shows up on the income statement. Looks pretty bare-boned, doesn't it?

Figure 10-4:
Computing COGS for a manufacturing company.

Beginning finished goods inventory	$	XXXX
Add: Costs of goods manufactured during the period		XXX
Equals cost of goods available for sale	$	XXXX
Minus: Ending inventory finished goods	(	XXX)
Equals cost of goods sold	$	XXXX

Here, I walk you through the preparation of the COGS line item "cost of goods manufactured during the period." Most of the terms I use in this calculation have already been explained in this chapter, but I throw in a couple new ones as well:

✔ **Direct labor:** This expense includes only what the company pays to workers who are directly involved in making the items the company manufactures. So if the company makes blouses, direct labor includes the payroll for the employees who make the blouse patterns, cut out the fabric pieces, and assemble the fabric pieces into a wearable garment.

✔ **Factory overhead:** This expense includes all manufacturing costs except those you include in direct materials and direct labor. It also includes indirect materials and labor:

- *Indirect materials:* These are materials that a manufacturer would use for more than one product. For example, your blouse manufacturer has to use thread to sew the pieces of the blouse patterns together to make a complete, wearable garment. If the thread is a generic color (such as black or white) that the company uses to make various other garments such as slacks or jackets, it would properly be classed as indirect materials. That's because the thread is not directly associated only with the blouses.

- *Indirect labor:* This item includes employee payroll that does not directly tie to a specific finished product. A good example of an indirect employee is a quality control inspector who makes sure the goods flowing down the assembly line are made properly.

Another example of factory overhead is *depreciation of factory equipment,* which is the process of spreading the cost of the factory equipment over its useful life. For example, you include the depreciation of the sewing machines the company uses to make the blouses in factory overhead. Depreciation of the computers that the number-crunchers use in the accounting department *isn't* included. I explain different methods of depreciation in Chapter 12.

Utilities you include in factory overhead are the heating and air conditioning, lights, power to run the factory machines, and factory water. These expenses are classed as overhead because while the business incurs them when manufacturing products, it cannot tie these expenses to one particular product (unless the company makes only one product).

Other overhead items can include any other manufacturing costs that can't be attributed to a specific product. One example is repair and maintenance expense to keep the factory machines running smoothly. A good example is if the company buys the same brand of lubricant to oil all the machines.

Now that you know all the terms you see when preparing the "cost of goods manufactured during the period," I walk you through the preparation itself in Figure 10-5.

Beginning direct materials inventory	$ XXXX	
Plus net purchases	XXX	
Equals total direct materials available	$ XXXX	
Less: Ending direct materials inventory	(XXX)	
Equals direct materials used		$ XXXX
Plus direct labor		XXX
Plus items of factory overhead:		
Depreciation of factory equipment	$ XXX	
Utilities	XXX	
Indirect factory labor	XXX	
Indirect materials	XXX	
Other overhead items	XXX	XXX
Equals manufacturing cost incurred during the period		$ XXXX
Add: Beginning work in process		XXX
Less: Ending work in process		(XXX)
Costs of goods manufactured during the period		$ XXX

Figure 10-5: The step-by-step preparation of cost of goods manufactured during a period.

Gross profit

Well, this is an easy one! On the multiple-step income statement (refer back to Figure 10-2), *gross profit* is what's left over after you subtract the cost of goods sold from net sales. Basically, gross profit shows you how much money the company makes if it doesn't have any other expenses such as office rent, salaries, and so on. (Note that this line doesn't appear on the single-step income statement format, such as the one shown in Figure 10-1.)

Gross profit is very important in financial accounting because it gives the users of the financial statements a measurement upon which to compare this company to others. (See Chapter 14 for info about ratio analysis.) A company showing a higher gross profit than others in its industry will be more likely to attract investors, as long as expenses other than COGS are kept in line.

Operating expenses

Two principal categories of operating expenses show up on the income statement:

✔ **Selling expenses:** Any expenses a company incurs to sell its goods or services to customers. Some examples are salaries and commissions paid to sales staff; advertising expenses; store supplies; and depreciation of a retail shop's furniture, equipment, and store fixtures. (See Chapter 12 for a discussion of depreciation.) Typical retail shop depreciable items include cash registers, display cases, and clothing racks.

✓ **General and administrative expenses:** All expenses a company incurs to keep up the normal business operations. Some examples are office supplies, officer and office payroll, nonfactory rent and utilities, and accounting and legal services.

Depending on the amount of detail shown on the income statement, these two categories are often combined. (I combine them in previous figures in this chapter, and your financial accounting textbook probably does as well.) However, the complete income statement (Figure 10-7) at the end of this chapter shows you how to present them separately.

Heading toward the bottom line

You've gone through a lot of different income statement accounts so far in this chapter. Bet you never thought that making money could be so complicated! However, you are fast approaching the finish line where you find out if the company has made or lost money during the accounting period.

Operating income

After you've totaled all your operating expenses, you subtract that figure from gross profit to figure your operating income. Suppose that a company's net sales are $10 million and its cost of goods sold is $4 million. Your gross profit is $6 million. If your selling plus general and administrative expenses are $1 million, your operating income equals $5 million.

But hold on to your hat! You're not done yet. Your next step is to add in and subtract back out other income and expenses.

Other income and expenses

In the earlier section "Two types of revenue," I explain that *gross sales* includes only the amount of money the company brings in doing whatever it is in the business of doing; it does not include any investment income. Well, you've finally arrived at the section of the income statement where you record all the other types of revenue.

This line of the income statement also includes expenses that the company incurs other than costs associated with normal operations. Here are two types of expenses you typically see reflected on this line:

✓ **Interest expense:** This includes the cost of using borrowed funds for business operations, expansion, and cash flow. Why wouldn't interest expense be included as an operating expense? Well, operating expenses are for the day-to-day activities involved in running a business. Per generally accepted accounting principles (GAAP, which I explain in Chapter 4), interest expense is not considered to be a day-to-day activity unless the company is in the business of loaning money.

✔ **Loss on disposal of a fixed asset:** I talk about "gain on disposal of an asset" earlier in the chapter (see the "Other income" section). Loss is the flip side of the coin. If a company sells an asset it no longer needs and loses money on the transaction, the loss reflects on the income statement as "loss on disposal of fixed asset" or whatever the company decides to name the account.

Income from continuing operations before taxes

Adding other revenue and subtracting other expenses from operating income give you *income from continuing operations before taxes.* Your financial accounting textbook may simply call this figure *income before taxes.* That's because if the company doesn't have any income or loss from *discontinued operations,* which are segments a company has disposed of, it's kind of overkill to add in the "from continuing operations" part. (Look for information about unusual income statement items like discontinued operations in the "Watching Out for Unusual Income Statement Items" section later in the chapter.)

Provision for income taxes

Before you figure the final total for net income or loss, you have to reduce income from continuing operations (or income before taxes) by subtracting a provision for the income tax the company will pay when it files tax returns. I discuss accounting for income taxes in Chapter 18. For now just remember that depending on many different factors, the business may owe just federal or both federal and state income taxes — or maybe other types of income taxes as well.

If your financial accounting professor assigns homework or has a question on a test regarding income taxes, you'll probably be asked to figure net income by calculating a provision for income taxes, and the facts of the question will provide the tax rate. Your job is the easy task of multiplying income from continuing operations before taxes by the given rate (I see 35 percent in a lot of financial accounting textbooks) and subtracting the tax figure from the income figure before taxes to arrive at your income from continuing operations after taxes.

So if income from continuing operations before taxes is $10,000 and you have an income tax rate of 35 percent, your provision for income taxes is $3,500. That makes income from continuing operations after taxes equal to $6,500 ($10,000 – $3,500).

Finally — net income!

If there are no unusual items on the income statement, such as discontinued operations, the income from continuing operations after taxes is called *net income*. That line on the income statement reflects all revenue less all expenses incurred in the production of that revenue.

If expenses are more than revenue, the company has a net loss rather than net income.

Earnings per share

Earnings per share (EPS) shows the spread of net income when you divvy it up among shares of stock *outstanding,* which means the stock has been issued and is in the hands of the investor. Potential investors in a corporation like to see this type of information so they can make educated investment decisions. If your motivation for buying stock in a corporation is to bring in some dividend income, you want to be able to compare what kind of dividends your top picks are paying their current investors.

Before I get into the discussion of earnings per share, it's important to understand the two types of stock an investor may own in a corporation:

✔ **Common stock:** People who own common stock are the ultimate owners of the corporation and have voting privileges. For example, common stockholders of record vote to elect the corporation's board of directors.

✔ **Preferred stock:** This type of stock gives stockholders a claim to the corporation's assets. In case of *liquidation* (when the corporation shuts its doors and disposes of all its assets), the preferred stockholders are paid back for their ownership in the corporation first, and any leftovers go to the common stockholders.

Preferred stockholders normally don't have voting rights, but they have a much more favorable position when it comes time to pay dividends. If a corporation decides it's going to pay dividends, the preferred stockholders normally get their piece of the pie first with any leftover cash then paid to the common stockholders.

See Chapter 9 for more information about stock, shareholders, and dividends. With the basic definitions of common and preferred stock in mind, here's an example of how to figure EPS when a corporation issues both types of stock:

At the end of the year, Penway Manufacturing Corporation has net income of $473,400. During the year the corporation has outstanding 38,000 shares of $4.50, $70 par value preferred stock and 205,000 shares of common stock.

This means that the owners of the 38,000 shares of preferred stock get a dividend of $4.50 per share first, which equals $171,000 (38,000 shares multiplied by $4.50 per share). This figure has to be subtracted from the company's net income prior to figuring earnings per share of common stock.

Doing so gives you a figure of $302,400 ($473,400 – $171,000). Dividing $302,400 by the shares of common stock outstanding (205,000) equals $1.48 in earnings per share of common stock.

Watching Out for Unusual Income Statement Items

You're almost done! Let's just get a handle on a couple of the unusual items you may see on income statements while taking your financial accounting course. I discuss two in this chapter: discontinued operations and extraordinary items. These items are broken out from "income from continuing operations" to give users of the financial statements a better idea of the probable results of future operations. Separating out nonrecurring events from regular recurring business results makes it easier for the users of the financial statements to form an accurate opinion about the company.

GAAP require that a company show discontinued operations on the income statement before extraordinary items, so I start with that topic.

Discontinued operations

Discontinued operations take place when a segment of a business is regarded as *held-for-sale*. This term means either that the business has some sort of legal obligation to sell the segment (for example, the shareholders voted on the sale) or that the segment has been disposed of during the accounting period and both the following criteria are met:

✔ The figures for "operational results" and "cash flow" (which are the sources and uses of cash; see Chapter 11) of the discontinued segment are or will shortly be removed from the ongoing operations of the business.

> ✔ The business will not have any significant involvement with the operations of the discontinued segment after it is disposed of.

Here's an example to breathe a little life into this concept for you. Say a company that manufactures shoes has four different segments: boots, tennis shoes, ladies' sandals, and men's loafers. The company decides to sell its tennis shoe segment to a well-known manufacturer of exercise shoes.

Financial accounting dictates that you report any anticipated operational losses that directly relate to getting rid of the tennis shoe segment (net of tax) and any loss or gain the company incurs when selling the asset portion of the tennis shoe segment (also net of tax) — for example, tennis shoe–making equipment — on the income statement after income from continuing operations.

Extraordinary items

To meet the criteria laid out by GAAP for *extraordinary item* treatment, the item in question must be something that occurs infrequently and is by its very nature unusual. To meet both criteria is very hard.

Examples that could possibly meet this strict criteria are the results from litigation. If the company is a defendant in a lawsuit and a final judgment of a specific amount of monetary damages is awarded to the plaintiff, and if this type of event is unusual and infrequent, GAAP allow it to be classified as an extraordinary item. However, being the subject of a lawsuit must be a highly abnormal event for the business and be unrelated to its ordinary business activities in order for this event to record as an extraordinary item.

The important thing to remember for your financial accounting class is the fact that you report the gain or loss on the extraordinary item net of income tax. Figure 10-6 shows how to represent unusual items on the income statement.

Figure 10-6:
Reporting unusual income statement items.

Income from continuing operations	$53,000
Loss from discontinued operations, net of tax	(15,000)
Earnings before extraordinary item	$38,000
Extraordinary gain from fire insurance proceeds, net of tax	14,000
Net income	$52,000

Recent events not considered to be extraordinary

Two of the most infamous events taking place in the United States in recent history were the terrorist attacks on September 11, 2001, and Hurricane Katrina on August 29, 2005. You may be startled to find out that neither event is considered to meet the extraordinary criteria. After consideration, the Financial Accounting Standards Board Emerging Issues Task Forces declared that no company sustaining damages from the 9/11 attack could treat any of its losses or expenses as extraordinary items. And while the destructive effect of Hurricane Katrina on Gulf states was chilling, hurricanes in that area are neither infrequent nor unusual.

Arriving at the Final Product

Ta-da! Here you are, ready to take everything you know from this chapter and use it to produce your final product: an income statement.

Every company may have a slightly different system to handle the financial accounting work that begins with invoices and bills and ends with all transactions being recorded in the accounting records. In the past, I've worked for a very large company where my only task was to manage accounts payable, and I've also worked for a business where I was the only accounting department employee doing everything from opening the mail to running the financial statements. How the accounting work happens varies from company to company. What doesn't vary is how the income statement looks on paper when using GAAP.

Figure 10-7 provides a multiple-step income statement for a merchandising company that has no extraordinary items or discontinued operations. Because these items are not present, rather than using "income from continuing operations," I use "net income."

So that you can clearly see how the accounting transactions you enter play out, in this figure I don't consolidate sales into the single line item "net sales" or the components of cost of goods sold (COGS) into a single line item for COGS. Keep in mind that the expenses you see on this income statement, while representative of normal business expenses, certainly do not show all expenses a business can possibly have.

Yeeoh Merchandising Company, Inc.
Income Statement
For the Year Ending December 31, 2012

Sales			
Sales			$300,000
Less: Sales discounts		$ 25,500	
Sales returns and allowances		1,000	(26,500)
Net sales			$273,500
Cost of goods sold:			
Beginning inventory			$ 5,000
Add: Purchases		125,000	
Freight-in		10,500	
Cost of purchases		135,500	
Less: Purchase discounts	$ 5,000		
Purchase returns and allowances	7,000	(12,000)	
Net purchases			123,500
Cost of goods available for sale			128,500
Less: Ending inventory			(10,000)
Cost of goods sold			118,500
Gross profit			$155,000
Operating expenses:			
Selling expenses			
Sales salaries	$ 5,000		
Commissions	2,000		
Advertising expense	550	$ 7,550	
General and administrative expenses			
Office salaries	$ 6,000		
Office supplies expense	200		
Insurance expense	600		
Utilities expense	150	$ 6,950	
Total operating expense			(14,500)
Operating income			$140,500
Other revenues:			
Interest income		$ 1,500	
Dividend income		3,200	4,700
Other expenses:			
Interest expense			(1,200)
Income before taxes			144,000
Provision for income taxes *			(50,400)
Net income			$ 93,600
Basic earnings per share of common stock **			$ 9.36

* assuming a 35% tax rate
** assuming 10,000 shares of common stock outstanding and no preferred stock

Figure 10-7:
An income statement for a merchandising business.

Quick and dirty income statement preparation

Many CPAs who own their own accounting practice provide write-up services preparing financial statements for clients who don't have a formal accounting department. Breaking write-up services down into their most elemental factor means that the CPA (or usually a clerk in the firm) uses the client's business check stubs and bank deposit information to record revenue and expenses.

The books are adjusted for any accounts payable or accounts receivable info and for any cash payments that should record as an asset instead of an expense (see Chapter 7). They're also adjusted for the opposite: moving any assets that are really expenses (see Chapters 12 and 13) from the balance sheet to the income statement.

It sounds like a lot more work than it actually is because most write-up work involves smaller companies that may write only 300 to 500 business checks (or less) per month and have little accounts receivable or payable activity.

Chapter 11

Following the Money by Studying Cash Flow

In This Chapter

▶ Separating cash from profit and costs from expenses

▶ Connecting the dots with the statement of cash flows

▶ Learning about the sections of the statement of cash flows

▶ Presenting cash flow using the direct or indirect method

*W*hile financial accounting is all about the *accrual* method, which means revenue is recorded when it is earned and realizable and expenses are recorded when they are incurred, the missing piece of the puzzle is cash changing hands. For the financial statements users to get a total picture of the health of the business, cash payments and receipts have to be reconciled with accrual transactions.

You accomplish this reconciliation by preparing a statement of cash flows. In this chapter, you find out about the three sections of the statement of cash flows — operating, investing, and financing — and what types of accounting information are reported in each.

To shake things up a little bit, there are currently two acceptable ways to prepare the statement of cash flows: using the direct method and the indirect method. (I say *currently* because this situation may change in the future.) The Financial Accounting Standards Board (FASB) prefers the direct method because it believes this method provides the user with more standardized info so companies can more accurately be compared. However, most companies use the indirect method because compiling the information is less expensive than when using the direct method.

Never fear! Before you finish the chapter, you find out how the statement of cash flows is prepared using both methods so you are ready for any homework assignments or text questions on this subject in your financial accounting class.

Understanding the Difference between Cash and Profit

Your financial accounting class is all about the accrual method of accounting. As I explain in Chapter 6, with the accrual method, you record revenue when it's earned regardless of whether money changes hands. Plus, you record expenses when you incur them regardless of whether they are paid. (As I also note in Chapter 6, there is another accounting method — the cash method — which uses the criterion of cash changing hands to record revenue and expenses.)

Because recognizing accounting transactions for financial accounting doesn't hinge on cash being exchanged, there most likely will always be a difference between a company's cash balances and profit shown on the income statement (see Chapter 10). That's because all costs aren't expenses, and until a cost *is* an expense, it doesn't hit the income statement.

In this section, I first show you how noncash transactions influence a company's net income. Then I illustrate the difference between costs and expenses.

Seeing how noncash transactions affect profit

The statement of cash flows homes in on the difference between cash a company receives and profit it has earned. Profit shows the real net income for the financial period — factoring in revenue earned but not yet collected from customers and expenses incurred but not yet paid — rather than reflecting only transactions involving cash.

For example, let's say that in June a company deposits $2,000 into its checking account and writes checks to pay bills for $1,800. If you look only at the cash flowing in and out of the business, the company spent $200 less than it made, so it shows a profit of $200. But what if, in June, the company also used a credit card it doesn't intend to pay for until August (or a loan it took out in May or any other noncash resource) to pay monthly bills in the amount of $1,000? Taking this transaction into account, the company actually spent more than it made, resulting in a loss of $800.

Distinguishing costs from expenses

Generally accepted accounting principles (GAAP; see Chapter 4) pretty much dictate the accrual method for financial accounting. There are some variations on this theme, which you can find out about in Chapter 22. However, your number-one focus for your financial accounting class when talking about costs and expenses is to remember that in the world of business, costs are not the same as expenses.

Let's say a company buys a new car for $25,000 cash. A company car is an example of a fixed asset (see Chapter 7), which goes on the balance sheet. When the company buys the car, the price it pays, or promises to pay, is a *cost.* Then as company employees drive the car on company business, the company depreciates the car.

Depreciation (see Chapter 12) is the process of reclassifying the cost of buying the asset as an expense of doing business. So over time, the resources (in this case $25,000 cash) that the company uses to purchase the car are reclassified from the balance sheet (where they're a cost) to the income statement (where they're an expense).

Assume that the amount the company depreciates the car in the year of purchase is $4,500. So in that first year, the company's *expense* is $4,500 and the *cost* is $25,000. Big difference, huh? That's why the statement of cash flows is so important; it ties together the costs shown on the balance sheet with the expenses shown on the income statement.

Make sure you don't get confused about the difference between costs and expenses! A *cost* is the value of money the company uses to produce or buy something — money that is not available to use anymore. Costs are the ways a company uses cash, be it to purchase inventory, make investments, or pay back debt. *Expenses* are costs that directly tie back to revenue the company earns during a financial period.

Realizing the Purpose of the Statement of Cash Flows

The primary purpose of the statement of cash flows is to show a company's cash sources and uses during the financial period. While cash can come from many different origins, such as customer payments, loans, and sales of assets and equity, uses of cash directly trace back to costs. This information is very interesting to the external users of the company's financial statements, who are not privy to the day-to-day operations of the business, because it provides a basis for understanding how wisely a company manages its cash.

A company can be a real go-getter in the business world, but if cash is thrown around like chewing gum, the business may not be able to give the external users what they are looking for, which is basically a return on their investment. This holds true both for potential investors looking for dividend payments and potential lenders wanting to make sure the company can pay back the principal portion of any loan plus any interest the lender charges.

A third category of external users of financial statements is governmental taxing agencies. Their main focus is whether the company is reporting taxable income correctly, a topic I discuss in Chapter 18. In that regard a statement of cash flows has limited value.

The statement of cash flows provides guidance for the following questions:

> ✔ **Does the company have the ability to generate positive cash flow in the future?** You don't want to invest in a one-hit wonder. Viewing a current statement of cash flows does give a hint as to the company's future prospects.

> ✔ **Does the company have enough cash to make loan or dividend payments?** Obviously, if you are a potential investor or lender for a corporation, it's probably not your idea of a good time to let the business use your money for free. You want to check out the statement of cash flows to see how the business manages its money and gauge the probability of the company having enough cash to satisfy its obligations and pay dividends.

> ✔ **Is the reason for the difference between net income and cash transactions indicative of a healthy business?** All cash is not created equal. Cash a company brings in from gross receipts is a lot more exciting to me as a potential investor than cash the company has left over because it sold some assets. After all, the business can own only a finite number of assets, while with a well-run business the sky's the limit for bringing in revenue from operations.

You ferret out this information by reviewing the different sections of the statement of cash flows. Each section ties back to how accounting transactions affect the income statement and balance sheet. So you're not looking at new information; instead, you're looking at the same information shown in a different way.

Walking through the Cash Flow Sections

A statement of cash flows has three sections: operating, investing, and financing:

- ✔ The sources and uses of cash in the **operating** section come from revenue, expenses, cash received from gains and losses shown on the income statement, and cash paid out for other costs.

- ✔ The **investing** section shows sources and uses of cash from debt and equity investment purchases and sales; purchases and sales of property, plant, and equipment; and collection of principal on debt.

- ✔ The **financing** section shows long-term liability (paying or securing loans beyond a period of 12 months from the balance sheet date) and equity items (the sale of company stock and payment of dividends).

Some of these terms may be unfamiliar to you. Don't worry, by the time you finish reading the rest of this section, you'll be an old pro on cash flow. First, I satisfy your curiosity about the operating section.

Figuring cash operating results

GAAP's guide to what shows up in the operating section is simply this: The operating section contains transactions not listed as investing or financing transactions — in other words, income statement items. Here, I offer examples of operating sources and uses of cash.

Operating sources of cash

Here are examples of operating sources of cash:

- ✔ **Cash receipts from the sale of goods or services:** This source is the cash that customers pay the company at the point of contact or what the company collects at a later date from existing accounts receivable. For example, I go into Target and buy a new DVD player. It costs $65 (hey, I'm too cheap to pay for the bells and whistles). I plunk over the cost of the purchase plus sales tax in cash. Target records this receipt as a source of cash.

    On the flip side, let's say that on October 12, I go into one of those scratch-and-dent appliance warehouses to buy a new washer and dryer. The warehouse is holding a "90 days same as cash" promotion, which means that as long as I cough up the cash for the washer and dryer within 90 days, I pay no interest. On October 12, the appliance warehouse has no cash source from me, and it won't have that source until I pay for my purchase on or before January 12.

✔ **Trading portfolio sales:** *Trading securities* are assets a business purchases to make a profit in the short term. How this normally happens is that a business has some spare cash lying around that it doesn't need access to in the immediate future. Rather than leaving the cash in the bank earning little or no interest, the company buys *highly liquid* (easily convertible to cash) stocks, bonds, or loans.

The business tries to invest in a sure thing — something that won't go down in value during the holding period. Then, when the company sells the investment, the cash it receives goes on the statement of cash flows in the operating section rather than investing. The key here for operating section placement is that the investment is *short term*. See Chapter 7 for more information about short-term investments.

✔ **Interest and dividends:** If the company makes loans to other businesses or individuals, any interest income it receives on those loans goes in the operating section. An example is a loan to a shareholder who is also an employee and needs cash beyond what she's receiving in her paycheck. This situation happens often in a closely held corporation.

Also, some companies make loans to key vendors needing a short-term infusion of cash to keep their doors open. A company will take this step if it's in the company's best interest to keep an essential vendor in business. After all, if you like to buy your widgets from Joe's Widget Shop and Joe goes out of business, you'll have to find another widget vendor, and maybe you won't like working with that vendor (or paying its prices) as much as you liked working with Joe.

As reported on the income statement, *dividends* are income paid to shareholders based on their proportional ownership of the corporation. For example, ABC Corp. owns 2,000 shares of XYZ, Inc. stock. ABC receives dividends from XYZ at $2 per share totaling $4,000 ($2 × 2,000 shares); this amount shows in the operating section as a source of cash. You can find out more about the process behind declaring and paying dividends in Chapter 9.

Operating uses of cash

Next, I look at uses of cash showing up in the operating section of a statement of cash flows. The cash outflows are kind of the flip side of the cash inflows. For example, accounts receivable from customers is an inflow, and accounts payable paid to vendors is an outflow.

Trading at a personal level

Even though you're not a business, you may have put the principles of trading securities to work for you. For example, let's say your great aunt Dottie was feeling flush while visiting your parents for Thanksgiving and gave you $5,000 to put toward your college tuition. (Such a thing has never happened to me, but one can dream.)

Your tuition is already paid through the next six months. So, since you know you won't need this money until then, you buy a certificate of deposit that matures just in time to make your next tuition payment. That way, you have both the $5,000 gift from Dottie and the interest you earn on the certificate of deposit at your disposal instead of just hiding the cash under your bed or allowing it to languish in a non-interest-bearing checking account.

Here are the operating cash outflows you'll see in your financial accounting textbook:

✔ **Satisfying accounts payable:** *Accounts payable* is the amount a company owes vendors for services and products the vendors render to the company. When the original purchase takes place, no money changes hands between the customer and the supplier. Rather, there is a promise to pay within a certain amount of time.

For example, I buy $500 of office supplies from a major supply house to refill the supply cabinet at my company. When I come back to the office with that $500 receipt in my grubby little hand, my company doesn't record this amount as a cash outlay. That's because the office supply house wasn't paid yet; it merely has my promise to pay within 10 days (or 30 days, or whatever). This $500 will be a cash outlay only after I sign and mail the payment check to the office supply store.

✔ **Trading portfolio purchases:** Just as sales of trading securities are a cash source, the amount of money the company pays to buy any trading security is a use of cash. No securities other than trading securities go in the operating section of the statement of cash flows. Again, the key here for operating section placement is that the investment is *short term.* See Chapter 7 for more information about short-term investments.

✔ **Payments for other business expenses:** This category includes any cash outlays to buy inventory, pay employees, remit income taxes due, or pay any other suppliers (such as utility providers or the telephone company). You can find out more information about inventory purchases in Chapter 13. Chapter 18 shows how to account for income taxes.

✔ **Interest payments:** Any cash paid to lenders in the form of interest also goes in the operating section. It doesn't make any difference what the purpose of the loan or source of the loan is. So interest paid to a related party, such as a shareholder, for an *operating capital* loan (cash made available for day-to-day business functions) is treated in the same fashion as interest paid to a vehicle financing company for the note on the company car.

What about dividends, which I list as a source of cash? Did I forget to add them here as a use of cash? Nope! Remember, the main thrust of the operating section of the statement of cash flows is to reconcile the cash versus accrual treatment of income statement items. Because paying dividends to shareholders is not a business expense, it does not show up on the income statement, so it's not an operating use of cash.

Showing cash investing transactions

Investing transactions are those involving the purchase and sale of noncurrent assets (see Chapter 7). *Noncurrent assets* are assets the company anticipates owning for more than one year past the date of the balance sheet. Examples of noncurrent assets are long-term debt and equity investments; property, plant, and equipment; and intangible assets such as patents and copyrights.

What exactly are "debt and equity investments"?

✔ Common stock is an example of an *equity* investment. Let's say you buy AT&T common stock. As a shareholder, you don't have a creditor and debtor relationship with AT&T. Instead, you are an investor who will be paid back for the purchase of the stock only if you sell it to someone else.

✔ Bonds are *debt* investments. For example, say a municipality sells bonds to the public for the purpose of financing a new hospital. The municipality eventually has to pay the bonds back plus interest. Corporations generally issue bonds to raise money for capital expenditures, operating expenses, and acquisitions. Bondholders receive interest payments at the bond's stated interest rate. When the bond matures, the company pays the bondholder back the face amount of the bond.

Investing sources of cash

Here, I show you specifically how investing transactions show up as sources of cash:

✔ **Long-term debt sales and collection:** A company's investments in debt may fall into three categories: straight-out loans, held-to-maturity debt investments, and available-for-sale debt portfolios. Here's how they differ:

- *Loans* are easy to understand; they're merely money the company loans to others that will not be paid off within 12 months of the balance sheet date. You know from your own personal debts (such as car loans) that when you owe money, you periodically have to make payments on the principal portion of the loan. The same holds true with businesses. So any collection of principal on loans is a cash source for the company lending the money.

- *Held-to-maturity* debt investments are those the company antici- pates holding onto until the debt matures. For example, ABC Corp. buys five-year bonds issued by the city of Orlando to build a new sports arena. When the bonds mature, the cash proceeds go in the investment section. See Chapter 8 for the whole story on bonds.

  This is not something to worry about for your financial accounting class, but keep it in the back of your mind for any other accounting or finance classes you take: Sometimes a company receives cash on held-to-maturity investments because of a prepayment of the principal or scheduled payments of principal and interest. Additionally, sometimes bonds are *called,* which essentially means that the issuer pays them off early.

- *Available-for-sale* debt investments are one of those accounting topics defined by what they aren't rather than what they are. They don't fall into the held-to-maturity or trading category. However, as with the held-to-maturity investments, any cash the company receives from their sale or collection of principal prior to or at maturity reflects as a cash source in the investing section of the statement of cash flows.

✔ **Sales of equity investments:** If the company sells stock it owns in other corporations, the cash it receives is an investment source. So suppose your company owns 500 shares of ABC Corp. common stock, and you decide to sell all 500 shares to finance another purchase. Any money you receive for the sale of your shares goes in the investing section.

✔ **Sales of property, plant, and equipment (PP&E) and intangibles:** The cash proceeds from any PP&E the corporation owns and sells (such as cars, buildings, or equipment) is an investment source of cash. Ditto if the company sells an intangible such as a patent. (A *patent* provides licensing for inventions or other unique processes and designs, thus lim- iting who can profit from them.)

Investing uses of cash

Here are the potential uses of cash that would appear in the investing section of the statement of cash flows:

- ✔ **Loans and debt purchases:** Any cash the company loans to another company is a cash outlay. So is any cash the company uses to buy bonds.

- ✔ **Purchase of equity investments:** This category includes any cash the company uses to buy stock in another corporation.

- ✔ **Purchase of PP&E:** If the business pays cash for any fixed asset acquisition or an intangible asset, this outlay of cash must appear in the investing section.

Accounting for financing activities

If your head is spinning like a top at this point, take heart! You're on the last section of the statement of cash flows. In addition to that good news, financing activities are the flip side of investing, so if you have a handle on investing you'll be able to whiz through financing activities.

Okay, so in a nutshell, what are these financing activities? Financing activities show transactions with lenders such as with long-term liabilities (paying or securing loans beyond a period of 12 months from the balance sheet date) and equity items (the sale of company stock and payment of dividends). Sound familiar from the investing section?

There is just one main financing cash source: **Cash proceeds if a business issues its own stock or debt.** For example, ABC Corp. sells $3,000 of its own stock to XYZ, Inc., The cash ABC receives from XYZ for this transaction is a financing source of cash on ABC's statement of cash flows.

Both short-term and long-term debt the company becomes liable for go in the financing section. How long the creditor plans to hold the debt determines whether it goes on the creditor's books as short- or long-term debt.

Now, here are the uses of cash that would appear in the financing section of the statement of cash flows:

- ✔ **Treasury stock transactions:** *Treasury stock* is shares of corporate stock that were previously sold and have since been bought back by the issuing corporation. The use of the cash is to buy back stock from shareholders. See Chapter 9 for more information about treasury stock.

✔ **Cash dividend payments:** *Cash dividends* are earnings paid to share-holders based on the number of shares they own. Dividends can also come in the form of stock dividends, which don't involve cash changing hands. So remember, only cash dividends go in the financing section. You find more information about cash and stock dividends, plus some info on stock splits (also a noncash transaction), in Chapter 9.

✔ **Paying back debt:** Any principal payment a company makes on bonds or loans is a financing activity. Principal payments on capital lease obligations are financing activities as well. *Capital leases* take place when the renter (lessee) assumes the benefits and liabilities of ownership of the leased asset; see Chapter 19.

Recognizing Methods for Preparing the Statement of Cash Flows

There are two ways to prepare a statement of cash flows: the indirect and direct methods. The Financial Accounting Standards Board (FASB; see Chapter 4) prefers the direct method, while the business community prefers the indirect method. Regardless of which method you use, the bottom-line cash balance is the same, and it has to equal how much cash you show on the balance sheet.

Change is in the wind regarding the preparation of the statement of cash flows. As of this writing, FASB staff have drafted proposals addressing many changes to the statement of cash flows, including a possible mandate requiring the use of the direct method. Many companies argue that the cost to prepare the statement of cash flows using the direct method (or any new method deviating from the indirect method) outweighs the potential benefit to the users. But the FASB's goal is to achieve standardization with this financial report, so stay tuned for possible changes!

At the end of this chapter, I show you how to prepare a statement of cash flows using both the direct and indirect methods. Should changes to the way you prepare the statement of cash flows take place in the future, it's doubtful that the FASB will require companies to restate prior years' financial statements. So no matter what happens, you need to have a handle on how to use both methods. Plus, your financial accounting textbook discusses both methods, so you can bet you'll be tested on both!

Using the direct method

The direct method of preparing the statement of cash flows shows the net cash from operating activities, so it shows all operating cash receipts and payments. Some examples of cash receipts you use for the direct method are cash collected from customers, interest and dividends the company receives, and other operating cash receipts such as cash received if the company sells an asset. Examples of cash payments are cash paid to employees and other suppliers and interest paid on notes payable, capital leases (see Chapter 19), or other loans.

Here are three key facts to remember about the direct method:

- ✔ You present cash received and paid — not net income or loss as shown on the income statement (see Chapter 10).

- ✔ Any differences reflecting when using the direct versus the indirect method take place only in the operating section of the statement of cash flows. The financing and investing sections are the same regardless of which method you use.

- ✔ The FASB prefers the direct method because it believes the direct method gives the users of the financial statements a more complete picture of the health of the business.

Starting indirectly with net income

When you use the indirect method of preparing the statement of cash flows, the operating section starts with net income from the income statement. You then adjust net income for any noncash items hitting the income statement. Your two biggies are depreciation (see Chapter 12) and amortization (see Chapter 7) expense, both of which are noncash transactions.

Other common items requiring adjustment are gains and losses from the sale of assets (see Chapter 10). This is because the gain or losses shown on the income statement for the sale will rarely if ever equal the cash a company receives. In other words, gain or loss is based on the difference between the asset's *net book value*, which is cost less accumulated depreciation, and the amount the item sold for — not how much cash the buyer hands over to the seller.

For example, say that a business has a machine it previously used for a product it no longer makes. Because it no longer needs the machine, the business sells it to another company for $1,500. The cash received is $1,500, but what about gain or loss on disposal? To figure out that amount, suppose the company originally paid $3,000 to purchase and install the machine. During the time it owned the machine, it *depreciated* the machine (spread the cost of ownership over the machine's useful life) in the amount of $2,000, making its book value $1,000 ($3,000 – $2,000). Gain on disposal is $500, which is the difference between book value and the purchase price ($1,500 – $1,000). So there is a $500 difference between gain on the income statement ($1,000) and the cash inflow of $1,500.

Interpreting the Statement of Cash Flows

Users of the statement of cash flows are primarily interested in whether the company has positive cash flows from operations. As a general rule, a company should be covering its costs by cash it brings in from the day-to-day running of the business rather than from borrowed funds. As a potential investor or creditor, I want to see that cash the company brings in through operations exceeds any cash brought in by selling assets or borrowing money. This is because selling assets or borrowing money can never be construed as a continuing event like bringing in cash from selling goods or services.

A company may issue stock or bonds in order to expand. The amount it generates may well exceed the net cash from operations. On a nonrecurring basis, that situation can be okay because successful expansion is a good thing for investors and creditors. However, unless cash from operations with regularity exceeds cash from other sources, a company will be paying back debt with debt, which is decidedly not a good thing.

Here's how an investor and lender uses the statement of cash flows:

- ✔ **Investor:** An investor wants to make sure the corporation has enough cash flow to pay an adequate return on investment. In other words, can the investor anticipate getting a cash dividend each year? Also important is using the statement of cash flows to evaluate how well the company is managing its cash because investors will eventually sell their shares of stock, something that won't be possible if the company mismanages its cash to such a point that it goes out of business.

- ✔ **Creditor:** The creditor also has a vested interest in making sure the company has sound cash management. After all, in addition to the interest income the debtor pays for the use of the loan, the creditor wants to make sure it also gets paid back the principal portion of the loan. It's never a good sign if a business is paying back debt by assuming more debt.

Looking at Two Sample Statements of Cash Flows

Here, I show you what the statement of cash flows looks like when you use both the direct and indirect methods of preparation. Figure 11-1 is the statement of cash flows using the direct method, and Figure 11-2 is the statement of cash flows using the indirect method. As you look at both, note that the cash balance at 12/31/2012 is the same for both methods.

The increase in cash of $10,212 is the sum of the net cash provided by operating activities, net cash used for investing activities, and net cash used for financing activities ($45,287 – $35,000 – $75).

When you prepare a statement of cash flows using the direct method, you also have to include a section reconciling accrual net income to cash provided by operating activities.

As you can see, the indirect method operating section is the same as the statement you prepare reconciling cash to accrual for the direct method. Cash flows from investing and financing remain the same regardless of which method you use.

Statement of Cash Flows
Direct Method
For the Year Ending 12/31/2012

Cash Flows from Operating Activities:

Cash received from customers	58,523
Cash paid to suppliers	7,884
Employee compensation	2,139
Other operating expenses paid	1,548
Interest paid	675
Taxes paid	990
Net cash provided by operating activities	45,287

Cash Flows from Investing Activities:

Proceeds from sale of equipment	25,000
Purchase of land	(60,000)
Net cash used for investing activities	(35,000)

Cash Flows from Financing Activities:

New long-term borrowing	350
Payment of long-term debt	(200)
Purchase of treasury stock	(175)
Payment of dividends	(50)
Net cash used for financing activities	(75)

Increase (decrease) in cash	10,212
Cash balance, January 1, 2012	35,620
Cash balance, December 31, 2012	45,832

Reconciliation of Net Income and Net Cash Provided by Operating Activities:

Net Income	
Add (deduct items) not affecting cash:	43,987
Depreciation expense	2,150
Gain on sale of equipment	(150)
Increase in accounts receivable	(3,500)
Increase in accounts payable	2,800
Net cash provided by operating activities	45,287

Figure 11-1:
A direct method statement of cash flows.

Statement of Cash Flows
Indirect Method
For the Year Ending 12/31/2012

Cash Flows from Operating Activities:
    Net income
    Add (deduct items) not affecting cash: 43,987
        Depreciation expense   2,150
        Gain on sale of equipment   (150)
        Increase in accounts receivable   (3,500)
        Increase in accounts payable   2,800
        Net cash provided by operating activities   45,287

Cash Flows from Investing Activities:
    Proceeds from sale of equipment   25,000
    Purchase of land   (60,000)
    Net cash used for investing activities   (35,000)

Cash Flows from Financing Activities:
    New long-term borrowing   350
    Payment of long-term debt   (200)
    Purchase of treasury stock   (175)
    Payment of dividends   (50)
    Net cash used for financing activities   (75)

Increase (decrease) in cash   10,212
Cash balance, January 1, 2012   35,620
Cash balance, December 31, 2012   45,832

Figure 11-2:
An indirect method statement of cash flows.

Chapter 12

Examining Depreciation Cost Flow Assumptions

*T*his chapter is your introduction to a company's *tangible* assets, which you can touch and feel — they have a physical presence. Tangible assets, also called *fixed* assets, include property, plant, and equipment (PP&E). Many fixed assets are used for years, and a company relies on a mysterious accounting tool called *depreciation* to keep its financial statements in line with the reality of how long those assets stay in use.

If you read this entire chapter, depreciation won't seem so mysterious anymore. I help you understand what depreciation is, how it affects all three financial statements, and how it connects a business's costs to its expenses. (Yes, costs and expenses are two different things in the business world.) I also show the various depreciation methods financial accountants use: the straight-line, declining balance, sum-of-the-years'-digits, and units-of-production methods. And I walk you through what information you find in a schedule of depreciation.

The presentation in this chapter follows the setup of most financial accounting textbooks, so you can relate the information you find here back to your financial accounting class resources. With this chapter's help, you should be able to discuss depreciation with confidence in the classroom.

Intangible assets, which are assets that you can't see or touch, receive an accounting treatment similar to depreciation that is called *amortization.* See Chapter 7 for the scoop on intangibles.

Discovering How Depreciation Affects All Financial Statements

Let me start with a simple definition of depreciation: It is a method of allocating a company's costs to the appropriate accounting period. Later in the chapter, I define the word *costs* and help you realize what the *appropriate accounting period* may be for a given item. For now, sit tight with this definition, and keep in mind that depreciation is *not* used to figure out an asset's *fair market value* (the amount of money the company could fetch upon sale of that asset). Companies depreciate fixed assets they own. (Only under certain circumstances, which I explain in Chapter 19, do they depreciate fixed assets they lease.)

Many financial accounting transactions affect more than one financial statement. Depreciation is a *noncash transaction* (no money changes hands when you book depreciation), and it affects all three financial statements: the balance sheet (see Part III), the income statement (see Chapter 10), and the statement of cash flows (see Chapter 11). So getting your depreciation calculations right is a major big deal in the world of financial accounting.

If you have already taken some tax accounting classes or have needed to depreciate some assets on your personal tax return (if, for example, you run a small business from home), you are probably familiar with accelerated depreciation methods used for tax purposes. But tax depreciation methods such as the Modified Accelerated Cost Recovery System (MACRS) are quite different from the financial accounting depreciation methods you learn about in this chapter.

How does depreciation take place and affect all three financial statements? When a company buys something that it anticipates being able to use for more than one year, generally accepted accounting principles (GAAP; see Chapter 4) dictate that this purchase not be taken as a reduction to income all at once. (Keep in mind that *income* is the operating and non-operating revenue the company brings in.) Accountants refer to the process of recording the cost of an asset on the balance sheet as *capitalization.*

When an asset it *capitalized,* here's how the purchase affects each financial statement:

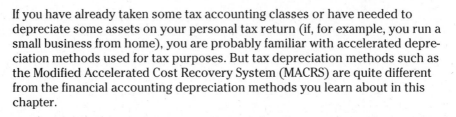

- ✔ **Balance sheet:** The purchase goes on the balance sheet as an asset.

- ✔ **Income statement:** Through the wonderful process of depreciation, the purchase eventually moves from the balance sheet onto the income statement. (The upcoming section "Distinguishing among Depreciation Methods" shows you exactly how this process happens.)

✔ **Statement of cash flows:** At the time of purchase, the item's cost goes on the statement of cash flows as a reduction in cash for the entire purchase price. (If cash doesn't change hands at the time of purchase, the transaction still shows up on the statement of cash flows — just in a slightly different manner.) As the asset is depreciated, the depreciation amount has to be added back onto the statement of cash flows if you use the indirect rather than direct method to prepare the statement of cash flows. (That's because it's a noncash transaction that has been included as an expense.) See Chapter 11 for the scoop on the indirect versus direct method of presenting the statement of cash flows.

When determining what items should be capitalized, common sense has to play a role. For example, I have a trash can in my office that I have used for over three years. Does that mean that the trash can should have been capitalized at the time of purchase? Well, unless this was some sort of pricey designer trash can costing a lot of money, the answer is no. Most companies have a capitalization policy setting a dollar limit for items to be capitalized rather than expensed — for example, items that cost under $100 are automatically expensed no matter how long a company will use them.

Items under $100 are automatically expensed

Mastering Costs

You probably use the terms *cost* and *expense* interchangeably to describe any situation where you're paying cash or a promise of cash in order to purchase a good or service. For example, you buy a gallon of milk at the grocery store and pay cash, or you fill up your car at the pump after swiping your credit card. In either situation, you may gripe about the *cost* of the item you're buying or how that *expense* seems too high. In the business world, costs and expenses are two separate things. I explain why in Chapter 11, and I start this section with a refresher about the difference.

Defining costs and expenses in the business world

Has a life!

In the world of business, day-to-day costs are not the same as expenses. When a business incurs a *cost,* it exchanges a resource (usually cash or a promise to pay cash in the future) to purchase a good or service that will allow the company to generate revenue. But in the future the cost will probably turn into an expense. That's because all expenses have to be matched with revenue for the financial period.

costs turn into expenses

(I can hear the "Huh?" escaping your lips right now. Keep reading, and I'll try to clear things up.)

Here's an example of how a common business transaction can initially record as a cost and eventually migrate into an expense.

Let's say you are the manager of the women's apparel department of a major manufacturer. You're expanding the department to add a new line of women's formal garments. You need to purchase five new sewing machines, which for this type of business are fixed assets.

When you buy the sewing machines, the price you pay (or promise to pay) is a cost. Then, as you use the sewing machines in the normal activity of your business, you *depreciate* them: You reclassify the cost of buying the asset as an expense of doing business. So the resources you use to purchase the sewing machines move from the balance sheet (cost) to the income statement (expense).

Your income statement shows revenue and expenses. The difference between those two numbers is the company's *net income* (when revenue is more than expense) or *net loss* (when expenses are higher than revenue).

Still wondering what the big deal is with financial accountants having to depreciate fixed assets? Well, the process ties back to the matching principle, which I discuss in the next section.

Satisfying the matching principle

In financial accounting, every transaction you work with has to satisfy the matching principle (see Chapter 5). You have to associate all recognized revenue (both earned and realizable) during the accounting period to all expenses you incur to produce that revenue.

Continuing with the sewing machine example, let's say the life of the sewing machine — the average amount of time the company knows it can use the sewing machine before having to replace it — is five years. The average cost of a commercial sewing machine is $1,500. If the company expenses the entire purchase price (cost) of $1,500 in the year of purchase, the net income for year one is understated and the net income for the next four years is overstated.

Why? Because while the company laid out $1,500 in year one for a machine, the company anticipates using the machine for another four years. So to truly match the sales the company generates from garments made using the sewing machine, the cost of the machine has to be allocated over each of the years it will be used to crank out those garments for sale.

Identifying product and period costs

How a company classifies a cost depends on the category it falls into. Using generally accepted accounting principles (GAAP), which I explain in Chapter 4, business costs fall into three general categories: product, period, and systematic. The subject of this chapter, depreciation, is a *systematic cost,* which means it's a cost expensed over time. I discuss depreciation more in the next section.

Here, let me briefly define product and period costs so you can see how they differ from a systematic cost such as depreciation:

- **Product costs:** Any costs that relate to manufacturing or merchandising an item for sale to customers. A common example is inventory (see Chapter 13), which reflects costs a manufacturing company incurs when buying all the different items or raw materials it needs to make the items it sells to its customers. For a merchandiser, the cost of inventory is what it pays to buy the finished goods from the manufacturer.

- **Period costs:** Costs that, while necessary to keep the business doors open, don't tie back to any specific item the company sells. Examples of period costs are shop rent, telephone expense, and office salaries.

Learning which costs are depreciated

When a company purchases a fixed asset (see Chapter 7) like a computer or machine, the cost of the asset is spread over its useful life, which may be years after the purchase. Therefore, depreciation is a *systematic cost:* It logically allocates to financial periods based on when the company receives the benefit of the cost.

Your next question may be this: "Which costs associated with purchasing a fixed asset do you add together when figuring up the entire cost? Just the purchase price? Purchase price plus tax and shipping? Other costs?"

Except for the allocation of cost between land and buildings, which I discuss in the next section, figuring depreciated cost is straightforward. Per GAAP, the business has to record all fixed asset purchases on its balance sheet at their original cost plus all the ordinary and necessary costs to get the fixed asset ready to use. The total cost of the fixed asset is referred to as its *depreciable base.*

Say, for example, the company makes pencils and buys a new machine to automatically separate and shrink-wrap ten pencils into salable units. Here are examples of various costs of the machine: the purchase price, sales tax, freight-in, and assembly of the shrink-wrapping machine on the factory floor. (*Freight-in* is the buyer's cost to get the machine from the seller to the buyer.)

Allocating costs between land and building

A frequent question I get in my financial accounting lectures is how to figure out the allocation between land and building. After all, you are taking an accounting class — not the real estate appraiser's exam! How do you figure out if the company appropriately allocates cost between the land and the building? The best verification is for the business to have an appraisal done during the purchasing process.

An *appraisal* occurs when a licensed professional determines the value of real property. If you've ever purchased a home and applied for a mortgage, you're probably familiar with property appraisals. Basically, the appraisal provides assurance to the mortgage company that you're not borrowing more than the property is worth.

Even if a business doesn't have to secure a mortgage to purchase a real property asset, it still gets an appraisal to make sure it's not overpaying for the property. Alternatively, the county property tax records may show an allocation of building to land. However, that allocation is just for property tax purposes; it may not be materially correct for depreciation purposes.

For your financial accounting class, the allocation information will be given. Just remember to subtract land cost from the total if doing a real property depreciation homework assignment or test question.

Handling real property depreciation

Now, what about *real property* — land and buildings? Both are clearly fixed assets, but the cost of the land a building sits on is not depreciated and has to be separated from the cost of the building. (See Chapter 7 for how this separation looks on the balance sheet.) Why? The answer is that GAAP mandates that separation — no *if*s, *and*s, or *but*s about it.

The cost of land is never depreciated either under GAAP or on the company's tax return. That's because the land a building stands on is assumed to retain its value. In other words, it won't be used up or run down through use over time.

So, if a company pays $250,000 to purchase a building to manufacture its pencils and the purchase price is allocated 90 percent to building and 10 percent to land, how much of the purchase price is spread out over the useful life of the building? Your answer is $250,000 multiplied by 90 percent: $225,000.

However, just to keep you on your toes, land *improvements* are depreciable. Examples of land improvements are fences, roads, and gates. Land improvements should be shown as a separate line item on the balance sheet (see Chapter 7).

If a business purchases a piece of raw land and constructs its own building, this accounting issue gets simple because you have a sales price for the land and construction costs for the building.

Expensing repairs and maintenance

Preventative repair and maintenance costs are expenses of the period in which they are incurred and not systematic depreciation costs. For example, on June 14, a florist business has the oil changed and purchases a new set of tires for the flower delivery van. The cost of the oil change and tires goes on the income statement as an operating expense for the month of June.

The next month, the delivery van's transmission goes completely out, stranding driver and flowers at the side of the road. Rebuilding the transmission significantly increases the useful life of the delivery van, so you have to add the cost of the new transmission to the net book value of the van on the balance sheet. *Net book value* (also shortened to just *book value*) is the difference between the cost of the fixed asset and its accumulated depreciation at any given time.

I discuss accumulated depreciation in the "Preparing a Depreciation Schedule" section later in this chapter. For now, just remember that *accumulated depreciation* refers to how much depreciation has been taken for a particular asset so far.

Distinguishing among Depreciation Methods

Financial accounting generally uses four methods of depreciation. Three are based on time: straight-line, declining balance, and sum-of-the-years'-digits. The fourth method, units-of-production, is based on actual physical usage of the fixed asset. Here's a brief explanation of each:

- ✔ **Straight-line method:** This method spreads out the cost of the fixed asset evenly over its useful life.

- ✔ **Declining balance method:** This is an *accelerated* method of depreciation, meaning the depreciation expense is higher in the earlier years of ownership.

- ✔ **Sum-of-the-years'-digits method:** With this method, you figure depreciation expense by assigning numbers (in declining order) to each year of the fixed asset's expected useful life. For example, an asset used for three years would require this calculation: 3 + 2 + 1 = 6. Your depreciation rate for any given year is the year's assigned number divided by that sum, so the year 1 rate would be 3/6 (or 1/2). This is another accelerated method of depreciation.

- ✔ **Units-of-production method:** Using this method, you compare the total estimated number of units the fixed asset will produce over its expected useful life to the number of units produced in the current accounting period.

Depletion, which is the annual expense for the use of natural resources, is also based on actual physical usage. Examples of natural resources subject to depletion are oil, timber, and minerals.

Don't worry, I walk you through an example of each of the above methods of depreciation in detail later in this section. And to show how the choice of a depreciation method can greatly affect the amount of depreciation expense taken in each year, I use the same asset facts and circumstances for each depreciation example.

First, however, you need to realize what information you need to know about each fixed asset before you calculate depreciation for your financial accounting class. For the purposes of calculating depreciation for this chapter, here are the facts and circumstances for your sample fixed asset — a delivery truck that the company buys on January 1, 2012:

- ✔ **The cost of the asset:** In the earlier section "Learning which costs are depreciated," I explain what costs have to be included in the *depreciable base* — the total cost of the fixed asset. The cost of the delivery truck is $30,000.

- ✔ **How long the company anticipates being able to use the fixed asset:** The company may measure the length in years, in production hours, or in miles driven. For our example, the business anticipates using the delivery truck for 5 years or 50,000 miles.

- ✔ **The value of the asset after the company is done using it (known as its *salvage value*):** The salvage value is an estimate that management makes for how much the fixed asset will be worth when it's retired. When the delivery truck is replaced, the company anticipates receiving $3,000 in trade-in value.

- ✔ **The depreciation method the company uses:** I introduce the four GAAP methods earlier in this section. The method the business uses is a matter of choice as long as the method is appropriate for the asset. For financial accounting, the standard of appropriateness is met if the company uses the method that most closely matches expenses to revenue.

  A business can't arbitrarily switch methods after it's started using one depreciation method for an asset. To do so would be a change in accounting method (see Chapter 15).

- ✔ **Date of purchase and whether the company is on a calendar or fiscal year-end:** The date is when the fixed asset is ready for use. Calendar year-end is on December 31. A fiscal year ends on the last day of any other month during the year. For example, a fiscal year can be April 1 through March 31. This business has a calendar year-end of December 31. The delivery van is purchased on January 1.

Ready? Well, start your engines and let's depreciate this delivery van!

Walking through the straight-line method

When using the straight-line method, the salvage value reduces the depreciable base. So the cost of the delivery truck ($30,000) less its salvage value ($3,000) gives you a depreciable base of $27,000.

The expected useful life is 5 years. So depreciation expense for the van would be $27,000/5 or $5,400 depreciation expense per year for each of the 5 years. Book value at the end of year 5 is $3,000.

Accelerating by using declining balance

Unlike the straight-line method, you do not deduct salvage value when figuring the depreciable base with the declining balance method. However, you do have to limit depreciation so that at the end of the day, net book value is the same as the salvage value. Clear as mud? Stick with me.

For your depreciation rate, you take a multiple of the straight-line rate (which will be given to you as part of the narrative for any financial accounting assignment or test question). In this example, I want you to use *double declining balance,* which is twice the straight-line rate.

Because the delivery van has a useful life of 5 years, shown as a percentage, the straight-line rate is 1/5 or 20 percent per year. Double that to get your double declining balance rate of 40 percent.

Figure 12-1 shows how to figure double declining balance depreciation. Note that in year 5, the rate doesn't matter because you have to limit the depreciation to salvage value. Because the ending net book value is $3,888 in year 4, depreciation is limited to $888 in year 5.

	Beginning Net Book Value	Rate	Depreciation Expense	Accumulated Depreciation	Ending Net Book Value
20X1	$30,000	0.4	$12,000	$12,000	$18,000
20X2	18,000	0.4	7,200	19,200	10,800
20X3	10,800	0.4	4,320	23,520	6,480
20X4	6,480	0.4	2,592	26,112	3,888
20X5	3,888	*	888	27,000	3,000

Figure 12-1: A double declining balance depreciation calculation.

Calculating sum-of-the-years'-digits

Using this method, you depreciate the asset by adding the useful life years together (5 + 4 + 3 + 2 + 1 = 15) to get your denominator for the rate fraction. In year one, your multiplier is 5/15 (1/3); in year two, the multiplier is 4/15; and so on. As with straight-line depreciation, you back out the salvage value before you start.

So here's how sum-of-the-years'-digits depreciation expense plays out for the delivery van:

- ✔ **Year 1:** $27,000/3 = $9,000 depreciation expense.

- ✔ **Year 2:** $27,000 multiplied by 4 and then divided by 15 = $7,200 depreciation expense

- ✔ **Year 3:** $27,000 multiplied by 3 and divided by 15 = $5,400 depreciation expense

- ✔ **Year 4:** $27,000 multiplied by 2 and divided by 15 = $3,600 depreciation expense

- ✔ **Year 5:** $27,000/15 = $1,800 depreciation expense

Check the math: Adding up all five years of depreciation expense equals $27,000, which is the cost of the delivery truck less the salvage value!

Using the units-of-production method

Unlike straight-line and declining balance, this method bases depreciation expense on actual physical use. It's very good for figuring depreciation for machinery and vehicles.

Here's how this method works with the delivery van purchase example: The business anticipates using the delivery truck for 50,000 miles. First, you have to figure the depreciation rate. Find the cost of the delivery van less salvage value: $30,000 – $3,000 = $27,000. Divide this figure by your anticipated usage: $27,000/50,000 miles equals $.54 per mile.

In essence, using this method for the delivery van is giving you a standard mileage rate. If you've ever done your own tax return and had to figure up your mileage expense for charitable work you've done, it's the same concept.

To figure depreciation expense year after year, you take the actual number of miles the delivery van is driven during the year times the depreciation rate. Say that in 2012, the van is driven 10,200 miles; depreciation is $5,508 (10,200 × $.54).

after the fact if material renovations are performed. (Think about the truck transmission example from the earlier section "Expensing repairs and maintenance.")

✔ **Life:** How long the company estimates it will use the fixed asset.

✔ **Method:** The method of depreciation the company uses for this fixed asset.

✔ **Salvage value:** The estimated value of the fixed asset when the company gets rid of or replaces it.

✔ **Date purchased:** The day the asset was purchased.

✔ **Current depreciation:** The depreciation expense booked in the current period.

✔ **Accumulated depreciation:** The total amount of depreciation expensed from the day the company placed the fixed asset in service to the date of the financial report.

✔ **Net book value:** The difference between the fixed asset cost and its accumulated depreciation.

Depending on the size of the company, the depreciation schedule may also have the fixed asset's identifying number, the location where the fixed asset is kept, property tax information, and many more facts about the asset.

Having a nicely organized depreciation schedule allows the company to keep at its fingertips a summary of activity for each fixed asset. Why is this information important? As you find out in Chapter 7 (when learning how companies account for fixed assets), this info cannot be ferreted out by looking at the balance sheet.

Check out Figure 12-3 to see the basic organization for a depreciation schedule.

Figure 12-3:
Example of a depreciation schedule.

Description	Cost	Life	Method	Salvage Value	Date purchased	Current year depreciation expense	Accumulated Depreciation	Net Book Value
Delivery van	30,000	5	Units-of-production	2,000	01/15/2012	3,060	6,200	23,800
Computer	1,500	3	Straight-line	0	05/20/2012	500	1,000	500
Furniture	2,500	3	Straight-line	300	09/15/2012	733	1,466	1,034
Fixtures	700	10	Straight-line	100	03/10/2012	60	240	460

See Chapter 18 if you are wondering how to account for the difference between GAAP and tax depreciation.

Chapter 13

Learning about Inventory Cost Flow Assumptions

Some people think that inventory is only the merchandise available for sale in a store. I discuss that kind of inventory (called *retail* or *merchandise inventory*) in this chapter, but I also introduce you to other kinds of *product inventory* used by manufacturers, which includes direct materials, work in process, and finished goods.

You also find out in this chapter about two methods a company may use to keep track of merchandise inventory, as well as the four methods businesses may use to value ending inventory: specific identification; weighted average; last-in, first-out; and first-in, first-out. Most financial accounting textbooks devote pages to these four methods.

Some businesses actually won't have *any* inventory, and I explain when you can expect this situation to occur and how to handle any minimal supply inventory this type of business may keep on hand.

Discovering How Inventory Valuation Affects the Financial Statements

In financial accounting, you are preparing financial statements for outside users, such as investors and lenders (see Chapter 1). They need accurate financial statements to make informed decisions on whether they want to invest in the company or loan it money.

For *manufacturing* companies (which make products) and *merchandising* companies (which sell the products made by the manufacturers), inventory can be a big part of the balance sheet. Actually, it may be their largest current asset account. So proper accounting for inventory is very important — including determining what costs go on the balance sheet rather than the income statement to make sure the client values its ending inventory properly. A company can inadvertently prepare a set of highly inaccurate financial statements by expensing purchases rather than keeping them on the balance sheet as inventory.

So what costs are okay to expense directly on the income statement, and which costs should stay on the balance sheet? Here's a quick and dirty answer: Any items a company buys to sell that it will put to use in periods beyond the current one are taken to inventory.

Inventory ties into the revenue process and to cost of goods sold (see Chapter 10). Associating inventory with cost of goods sold makes common sense — you have to buy something before you can sell it. But you may be wondering how revenue and inventory relate to each other. Well, remember that you need to use generally accepted accounting principles (GAAP), which I introduce in Chapter 4. GAAP dictate that expenses are matched with revenue earned for the period.

How does inventory come into the revenue equation? In Chapter 10 I show how to prepare a cost of goods sold for a merchandising and manufacturing company. Product costs are part of the cost of goods sold. Product costs that relate to inventory are any costs that a company incurs when purchasing or manufacturing an item for sale to customers. The cost of goods sold on the income statement is what the company pays to buy or manufacture the goods that it sells to its customers *in that specific period only*. The rest of the cost of the product purchases stays on the balance sheet as a current asset.

Do Service Companies Have Inventory?

While discussions of inventory focus on manufacturing and merchandising companies, you also need to consider *service companies:* those that don't provide a tangible good and normally won't have any type of appreciable inventory. Service companies provide more of a knowledge-based work product. (Think about what you get from your dentist or family physician.) However, if a service company keeps a large amount of office or other supplies on hand, it may inventory them instead of just taking the cost of supplies purchased to the supply expense each month.

All financial accounting textbooks I have taught from have a favorite homework and test question based on supplies inventory. Here's how to approach it to look like a star in your financial accounting class:

The facts will generally be that the company purchases a certain amount of supplies in a month. The question will ask you to set up the journal entry to record both the purchase and expense of the supplies in that month. In this example, let's say the company purchases supplies *on account,* which means the company promises to pay for them at a later date. The supplies cost $700 at the beginning of September. On the last day of September, an inventory is taken and supplies in the amount of $230 remain in the supply cabinet.

Your journal entry to record the purchase is to debit "supplies" (an asset account) and credit "accounts payable" for $700. So far you have not affected the income statement.

Now at the end of the month, you have to adjust supplies inventory to the actual on hand, which involves expensing the portion of supplies used. The company purchased $700 of supplies and only $230 remain, so you know that $470 ($700 – $230) of supplies were used and should be expensed for the month of September. So your journal entry is to debit "supplies expense" (an income statement account) and credit "supplies" (the asset account). A lot of students get this question wrong, so just remember the above and you'll be fine.

Technically, anything the company purchases that will not be used up in the current period should go to some sort of inventory account. However, retail shops sometimes take shop supplies (such as bags, tags, and cash register receipts) to the income statement expense when they are purchased instead of to a balance sheet account such as shop supplies inventory. Doing so is normally not a big deal unless the expense is a material amount. For a larger retailer like Target, the amount would be material because it purchases everything in tremendous volume.

Classifying Inventory Types

Depending on the type of business, you'll encounter different types of inventory. To make it easier for you to understand, in this section I break the subject out between inventory for merchandising companies and inventory for manufacturing companies.

Accounting for merchandising company inventory

Accounting for merchandise inventory, while it has its moments, is easier than accounting for manufacturing inventory. That's because a merchandising company, such as a retail store, has only one class of inventory to keep track of: goods the business purchases from various manufacturers for resale.

Here's an example of the basic flow of inventory for a retailer: A linen sales associate at a major department store notices and informs the manager of the department that the department is running low on a certain style of linen. The manager follows the department store's purchasing process, and the end result is that the department receives a shipment of linens from its vendor.

This transaction is a purchase (cost), but it's not an expense until the department store sells the linens. So the business records the entire shipment of linens on the balance sheet as an addition to both inventory and accounts payable (see Chapter 8). I use *accounts payable* instead of *cash* because the department store has payment terms with this vendor and money has yet to change hands during this transaction.

Say that in August, the store sells linens to customers for $150 that cost the company $75 to purchase from the vendor. Sales revenue increases by $150, cost of goods sold increases by $75, and inventory decreases by $75. Matching the expense to revenue, the effect to net income is $75 ($150 – $75).

Pretty basic stuff. The company buys inventory and sells it. Next, I talk about how retail shops normally track inventory. Two major types of inventory systems exist: perpetual and periodic.

Perpetual system

Most larger retailers have electronic cash registers (ECRs). If you've ever used the self-checkout, you've used one. The checkout features a glass window with a red beam of light. You run the bar code of a product over the red beam, and the selling price of the item automatically records as a sale for which you are charged and the business receives revenue.

If the business also uses a *point-of-sale system,* which means transactions at the register automatically update all accounting records, the inventory count is updated constantly, *perpetually,* as the ECR records the item sold. This means that the cost of the item sold is taken out of the asset inventory account and moved to cost of goods sold (COGS).

With point-of-sale systems, transactions taking place at the cash register update all inventory, COGS, and sales information throughout the system in real time as the transactions occur.

Let's say you go into Target and buy a birthday card for a friend. As you check out, the point-of-sale software is updating the greeting card department records showing that one less birthday card is available for sale. The software is also updating COGS showing the cost for the card, and it's updating revenue to reflect the retail price (what you just paid) for the birthday card.

Even if a company uses a point-of-sale system, taking a physical inventory at year-end (or periodically) is still very important to verify that the perpetual system is working correctly. Taking a physical inventory is also the best way to identify breakage and employee or customer theft issues.

Periodic system

With a periodic system, the physical inventory is taken periodically, and the resulting figure is used to adjust the balance sheet "inventory asset" account. Retail shops using periodic inventory usually take inventory at their particular year-end. However, inventory could be taken more often, such as quarterly or at the end of every heavy sales season (such as Valentine's Day, Mother's Day, and the December holidays).

Here's how the periodic system works: The business takes *ending inventory,* coming up with a dollar amount for all unsold inventory as of the last day of the accounting period. Next, the company's accounting department subtracts ending inventory totals from the beginning inventory after adding in all inventory purchases made during the period. The resulting number is cost of goods sold (COGS). The balance sheet inventory account is reduced and the income statement expense account COGS is increased by that number to match expenses with revenue.

Using the periodic system, COGS can be determined with accuracy approaching 100 percent only after the physical inventory is taken. When companies prepare financial statements and a physical inventory is not taken, they use an estimate, which is basically the best guess for inventory and COGS (see Chapter 15). For example, they may use prior experience to estimate COGS. If in prior years COGS for May was 75 percent of gross sales, the company uses the same percentage for current COGS, adjusting that figure to actual at year-end using the physical inventory figures.

Consignment goods, those a merchandising business offers for sale but does not officially own, are not included in inventory. With a consignment arrangement, the merchandiser (consignee) is acting as a middleman between the owner of the goods (consignor) and the customer.

Accounting for manufacturing company inventory

To account for all expenses it incurs while making products for resale, a manufacturing company has a "cost of goods manufactured." (See Chapter 10 for a visual on preparing the cost of goods manufactured section of the income statement.) The cost of goods manufactured contains three types of inventory: direct materials, work in process, and finished goods.

Direct material inventory

The *direct material* (also known as *raw materials*) inventory reflects all the materials the company uses to make a product. For example, for a car manufacturer this includes the steel to form the body, leather or fabric for the seat, and all those other gizmos and parts that go under the hood. (Hey, I'm an accountant — not a mechanic.) In essence, any materials that you can directly trace back to making the car are direct material inventory.

For your coursework, keep in mind that manufacturing companies can use the perpetual inventory tracking method I describe in the previous section to keep track of their direct material inventory. For example, components that a computer manufacturer needs to assemble laptops for sale to retail stores will have serial numbers that are scanned in when purchased from the component manufacturer and scanned back out when incorporated into the computer made by the computer manufacturer. Thus, the manufacturer keeps a running total of components in inventory.

Work-in-process inventory

At any point in time during the manufacturing process, the company probably has items that are in the process of being made but are not yet complete, which is *work in process.* With a car manufacturer, imagine the car going down the production line. At the stroke of midnight on the last day of the accounting period, there will be cars up and down the line in various stages of completion. The company values its work-in-process inventory based on how far each product has been processed.

Figuring up the value of the work-in-process inventory is an exciting subject you'll cover when and if you take managerial or cost accounting. For your financial accounting class, any work-in-process figures will be given to you.

Figuring ownership of finished goods

Obviously, any finished goods that haven't been matched with a customer are part of the manufacturer's inventory. But suppose the finished goods have a buyer and are in transit to that customer. Who owns the finished goods then?

To make this determination, you need to find out whether the terms of the sale are for *free on board (FOB) shipping point* or *FOB destination*.

FOB shipping point means the customer owns the merchandise as soon as it leaves the manufacturer's loading dock; ownership transfers to the buyer at the shipping point to the common carrier. FOB destination is the opposite: The customer owns the inventory only after it has hit its own loading dock; any merchandise in transit to the customer is still counted as part of the seller/manufacturer's inventory.

Finished goods inventory

Finally, the costs you associate with goods that are completely ready for sale to customers, but have not yet been sold, are classified as *finished goods inventory*. For the car manufacturer, this category consists of cars not yet sold to individual dealerships.

Getting to Know Inventory Valuation Methods

Your financial accounting textbook discusses four methods to value ending inventory: specific identification; weighted average; first-in, first-out (FIFO); and last-in, first-out (LIFO). Like depreciation (see Chapter 12), depending on the method the company uses, the amount transferring from the balance sheet inventory account to the income statement cost of goods sold can vary wildly.

Because of this fact, the user of the financial statements must know which inventory valuation method a company uses. The method is always spelled out in the notes to the financial statements; see Chapter 15. If the method used is unclear, any comparison of one company's financial statements to another will be inaccurate because the user may be comparing financial results from dissimilar valuation methods.

In this section, I walk you through each method, show you how to calculate it for your financial accounting homework assignments or test questions, and show you the dollar amount differences when the same number of items in ending inventory is treated using three of the methods: weighted average, FIFO, and LIFO.

Specific identification

This method is probably mentioned only briefly in your financial accounting textbook. Using the *specific identification method*, it's possible to trace back to the exact cost of each individual item in inventory. Usually that's because each item in inventory is special and unique or is equipped with a serial number that can be traced back to its purchase price. So ending inventory is the total of all payments made to the particular vendors from whom the company purchases the inventoried goods.

For example, an art gallery selling a bronze casting by a particular artist can quickly identify how much it cost them to originally purchase the casting by checking out that particular invoice from the artist. So if the gallery paid the artist $500, when the item is sold, the accounting department debits cost of goods sold for $500 and credits inventory for the same amount — reducing ending inventory by $500.

Weighted average

When a company uses the weighted average method, inventory and the cost of goods sold are based on the average cost of all units purchased during the period. This method is generally used when inventory is substantially the same, such as grains and fuel.

If the company sells running shoes, the total cost of all running shoes available for sale is divided by the total pairs of running shoes available for sale. Multiply that figure by the number of running shoes remaining in inventory at the end of the period to get your ending inventory figure.

In the upcoming section "Comparing inventory cost-flow assumptions," you can find an example of this method at work.

First-in, first out (FIFO)

Using the FIFO method, the company assumes that the oldest items in its inventory are the ones first sold. Consider buying milk in a grocery store. The cartons or bottles with the most current expiration date are pushed ahead of the cartons that have more time before they go bad. The oldest cartons of milk may not always actually be the first ones sold (because some people dig around looking for later expiration dates), but the business is basing its numbers on the oldest cartons being sold first.

The *inventory cost flow assumption* states that under FIFO, the oldest units are presumed to be sold first, regardless of whether they actually were.

Last-in, first-out (LIFO)

With this method, the company assumes that its newest items (the ones most recently purchased) are the first ones sold. Imagine a big stack of lumber in a hardware store. If a customer wants to buy a plank, for convenience sake, he takes one off the top. As customers purchase the planks, more planks are added on top of the old ones instead of redistributing the old planks so they move to the top of the pile. Therefore, the newest planks are consistently sold to customers rather than the older ones.

Many manufacturing companies use LIFO because it more closely matches expenses to revenue than FIFO does. Why? The cost of the item being sold has been incurred more closely time-wise to the sale, so there is a better matching of dollar to dollar value.

Your financial accounting book may briefly mention *LIFO reserve*. When a company uses the LIFO method, it may have to include a LIFO reserve amount in its notes to the financial statement. This reserve amount gives the dollar difference between ending inventory when using FIFO and LIFO. I discuss notes to the financial statements in Chapter 15.

Comparing inventory cost-flow assumptions

It's easier to understand how to value ending inventory using weighted average, FIFO, and LIFO if you have an example of each method. (The specific identification method is pretty straightforward, so I don't include it here.) In this section, I offer some practical calculations that should mimic what you see in your financial accounting textbook.

For the ending inventory calculation examples, I use a retail sporting goods shop called Fast Feet Sporting Goods, which sells a variety of items — specifically running shoes. Ready to start? Let's figure out this shop's ending running shoe inventory!

Figure 13-1 shows beginning inventory and purchases from July 1 to the end of the calendar year (there were no purchases in December). Your job is to figure ending inventory and cost of goods sold as of December 31.

Date of Purchase	Number	Cost per Unit	Total Cost
July 1 (beginning inventory)	200	$ 10	$ 2,000
July 15	250	12	3,000
August 5	100	15	1,500
September 6	450	9	4,050
October 3	325	13	4,225
November 21	50	11	550
Total available for sale	1,375		$15,325
Pairs sold	600		
Pairs remaining in December 31 inventory	775		

Figure 13-1: Fast Feet inventory analysis.

Figuring ending inventory and cost of goods sold using FIFO

Using FIFO, you start at the top of the running shoe list because the shoes in beginning inventory are first in, followed by the shoes purchased on July 15, those purchased on August 5, and 50 of the 450 purchased on September 6. As you can see from Figure 13-2, cost of goods sold is $6,950. That means ending inventory is $8,375 ($15,325 − $6,950).

FIFO

Date of Purchase	Number	Cost per Unit	Total Cost
July 1 (beginning inventory)	200	$ 10	$ 2,000
July 15	250	12	3,000
August 5	100	15	1,500
September 6	50	9	450
Total	600		$6,950

Figure 13-2: FIFO cost-flow assumption.

Figuring ending inventory and cost of goods sold using LIFO

Using LIFO, you start at the bottom of the running shoe list because the company assumes that the last shoes purchased are the first ones sold. That gives you the running shoes purchased on November 21, October 3, and 225 of the shoes purchased on September 6. As you can see from Figure 13-3, cost of goods sold is $6,800. That means ending inventory is $8,525 ($15,325 − $6,800).

LIFO liquidation layers

The authors of your financial accounting textbook probably discuss liquidation layers. The point the authors are trying to make is that changes in the number of items in ending inventory combined with fluctuations in cost per item affect cost of goods sold and net income.

Using LIFO more closely matches expenses to revenue because the sales price of the items are more closely matched to the purchase price of the items; both transactions usually take place within 30 to 45 days of each other.

When inventory levels rise (that is, inventory doesn't move as quickly as anticipated), these "layers" the authors refer to are just the additional valuation of inventory that is eventually moved to cost of goods sold when inventory quantities drop.

Here's what you need to do:

✔ Understand the difference between calculating ending inventory using LIFO and FIFO.

✔ Realize that in times of escalating costs, LIFO will give a higher cost of goods sold than FIFO. (And in times of decreasing costs, LIFO will give a lower cost of goods sold than FIFO.)

✔ Keep in mind that LIFO more closely matches revenues to cost of goods sold than FIFO.

LIFO Date of Purchase	Number	Cost per Unit	Total Cost
November 21	50	11	$ 550
October 3	325	13	4,225
September 6	225	9	2,025
Total	600		$ 6,800

Figure 13-3: LIFO cost-flow assumption.

Figuring ending inventory and cost of goods sold using weighted average

Last but not least, here's the calculation for weighted average: The total cost of $15,325 divided by the total number of running shoes available for sale (1,375) equals $11.15 per unit. The shop sells 600 pairs of shoes in the second half of the year. Multiply 600 pairs sold times an average cost of $11.15 to get a cost of goods sold of $6,690. Ending inventory is $8,635 ($15,325 – $6,690).

Depending on which method a business uses, ending inventory for the same facts and circumstances ranges from $8,375 to $8,635. While this isn't a dramatic difference, consider what a difference the accounting method makes when a company has sales in the thousands or millions of units!

The accounting inventory methods shown in this example assume the inventory is valued at cost rather than *market,* which is the price the company can charge when it sells its merchandise. If your client sells items whose market value is less than what the company paid for the inventory, your client may have to value its inventory using the lower of cost or market. You can save this topic for an advanced financial accounting course. But if you'd like to find out more about it now, check out Accounting Research Bulletin No. 43 at the Financial Accounting Standards Board Web site (www.fasb.org).

Preparing an Inventory Worksheet

Closing out this chapter, I want to show you what a simple inventory worksheet looks like. Using Fast Feet as an example, Figure 13-4 shows all running shoes theoretically in stock as of December 31. The last column, "Actual Count," is filled in by Fast Feet employees while taking a physical inventory.

Fast Feet Sporting Goods
Physical Inventory Worksheet

Figure 13-4:
Partial
inventory
worksheet.

Item Name	Item Description	Qty. on Hand	Actual Count
Running shoes			
Ladies	Ladies XYZ brand running shoes	210.00	_____
Ladies	Ladies ABC brand running shoes	125.00	_____
Men's	Men's XYZ brand running shoes	250.00	_____
Men's	Men's ABC brand running shoes	115.00	_____
Children	Children's Lil' Tike running shoes	75.00	_____
		775.00	

Even if a retail shop uses the perpetual method, it's important to take a physical inventory at year end to identify theft and breakage. If, after totaling up the "Actual Count" column, the company has a figure less than 775, it'll know that running shoes left the shop in other ways than by being carried out by paying customers. Under GAAP, the company has to prepare a journal entry (see Chapter 5) to record the cost of the missing footwear — in other words, it adjusts the inventory balance to the actual count.

Part V

Analyzing the Financial Statements

The 5th Wave   By Rich Tennant

"I like the numbers on this company. They show a very impressive acquittal to conviction ratio."

In this part . . .

*E*ver wonder why financial accounting rules are so nit-picky? In this part, you see that the proper classification of accounting transactions is necessary so the users of the financial statement can accurately judge the relative merits of a company. Among the tools investors use are three financial statement measurements: liquidity, activity, and profitability. Liquidity shows how well a company can cover its short-term debt. Activity reports how well a company uses its assets to generate sales. Profitability is measured by whether the company made or lost money during the financial period.

No examination of the financial statements is complete without knowledge of the facts supporting the figures. Chapter 15 walks you through the explanatory notes and other information found in most corporate annual reports. So that you can ace this part of your financial accounting course, I walk through common explanatory notes and disclosures, such as the method of depreciation the company uses and how a company values its ending inventory.

In Chapter 16, you get the scoop on corporate annual reports and the *Form 10-K,* an annual report required by the U.S. Securities and Exchange Commission (SEC).

Chapter 14

Using Ratios and Other Tools

*T*he information in this chapter helps you understand why financial accounting rules are so nit-picky. Properly classifying accounting transactions is key for user analysis, which is the topic of this chapter. Here, you learn about key measurements that financial statement users perform to gauge the effectiveness and efficiency of the way management is running the company.

Three major measurement categories are a company's liquidity, profitability, and activity. You may assume that all investors care about is how profitable a company is, but that's not necessarily true. *Liquidity,* which indicates how well a company can cover its short-term debt, and *activity,* which shows how well a company uses its assets to generate sales, have to be considered along with profitability to form a complete picture of how well the business is performing.

Wrapping up this chapter, you find out about horizontal and vertical analyses of the income statement, which is an excellent way to zoom in on profitability issues.

Ready to get started? The next stop on your exciting financial accounting journey is . . . liquidity measurements!

Learning about Liquidity Measurements

Liquidity is a company's ability to free up cash to meet its business obligations. Liquidity measurements reflect a company's ability to meet its short-term obligations. These measurements are important because a company that can't pay its bills in the short-term more than likely has going concern problems. The phrase *going concern* means the company is likely to continue in business for at least 12 months beyond the date of the balance statement. If a company has going concern problems, you can't be certain it's going to stay in business for very long.

The accounts you use to measure liquidity are taken from the balance sheet. Because liquidity is concerned with the short run, the accounts you use for these measurements are all current rather than long-term.

A quick heads up: Later in this chapter (in the section "Measuring Profitability"), I talk about *trend analysis,* which is looking at ratios over a period of years. Trend analysis isn't normally applicable to liquidity measurements because when it comes to liquidity, financial statement users are looking at what's going on in the short term — not over a long period of time.

Your financial accounting textbook discusses three principal evaluations to measure liquidity: current ratio, acid-test ratio, and working capital. The first two show up in the form of (you guessed it!) ratios. You express working capital as a dollar amount. These measurements are all easier to understand if you use account balances to work through them, so let's get to work computing some figures!

Figuring the current ratio

You find a company's current ratio by dividing its current assets by its current liabilities. I discuss current assets in Chapter 7 and current liabilities in Chapter 8, but here are some quick examples of each:

- **Current assets:** Accounts such as cash, accounts receivable, merchandise inventory, and short-term investments

- **Current liabilities:** Accounts payable and all other debt that is due within 12 months of the balance sheet date, such as *accrued payroll,* which is wages employees have earned but not yet been paid

So, let's say you are looking at a balance sheet. A company's current assets are $120,000, and its current liabilities are $57,000. The current ratio is 2.1 ($120,000 divided by $57,000).

The current ratio tells you a lot about how liquid a company is because current assets are either cash or are easily converted to cash in the short term; in theory, they can be used to pay the short-term obligations. Being able to meet short-term obligations is crucial to a company remaining a going concern.

The theory behind the current ratio is pretty darn simple, so if your financial accounting instructor is anything like me, she is going to test your understanding of the current ratio by giving you facts and having you back into a figure for current assets or current liabilities.

Here's an example similar to what you may encounter in your financial accounting class: Village Shipping, Inc., has current liabilities on December 31 of $140,000, and its current ratio at that time is 2.2. What are the company's current assets? Okay, you know that current assets divided by current liabilities equals the current ratio. You are solving for current assets (the unknown variable x), so your equation is x divided by $140,000 equals 2.2.

$$x/140,000 = 2.2$$

Isolating x on one side of the equation gives you $140,000 times 2.2.

$$x = 140,000 \times 2.2$$

So your current assets are $308,000 ($140,000 × 2.2).

Test your work by plugging that figure into the first equation: $308,000 divided by $140,000 does equal 2.2. Great work!

Don't forget that the method a company uses to value its ending inventory affects the carrying amount of inventory on the balance sheet. (I discuss inventory valuation methods in Chapter 13.) That is one of the reasons why spelling out inventory valuation methods is a required footnote to the financial statements, as I explain in Chapter 15.

Putting the acid test to work

As I explain in the previous section, a company whose current assets are $120,000 and whose current liabilities are $57,000 has a current ratio of 2.1. This business appears to have more than adequate sources from which to pay any short-term debt. However, one current asset account, *merchandise inventory* (inventory a company holds for resale to customers), isn't always all that easy to convert to cash quickly because the company would first need to sell it and then collect any accounts receivable resulting from the sale. So the acid-test ratio is used in conjunction with the current ratio to evaluate the worst-case scenario: that in which the company can't sell any of its existing inventory. If it can't sell any of its existing inventory, can it still pay its bills?

To figure the acid-test ratio, you first add together cash, all temporary cash investments, and accounts receivable. *Temporary cash investments* are those that the company is willing and able to sell within one year of the balance sheet date. (Luckily, you won't have to make a judgment call on what constitutes a temporary cash investment for your financial accounting class. For any homework assignments or test questions, temporary cash investments will be clearly identified.) Next, you divide that figure by the company's current liabilities.

So let's say our company has current assets worth $120,000 and merchandise inventory valued at $40,000. That means its other current assets (cash, temporary cash investment, and accounts receivable) are $80,000 ($120,000 – $40,000). Dividing $80,000 by the company's current liabilities of $57,000 gives you an acid-test ratio of 1.4.

As a general rule, if a company has both a current ratio of at least 2.0 and an acid-test ratio of at least 1.0, that shows it has adequate liquidity to pay current obligations as they come due. You may be asking, "What if ratios are less than these targets — should the investor or lender walk away?" This question is difficult to answer; it depends on the investor and that person's goals. Certainly an interested party should consider doing trend analysis before making a firm decision (see the upcoming section "Measuring Profitability").

Working with working capital

The working capital measurement is simply current assets less current liabilities. If our sample company has current assets of $120,000 and current liabilities of $57,000, working capital is $63,000 ($120,000 – $57,000).

It's not rocket science to realize that most healthy companies have positive working capital. In your personal life, you work to maintain positive working capital so you can pay your bills. Likewise, a business very much wants and needs to have enough cash rattling around in the bank accounts to pay its bills. When the coffers get too low, some businesses take out what are called *working capital loans:* short-term loans that carry companies over a rough patch.

Many businesses won't have enough cash on hand to cover all their short-term debts. The assumption is usually that its accounts receivable will be collected and its merchandise inventory sold, thus converting those current assets to cash.

Always keep in mind for your financial accounting class that you express the working capital measurement as a dollar amount, not a ratio. My students who aren't familiar with working with accounting data tend to confuse the current ratio and working capital — a mistake that can cost valuable points on a quiz or test.

A much-used financial accounting test question asks you to explain how working capital is affected by the payment of short-term debt. Always remember this immutable fact of accounting: Working capital is never affected by the payment of short-term debt because both current assets and current liabilities decrease by the same amount.

Let me give you an example: On December 1, Village Shipping, Inc., has current assets of $50,000 and current liabilities of $10,000. Working capital is $40,000 ($50,000 – $10,000). Now let's say that Village Shipping pays $5,000 of the current liability balance on December 15. Does this payment affect its working capital? No, it does not, because now current assets are $45,000 ($50,000 – $5,000) and current liabilities are $5,000 ($10,000 – $5,000). Working capital remains $40,000 ($45,000 – $5,000).

While the payment of short-term debt doesn't affect working capital, it does affect the current ratio. Using the same example, on December 1, Village Shipping's current ratio is 5 ($50,000 divided by $10,000). On December 15, Village Shipping's current ratio is 9 ($45,000 divided by $5,000). Quite a difference!

Measuring Profitability

In addition to having a handle on how well a company covers its current debt with current assets, just about all financial statement users want to be able to evaluate the relative robustness of a company's income over a series of years or financial periods. Looking at a company's performance over a long period of time is called *trend analysis.*

In this section, I explain how trend analysis works and why it's so important when evaluating profitability. Then, I move on to explain two profitability measures: return on investment and return on equity.

Explaining trend analysis

A single profitability measure standing alone doesn't really tell you much about a company or how it is performing compared to its competition. This is true for two reasons:

- ✔ **The company may have had an exceptionally good or bad year.** Unless a company's performance is static from year to year, looking at only one set of figures gives the financial statement user an inaccurate vision of the company as a whole.

    Consider a personal example. Let's say you have a windfall in 2012: You win $50,000 in the lottery, making your total income (after adding in your earnings from your part-time job) $62,000. The next year and the year after that, you don't have any winning lottery tickets (darn it!), and your average income is $13,000 per year. Clearly, looking only at your income for 2012 doesn't give anything near an accurate picture of your income because that year's income includes an unusual, nonrepeating event.

- ✔ **Under generally accepted accounting principles (GAAP), companies are allowed to use various methods to estimate some expenses.** If a financial statement user is trying to compare Company A to Company B by using a single set of profitability ratios, he's not going to see the whole picture.

    For example, Chapter 13 talks about inventory valuation methods. A company's decision to use one method versus another can cause a wild variation in net income. The same holds true for depreciation of long-term assets, which I discuss in Chapter 12. There are also different options available for booking an estimate for _bad debt_ expense, which is the money the company reckons it won't be able to collect from credit customers (see Chapters 7 and 10). There can be many more differences using allowable GAAP methods, but you get the picture.

    Trend analysis gives much more meaningful information to the financial statement user because differences in accounting methods tend to smooth out over time. For example, while which method a company uses for depreciation affects the amount of depreciation expense by year, it never affects historic original cost. In other words, an asset costing $1,000 can never be depreciated for more than $1,000. So, factoring in any alternative financial accounting methods in use, ratios over a period of several years should be somewhat consistent, which permits the financial statement user to do some useful trend comparisons.

Using trend analysis means looking at profitability ratios over a number of years. Doing so is usually more helpful to the financial statement user than any single ratio is because everything is relative. Seeing how profitability ratios go up and down (when comparing current performance to past performance and when comparing the company with other companies in the same industry) is more meaningful than just looking at one stand-alone ratio. Most investors consider at least five years — sometimes up to ten.

Focusing on return on investment

Return on investment (ROI) is a measuring tool investors use to see how well their investment in a particular company is faring — and to help them make that important decision to sell a stock and move on or to stick with it. Potential investors also use ROI when trying to make a decision among different companies in which to plunk their spare cash.

Basically, investors want to see how well company management is using the company assets to make money. This information gives the investor some idea of the competency of management and the relative profitability of a business when compared to others the investor is considering.

Investors can calculate ROI, which is expressed as a percentage, a few different ways. All the methods involve using some form of comparing income to assets. Here are two methods your financial accounting textbook most likely illustrates:

- ✔ **Net income divided by average total assets:** *Net income* (see Chapter 10) is the bottom-line total of what's left over after you deduct all business expenses and losses from all revenue and gains for the same financial period. I discuss *assets* in Chapter 7; in a nutshell, they are all the resources a company owns. So if a company has net income of $27,000 and average total assets of $100,000, its ROI is 2.7 percent ($27,000 divided by $100,000).

    For any questions in your financial accounting class using the average of any account, you figure it by adding the account balance at the beginning of the financial period to the ending balance and dividing that figure by two. So, if total liabilities are $50,000 at January 1 and $75,000 at December 31, average total liabilities are $62,500 ($125,000 divided by 2).

- ✔ **Operating income divided by average operating assets:** This form of ROI calculation starts with income before income taxes and interest (see Chapter 10 for more info) and divides it by average *operating assets,* which are long-lived assets such as property, plant, and equipment (see Chapter 7). So if a company's operating income is $82,000 and its average operating assets are $12,000, ROI using this method is 6.9 percent.

In real life, does it make any difference which method an investor uses? As long as the chosen method is used consistently, trend analysis using any ROI method will give the investor a significant resource for making a decision as to which company to invest in.

Expanding on ROI with the DuPont model

Your financial accounting textbook probably mentions the *DuPont model,* which was developed in the late 1930s and calculates ROI by multiplying margin by turnover. *Margin* is the ratio found by dividing net income by sales. So if net income is $10,000 and sales are $135,000, margin is 7.4 percent ($10,000 divided by $135,000). In other words, the company's net income equals 7.4 percent of sales. I discuss turnover in this chapter in the section "Exploring Activity Measures." Briefly, *turnover* measures how well a company uses its assets to make money. You figure turnover by dividing sales by average assets.

Taking the margin figure of 7.4 percent and assuming that a company's turnover is 1.6, figuring ROI using the DuPont model gives you 11.8 percent (.074 multiplied by 1.6).

Homing in on return on equity

Return on equity (ROE) measures the profit earned for each dollar invested in a company's stock. You figure it by dividing net income by average *owners' equity* (see Chapter 9), which is what's left over in the business after all liabilities are subtracted from all assets.

The higher the ROE ratio, the more efficient management of the company is at utilizing its equity base. This measurement is important to stockholders and potential investors because it compares earnings to owners' investments. Particularly because it takes into account *retained earnings* — the company's cumulative net income less dividends — it gives the investors much-needed data as to how effectively their capital is being used. Having net income grow in relation to increases in equity presents a picture of a well-run business.

Let's walk through a quick calculation. If a company's net income is $35,000 and the average owners' equity is $250,000, ROE is 14 percent ($35,000 divided by $250,000). Once again, to make wise investment decisions, users of this information will look at ROE as it trends over a series of years and will compare it to the ROE of other companies.

Exploring Activity Measures

In this section, I discuss *activity measures* that quantify the relationship between a company's assets and sales. Your financial accounting textbook probably mentions a few activity measures. In this section, I discuss the ones most commonly used: those measuring accounts receivable and inventory activity.

Ratio analysis that studies activity shows you how well a company is using its assets to make money. This calculation is an expansion of the return on investment (ROI) measurement. Basically, the premise is that how well a company uses its assets to generate revenue goes a long way toward telling the tale of its overall profitability. That's because a business that is effectively and efficiently operated, which activity measures show, will generally be more successful than its less effective and efficient competition.

Turnover analysis shows how quickly an asset comes in and goes out the door. The quicker the better! By this, I mean that in normal circumstances, efficiently moving assets indicates a well-run business. The basic formula to calculate turnover is this: turnover equals sales divided by average assets.

Your financial accounting textbook will specifically mention the relationship between sales and what are probably the two most important current assets for the majority of businesses: inventory and accounts receivable. I explain each in turn.

Accounts receivable turnover

This measurement shows the average number of times accounts receivable is turned over — that is, booked and paid — during the financial period. The sooner a company collects receivables from its customers, the sooner the cash is available to take care of the needs of the business. Why is this rate such a big deal? Well, the more cash the company brings in from operations, the less it has to borrow for timely payment of its liabilities.

Here is an example of how to figure accounts receivable turnover: Village Shipping has sales of $35,000 for 2012. Accounts receivable (A/R) was $2,500 at January 1 and $1,500 at December 31. The average A/R is $2,000 ($2,500 + $1,500 divided by 2). The basic formula for any type of turnover calculation is sales divided by average assets. So, accounts receivable turnover is 17.5 times ($35,000 divided by $2,000).

Another often-used accounts receivable activity measure is the average collection period for accounts receivable. This measure calculates the average number of days that credit sales remain in accounts receivable — a valuable aid in helping companies set credit and collection policies. It's figured by dividing accounts receivable as of the last day of the financial period by the average day's sales (all sales in the financial period divided by 365 days).

Inventory turnover

This activity measure shows how efficiently the company is handling inventory management and replenishment. The less inventory a company keeps on hand, the lower the costs are to store and hold it, thus lowering the cost of inventory having to be financed with debt or *owners' equity* (the ownership rights left over after deducting liabilities).

However, keep in mind that running out of inventory is not a beautiful thing either. Depleting inventory could cause a company to deliver an order late to a customer and perhaps strain the company's relationship with the customer. Also, running low on inventory may cause the company to panic and buy the same inventory for a higher price to get it *right now*. Too much of that sort of hilarity can play havoc with the bottom line.

To figure inventory turnover, you divide sales by average inventory value. Continuing with the Village Shipping example, sales are $35,000, and let's say average inventory is $8,500. Inventory turnover is 4.12 times ($35,000 divided by $8,500).

Some financial analysts use cost of goods sold instead of sales when figuring inventory turnover. That's because inventory is reported at cost, not at its selling price. Check out your financial accounting textbook to see which way the author prefers to calculate this activity measure so you know what's expected in your class.

Analyzing Financial Statements

A good way to do some ratio and trend analysis work is to prepare both horizontal and vertical analyses of the income statement. Both analyses involve comparing income statement accounts to each other in dollars and in percentages.

If you plan on taking a managerial accounting class, you'll definitely delve into horizontal and vertical analysis. That's because these types of analyses are very useful to *internal* users of the financial statements (such as company management), as well as to external users. If this type of analysis reveals any unexpected differences in income statement accounts, management and accounting staff at the company should isolate the reasons and take action to fix the problem.

Using horizontal analysis

Horizontal analysis compares accounts over different periods. For example, you compare a company's sales in 2011 to its sales in 2012.

Figure 14-1 is an example of how to prepare a horizontal analysis for two years. For useful trend analysis, you need to use more years (most investors use five), but this example gives you all the info you need to prepare one for an unlimited number of years. In this figure, all expenses are expressed as a percentage of sales. Net income is 6.67 percent of sales in 2011 and 4.05 percent of sales in 2012 — not a stunning difference, but of concern may be that cost of goods sold increases by almost 2 percent from 2011 to 2012. Whether any of these percentages is significant depends upon the company and management expectations.

Village Shipping Inc. Income Statement Horizontal Analysis For the years ending December 31, 2011 and December 31, 2012	2011	2012	% Change 2012 from 2011
Sales	500,000	475,000	-5.00%
Cost of goods sold	269,000	265,000	-1.49%
Gross profit	231,000	210,000	-9.09%
Wages	163,000	154,000	-5.52%
Repairs	4,150	5,800	39.76%
Rent	12,000	13,000	8.33%
Taxes	17,930	16,940	-5.52%
Office expenses	587	1,023	14.14%
Total expenses	197,667	190,763	-3.49%
Net Income	33,333	19,237	-42.29%

Figure 14-1: Income statement horizontal analysis for 2011 and 2012.

Comparing with vertical analysis

Vertical analysis goes up and down the income statement for one year comparing all other accounts to sales. This analysis gives the company a heads up if cost of goods sold or any other expense appears to be too high when compared to sales. Reviewing these comparisons allows management and accounting staff at the company to isolate the reasons and take action to fix the problem.

Figure 14-2 is an example of how to prepare a vertical analysis for two years. As with the horizontal analysis, you'll need to use more years for any meaningful trend analysis. This figure compares the difference in accounts from 2011 to 2012, showing the percentage change from one year to the next. Of concern should be that, while gross profit decreased by only 9 percent, net income decreased by 42 percent. Whether any of these percentages is significant depends upon the company and management expectations.

Village Shipping Inc.
Income Statement Vertical Analysis
For the years ending December 31, 2011
and December 31, 2012

	2011		2012	
Sales	500,000	100.00%	475,000	100.00%
Cost of goods sold	269,000	53.80%	265,000	55.79%
Gross profit	231,000	46.20%	210,000	44.21%
Wages	163,000	32.60%	154,000	32.42%
Repairs	4,150	0.83%	5,800	1.22%
Rent	12,000	2.40%	13,000	2.74%
Taxes	17,930	3.59%	16,940	3.57%
Office expenses	587	0.12%	1,023	0.22%
Total expenses	197,667	39.53%	190,763	40.16%
Net Income	33,333	6.67%	19,237	4.05%

Figure 14-2: Income statement vertical analysis for 2011 and 2012.

You can do the same types of analyses for balance sheet accounts. For a horizontal analysis, you compare like accounts to each other over periods of time — for example, accounts receivable (A/R) in 2011 to A/R in 2012. To prepare a vertical analysis, you select an account of interest (comparable to total revenue) and express other balance sheet accounts as a percentage. For example, you may show merchandise inventory or accounts receivable as a percentage of total assets.

Using Common Size Financial Statements

One way to visually zero in on potential problems and missteps taking place within a business is to prepare and study common size financial statements. *Common size financial statements* get rid of the dollars and cents, reflecting account balances as percentages only. For example, with the vertical analysis of income statement items, all income statement items are shown as a dollar amount and percentage of total revenue. With a common size income statement, you omit completely any references to the dollar figures.

Who would you rather loan money to?

Maybe the idea of preparing common size financial statements seems tedious and unnecessary. Consider an example of how useful the effort can be. Let's say you have two friends coming to you for a loan to help them weather a rough patch. (Okay, I know that common sense says you don't lend relatives or friends money — you should consider it to be a gift because you're probably not going to be paid back — but just play along with me here.) Who are you going to lend the money to? Here are your choices:

✔ **Good-Time Charlie:** His take-home salary is huge ($200,000), but his total personal living expenses are 110 percent of his take-home salary.

✔ **Frugal Sally:** She earns much less take-home pay ($30,000), but her total personal living expenses are only 75 percent of that take-home amount.

By eliminating dollar values and showing only percentages, you quickly realize that you have more of a chance of being paid back by Frugal Sally, who lives within her means. Had you not taken the dollars out of the comparison, you may have been totally dazzled by the fact that Charlie brings home $200,000 — a lot more than Sally's $30,000.

The big deal about common size financial statements is that the distraction of the dollar amounts is taken away. Cleaning up the statements this way allows the user to compare different companies in the same industry in a more equitable manner.

For example, just because one company has higher total revenue than another doesn't necessarily make it a better company to invest in or loan money to. Showing accounts as a percentage of another account of interest rather than a dollar amount really allows you to see the big picture of how the business is doing rather than obsessing about the difference in dollar amounts.

Chapter 15

Got Your Dictionary Ready? Reading Explanatory Notes and Disclosures

In This Chapter

▶ Touching on corporate governance

▶ Studying the characteristics of a corporation

▶ Finding out more about a company by reading its notes and disclosures

▶ Figuring out who is responsible for full disclosure

*T*his chapter begins with a quick overview of corporate governance and ends by shedding light on the explanatory notes and other information found in most corporate annual reports. I provide the complete picture on corporate annual reports in Chapter 16. Basically, they educate the shareholders about corporate operations for the past year.

Also in this chapter, you learn how a business becomes a corporation, and you review the four characteristics of a corporation: continuity, easy transferability of shares, centralized management, and (the biggie) limited liability.

The complete list of notes and disclosures that may appear on a corporate annual report is quite long, so I can't cover every one here. Instead, I focus on the most common explanatory notes and disclosures popping up on corporate annual reports. Rest assured that this chapter covers all the information you'll see in your financial accounting textbook.

Realizing How Corporations Should Govern Themselves

Simply put, *corporate governance* is the framework under which a corporation operates. At its core, this framework involves establishing financial *controls* (policies and procedures that govern how the company's finances are handled), showing accountability to the shareholders, and making sure corporate management acts in the best interest of the shareholders and the community in which it operates. I talk about financial controls and accountability in the upcoming sections "Reviewing Common Explanatory Notes" and "Looking for important event disclosures."

Part of a corporation's self-regulation includes fully disclosing information on its financial statements. Hence the focus on corporate governance in a chapter about financial statement notes and disclosures.

I cannot cover the subject of corporate governance in depth here; I'd need another book to do so. But here are just a couple examples of ways that corporations need to self-regulate:

- **Acting in the best interests of the shareholders:** The corporation should operate so that the shareholders can expect a reasonable rate of return. For example, the corporation doesn't pay excessive bonuses to corporate officers that reduce cash flow to such a point the business can't effectively operate.

- **Being sensitive to environmental concerns:** The corporation shouldn't pollute or cause health issues through its business waste or other by-products for those living in the communities in which the business operates.

Identifying Corporate Characteristics

Many of my students have only a murky understanding of how a business becomes a corporation and what it means to be a corporation. I quickly walk you through the process in this section and explain the characteristics of a corporation to provide a broader context for understanding corporate governance and financial statement disclosures.

Incorporation — the process of turning a regular old business into a corporation — is governed by state statute. If a company wants to set up shop as a corporation, it must play by the rules of the state in which it operates.

Enron: A cautionary tale of corporate governance at its worst

I find that my students are still fascinated with the Enron fiasco, and many aren't quite sure how it happened. Here's just a thumbnail sketch of what went down at Enron.

A primary contributor to the problem was the use of *mark-to-market accounting,* which essentially means booking expected profits before they are earned. It's actually a fairly easy concept to understand if you break it down to its lowest common denominator. Here is the example I give in my financial accounting classes:

Let's say I invent a machine that will rearrange the molecules in the fabric of a pair of jeans so that the jeans fit your body perfectly every time you wear them. I have a five-year contract with a merchandiser for the sale of this machine. My best guess is that sales over five years will be $50 million. Instead of waiting to book the profits as the machine is sold, under mark-to-market accounting I can book the entire $50 million at the time the contract is signed with the merchandiser.

You may be wondering, why would I want to do this? What would be the purpose? After all, the $50 million was just my best guess — a figure I wrote down on a napkin at the local Starbucks while drinking a cup of coffee. Why not wait and see what sales are really going to be?

Here's the deal: High-ranking employees at most publicly traded corporations are rewarded by methods other than their agreed-upon salaries. This reward system allows for millions

of dollars of incentive payments and stock options to be given to those employees as they deliver faster and faster revenues and earnings growth. Meeting and exceeding revenue projections has only one effect on the price of stock as traded on the open market: The price goes up. The increase in stock price will have a direct effect on the amount of money I make when I exercise and sell any stock options tied to an incentive plan.

Of course, I'm talking about a shell game here: New ideas must be constantly generated and theoretical profits booked to keep the action in process.

At Enron, mark-to-market accounting treatment was a condition of then-CEO Jeffrey Skilling accepting employment at Enron. Enron's accounting firm, Arthur Andersen, signed off on the treatment, and the U.S. Securities and Exchange Commission (SEC) approved it. Unfortunately for the lower-ranking employees at Enron, Enron's upper management lacked corporate governance. Large bonuses were paid to upper management based on grandiose revenue stream projections that never came to fruition.

In the end, all employees at Arthur Andersen and Enron lost their jobs and health insurance benefits. Many Enron employees and retirees lost their entire retirement savings, having been invested in Enron stock whose value bottomed out at 40 cents per share.

In most states, the whole process kicks off when the company files a *corporate charter* or *articles of incorporation* with the Secretary of State. This document contains all pertinent facts about the new corporation, including its name, address, and information about the type and number of stock shares it's authorized to issue. The person who initiates the process and files the charter is called the *incorporator*. The corporation must also name a *registered agent*: the person the Secretary of State contacts with questions about the corporation. After the charter is accepted by the Secretary of State, there is a meeting of parties interested in purchasing shares of stock in the business. These new shareholders then elect a board of directors, and the corporation is off and running!

This is a very simplified version of the whole process, which can also vary by state. An initial public offering (IPO) — when a company offers shares of common stock to the public for the first time — is much more complicated than the previous paragraph may lead you to believe. However, these basic facts are what you need to know for your financial accounting class.

Every corporation has four characteristics:

- ✔ **Limited liability:** This term means that investors in a corporation normally can't be pursued for corporate debt. If the corporation is sued by a vendor, a lender, or some other entity to which it owes money, the individual investors are generally off the hook.

  However, there can be exceptions to this general rule, which hinge on the corporation managing itself according to state statute. Also, the federal government and state departments of revenue can go after shareholders or corporate officers for certain types of unpaid taxes. One example is the *trust fund* portion of the payroll taxes, which includes the employee portion of federal withholding tax, Federal Insurance Contributions Act tax (FICA), and Medicare.

- ✔ **Easy transferability of shares:** This characteristic means that if a person has the money, he can purchase shares of stock in any corporation — with the expectation of selling the shares in the future if he needs the money. However, for *closely held* corporations (those with few shareholders), this characteristic doesn't quite ring true. If you are the majority shareholder in a private corporation, you don't have to sell shares to just anyone.

  Easy transferability of shares applies more to the purchase and sale of shares of publicly traded stock. For example, if you want to buy shares of AT&T stock, you don't have to get permission from good ole' Ma Bell. You just call up your friendly neighborhood stock broker — or go online — and plunk down the cash.

- ✔ **Centralized management:** The management of a corporation should not be divided among many different groups. Therefore, for the corporation to function at full efficiency, shareholders give up the right to chime in on every decision it makes. The shareholders elect the board of directors, who oversee the corporate operations and choose officers to handle the day-to-day business operations.

> ✓ **Continuity:** Until the corporation is formally dissolved, it is assumed to have unlimited life, continuing out into perpetuity. The members of the board of directors can change, corporate officers can change, or there can be a different mix of shareholders, but the corporation just rolls on and on.

Reviewing Common Explanatory Notes

As I note earlier in the chapter, one aspect of corporate self-governance is giving financial statement users the complete information they need in order to accurately gauge the company's performance and financial health. Some of that information comes in the form of explanatory notes.

Leveling the playing field among financial statements

Explanatory notes are discussions of items accompanying the financial statements; they contain important disclosures that aren't presented in the financial statements themselves. The financial statements are the income statement (see Chapter 10), balance sheet (see Part III), and statement of cash flows (see Chapter 11).

Another term for an explanatory notes is *footnote* or just *note*. I use all three terms in this chapter so you get used to seeing them used interchangeably.

Such notes are essential to fulfill the needs of the external users of the financial statements: people like you and me who may be interested in investing in the business, banks thinking about loaning the company money, or governmental agencies making sure the company has complied with reporting or taxation issues. External users don't work for the company, so they aren't privy to the day-to-day accounting transactions taking place within the business.

Information that can't easily be gleaned from reviewing the financial statements has to be spelled out in notes and disclosures, which explain how or why a company handles a transaction. Full disclosure allows external users to understand what is going on at the company and creates a level playing field so an external user can compare the financial statements of one company with those of another company.

Such notes are part of the corporate annual report, which provides shareholders with both financial and nonfinancial information about the company's operations in past years. I discuss this report in Chapter 16.

The notes come after the financial statements in the corporate annual report and are ordered to mirror the presentation of the financial statements. In other words, notes for income statement accounts come first, followed by balance sheet notes and then items reflecting on the statement of cash flows.

In the next section, I explain the six explanatory notes commonly addressed in financial accounting textbooks. Most of these subjects are presented elsewhere in this book in more detail, so I offer just a brief overview here and let you know where you can find more info.

Keep in mind that I give you just a light-bite (truncated) version of each of these explanatory notes. Depending on the company and the complexity of the underlying accounting transaction, explanatory notes can be long and boring to wade through for all but the most diligent and experienced investor. For each type of note, I give you a simple version of what you see in real life, which is more than sufficient for your financial accounting course requirements.

Some explanatory notes are required only for publicly traded companies by the U.S. Securities and Exchange Commission (SEC), which I introduce in Chapter 4. However, as a best practice, many preparers of financial statements for private companies follow SEC guidelines.

Explaining significant accounting policies

The first order of business when a company prepares its explanatory notes is to explain in general the business and its significant accounting policies. Some businesses break the two broad topics into different notes. The first could be called "Basis for Presentation" and the second "Accounting Policies." Alternatively, the company could have just one note called "Summary of Business and Accounting Policies."

Taking this first step creates a more fair presentation of the financial statements. Information about accounting policies helps financial readers to better interpret the statements. A footnote is needed for each significant accounting choice made by the company.

At the very least, the explanatory notes should include what depreciation methods are in use, how a company values its ending inventory, its basis of consolidation, how it accounts for income taxes, information about employee benefits, and accounting for intangible assets. I touch on each of these subjects in turn.

Reviewing depreciation and inventory valuation methods

In Chapter 12, I discuss *depreciation:* spreading the cost of a long-term asset over its useful life, which may be years after the purchase. *Inventory valuation methods,* which detail how a business may value its ending inventory, are the topic of Chapter 13.

The methods a company opts to use for both depreciation expense and inventory valuation can cause wild fluctuations for the amount of assets shown on the balance sheet and the amount of net income (or loss) shown on the income statement. Because of this fluctuation, the financial statement user needs to know which methods the company uses in order to more fairly compare one company's financial statement figures to another's. Differences in net income could merely be a function of depreciation or valuation methodology — a fact the user would be unaware of without the footnote.

Assuming that depreciation and inventory are addressed in note 1, here's a truncated example of how such a note looks:

NOTE 1: SUMMARY OF BUSINESS AND ACCOUNTING POLICIES

We compute inventory on a first-in, first-out basis. The valuation of inventory requires we estimate the value of obsolete or damaged inventory.

We compute depreciation for financial reporting purposes using the straight-line method, generally using a useful life of 2 to 5 years for all machinery and equipment.

Consolidating financial statements

Consolidation is what happens when companies merge or when a larger company acquires one or more smaller ones. In the context of GAAP and financial accounting, *consolidation* refers to the aggregation of financial statements of two or more companies so those statements can be presented as a consolidated whole. In this section of the footnotes, the company confirms the fact that the consolidated financial statements do indeed contain the financial information for all its subsidiaries. Any deviations from including all subsidiaries would have to be explained. See Chapter 17 for more information about consolidation.

Here's a truncated example of how a note addressing consolidation appears:

NOTE 1: SUMMARY OF BUSINESS AND ACCOUNTING POLICIES

Our consolidated financial statements include our parent account and all wholly owned subsidiaries. Intercompany transactions have been eliminated, and we use the *equity method,* which means we report the value based on our proportionate ownership, to account for investments in which we own common stock.

Accounting for income taxes

There is a difference between financial statements prepared using generally accepted accounting principles (GAAP) and those prepared for tax purposes. The former are created using what's called *book* accounting, and the latter use *tax* accounting. Temporary and permanent differences can exist between the book and tax figures, which I explain in Chapter 18.

Here's an example of a permanent difference: Using book accounting, a business can expense 100 percent of meals and entertainment costs it incurs in the normal course of business. For tax purposes, however, it can expense at most 50 percent of that same cost. This is a permanent difference because under the Internal Revenue tax code, the business will never be able to expense the whole 100 percent.

An example of a temporary difference is that for book purposes the company may use straight-line depreciation (see Chapter 12) and for tax purposes a more accelerated method. Eventually, over time, the amount of depreciation the company expenses for an asset using the straight-line versus accelerated method will balance out so that under either method the total amount of depreciation is the same.

The company must address the differences between book and tax, called *deferred tax assets and liabilities,* in the footnotes to the financial statements. Here's a truncated example of how such a note may look:

> NOTE 15: TAXES
>
> Income before taxes was $7.68M, and the provision for federal taxes was $2.78M, an effective tax rate of 31.1%. Deferred income taxes reflect the net tax effects of temporary differences between the carrying amounts of assets and liabilities for financial reporting versus for tax reporting purposes.

Spelling out employee benefits

Details about the company's expense and unpaid liability for employees' retirement and pension plans are also spelled out in the footnotes. The obligation of the business to pay for postretirement health and medical costs of retired employees must also be addressed.

Accounting for employee benefits is a somewhat advanced accounting topic that won't be discussed at length in your financial accounting textbook. For homework or testing purposes, just remember that employee benefits require an explanatory note, and you'll be fine.

Here's a truncated example of how such a note looks:

NOTE 18: RETIREMENT BENEFIT PLANS

We provide tax-qualified profit sharing retirement plans for the benefit of our eligible employees, former employees, and retired employees. As of December 31, 2012, approximately 80% of our profit sharing fund was invested in equities with the rest in fixed-income funds. We have unrelated external investment managers.

Walking through intangibles

Intangible assets aren't physical in nature like a desk or computer. Two common examples of intangibles are *patents,* which license inventions or other unique processes and designs, and *trademarks,* which are unique signs, symbols, or names that the company uses. (See Chapter 7 for more information about intangibles.) Besides explaining the different intangible assets the company owns via an explanatory note, the business also needs to explain how it has determined the intangible asset's value showing on the balance sheet.

Here's a truncated example of how such a note looks:

NOTE 14: INTANGIBLE ASSETS

We classify intangible assets with other long-term assets. As of December 31, 2012, our intangible assets consisted of the following: patents, copyrights, and goodwill. They are generally amortized on a straight-line basis. We perform a yearly review to determine whether useful life is properly estimated.

Looking for important event disclosures

A company must also provide information in its annual report explaining the following topics: accounting changes, business combinations, contingencies, events happening after the balance sheet date, and segment reporting.

Your financial accounting textbook likely talks about event disclosures separately from the discussion of explanatory notes that accompany financial statements. But keep in mind that event disclosure information goes in the footnotes to the financial statements right along with the accounting method information I discuss in the previous section.

Accounting changes

A company may have up to three types of accounting changes to report: a change in accounting principle, a change in an accounting estimate, or a change in a reporting entity. Narrative descriptions about accounting changes go in the explanatory notes to the financial statements very early in the game — usually in the first or second note.

To follow is an explanation of each type of accounting change:

✔ **Accounting principles** guide the way the company records its accounting transactions. Under generally accepted accounting principles (GAAP), a company is usually allowed different ways to account for transactions. For example, in Chapter 12, I discuss depreciation, which is the way a company expenses the cost of long-lived assets. That chapter lays out the various depreciation methods allowable under GAAP.

For the financial statements, changes in accounting principle have to be shown by retrospective application to all affected prior periods (unless doing so is not practical). This process involves three steps:

- Adjust the carrying amounts of affected assets and liability accounts for the cumulative effect of the change.

- Take any offset to beginning retained earnings.

- If the financial report shows multiple years for comparison, show the effect of the new accounting principle in each of the reported years.

I discuss each of these steps in more detail in Chapter 20.

✔ **Accounting estimates** are numbers a company enters into the financial records to reflect its best guesses as to how certain transactions will eventually shake out. For example, going back to the depreciation example, consider the estimate for *salvage value,* which is how much a company assumes it will be able to get for a long-lived asset when it comes time to dispose of it. If something happens to make you believe your original estimate of salvage value was wrong and you change it, that is a change in accounting estimate.

A change in accounting estimate has to be recognized currently and prospectively. For example, if salvage value is recalculated, the current and future financial statements show the salvage value as corrected. No change is made to prior period financial statements. More about this topic in Chapter 20.

✔ **Reporting entities** reflect what combinations of businesses are shown combined on the financial statements, also known as *consolidated* financial statements. When a business owns more than 50 percent of another business, the investor business is called a *parent* and the investee is the *subsidiary.* If something changes in the way the subsidiaries show up on the financial statements, that is a change in reporting entity.

Changes in reporting entities are shown retrospectively to the financial statements of all prior periods. This means you have to show the dollar amount effect of the change of reporting entities in the balances of all related assets and liabilities. Any offsetting amount goes to the beginning balance of retained earnings. If you're interested in slightly advanced financial accounting, I talk more about changes in reporting entities in Chapter 20.

Business combinations

Your financial accounting textbook goes over basic *business combinations,* which include these three:

- ✔ **Mergers:** Two or more companies combine into a single entity. Mergers are usually regarded as friendly combinations — not hostile takeovers.

- ✔ **Acquisitions:** One company acquires another business. The business doing the acquiring takes over, and in essence the *target* (acquired) company ceases to exist. Acquisitions are usually not quite as friendly as mergers.

- ✔ **Dispositions:** A company transfers, sells, or otherwise gets rid of a portion of its business. For example, a shoe manufacturer makes dress shoes, slippers, and tennis shoes and decides to sell its slipper division to another company.

If a company involves itself in any of these three activities during the financial reporting period, it has to explain the transaction and spell out the effect of the business combination on the financial statements. Business combination information goes in the explanatory notes to the financial statements very early in the game; it first crops up in the first or second note, and then it's addressed as needed in subsequent notes.

Your financial accounting textbook does not go into this subject in any great length. If you decide to take an advanced financial accounting class, be sure to check out Chapter 17, where I go over this topic in quite a bit more detail.

If a company is involved in a disposition, GAAP dictate that it disclose not only the facts and circumstances surrounding the disposition but also any anticipated operational losses from getting rid of a portion of its business. The losses are calculated *net of tax,* which means you factor in any increase or decrease in tax due because of the disposition. The company must also show any loss or gain on the sale of that portion of the business (also net of tax) on the income statement. These results are pulled out and reported separately because they won't continue into the future. See Chapter 10 for more information on how this type of event shows up on the income statement.

Contingencies

A *contingent liability* exists when an existing circumstance may cause a loss in the future depending on other events that have yet to happen (and, indeed, may never happen). For example, the company is involved in an income tax dispute. Disclosing this contingent liability is a requirement if the company will owe a substantial amount of additional tax penalties and interest should the unsolved examination end up in the government's favor. See Chapter 8 for more information about reporting contingencies.

Here's a truncated example of how a contingency note looks:

NOTE 10: COMMITMENTS AND CONTINGENCIES

As of December 31, 2012, we were contingently liable for guarantees of indebtedness owed by third parties in the amount of $3 million. These guarantees relate to third-party vendors and customers and have arisen through the normal course of business. The amount represents the maximum future payments that we could be responsible to make under the guarantees; however, we do not consider it probable that we will be required to satisfy these guarantees.

A contingent liability needs to be reported not only as a disclosure via a footnote to the financial statements but also in the financial statements if it is probable and the amount of loss that can be sustained is reasonably estimated (see Chapter 8). This disclosure specifically states the company does not consider the loss contingency probable, so footnote disclosure without inclusion in the financial statements is all that is required for this example.

Events happening after the balance sheet date

The company also has to address any subsequent events happening after the close of the accounting period but before the financial statements are released. Like contingent liabilities, depending on their nature, subsequent events may just need a disclosure in the footnotes to the financial statements, or they may require both a disclosure and an adjustment to the figures on the financial statements to reflect the dollar amount effect of the subsequent event.

How the company handles the event happening after the balance sheet date depends on whether the event is classified as a Type I or Type II event:

- **Type I events:** These events affect the company's accounting estimates reflecting on the books but not confirmed as of the balance sheet date. (See the earlier section "Accounting changes" for an explanation of accounting estimates.) A good example is the estimate for uncollectible accounts. This estimate exists on the books at the balance sheet date, but the company can't be sure of the resolution of the estimate until a subsequent event occurs, such as a customer filing for bankruptcy. At that point, the company confirms that the amount is actually uncollectible.

  If the confirming event (such as the bankruptcy) occurs after the balance sheet date but before the financial statements are finalized, the company has to adjust its financial statements. Footnote disclosure can be used to explain the event as well.

- **Type II events:** These events aren't on the books at all before the balance sheet date and have no direct effect on the financial statements under audit. The purchase or sale of a division of the company is a classic example of a Type II event.

These events are also called *nonrecognized events*. This means that if they are material, they have to be disclosed in footnotes to the financial statements, but the financial statements don't have to be adjusted.

Here's a truncated example of how a note on an event taking place after the balance sheet date looks:

NOTE 21: SUBSEQUENT EVENT

On February 1, 2013, we entered into an agreement to sell our ownership interests in our ABC division to XYZ Manufacturing for approximately $5 million in cash. The transaction is subject to certain regulatory approvals. We expect the transaction to close in the 4th quarter of 2013.

Segment reports

Business segments are components operating within a company. For example, a ladies clothing manufacturer makes dresses, blouses, pants, and sweaters; these are all business segments. If a business has various segments, it must disclose info about each segment such as its type, geographic location, and major customer base so that the users of the financial statements have sufficient information. Here's a truncated example of how such a note looks:

NOTE 25: SEGMENT REPORTING

As of December 31, 2012, our organizational structure consisted of the following operating segments: North America and Europe. Our North American segments derive the majority of their revenue from the sale of finished ladies clothing. Our European segment derives the majority of their revenue from the sale of fabric and notions to other European companies.

Putting the Onus on the Preparer

Here's the million-dollar question: Who the heck is responsible for preparing the notes and disclosures to the financial statements? If you decide to pursue accounting as your career field, are you going to be stuck writing footnotes for the rest of your life?

Well, it depends. The answers to these questions take us back to the very purpose of financial accounting, which is the preparation of financial statements for a business. The explanatory notes and disclosures, like the financial statements themselves, are the responsibility of the company's management and its accounting staff. Management and the internal accounting staff prepare the explanatory notes and disclosures using the applicable American Institute of Certified Public Accountants (AICPA) disclosure checklist.

All generally accepted accounting principles (GAAP) guides contain a comprehensive appendix listing the full AICPA disclosure checklist. The good news is that the only disclosures you'll be tested on for your financial accounting class are those included in your financial accounting textbook. I'd venture to guess that I cover just about all of them in this chapter.

After management prepares the financial statements and explanatory notes and disclosure information, the company often hires an independent certified public accountant (CPA) to evaluate management's work. The CPA is *independent,* which means she has no special relationship to or financial interest in the company (see Chapter 1).

Independent CPAs perform three major types of financial statement work:

- ✔ **Audits:** *Auditing* is the process of investigating information that is prepared by someone else, usually company management and the financial accountants the company employs, in order to determine if the information is fairly stated. CPAs performing audits must investigate the assertions that a company makes on its financial statements, including any notes and disclosures.

    Financial statement assertions often relate to how the company conducts business, such as how it makes and spends money and how it records financial information about its property, plant, and equipment; its long-term liabilities and equity; and its cash and investments.

    An audit provides a reasonable level of *positive assurance,* which means the financial statements are free of material errors and fraud and are stated in accordance with GAAP. An audit does not, however, provide an absolute guarantee that the financial statements contain no mistakes.

    While financial accountants employed by the business prepare the financial statements (including the notes and disclosures), only an independent CPA can audit them. If auditing is a subject that interests you, check out my book *Auditing For Dummies* (Wiley).

- ✔ **Reviews:** When a CPA conducts a *review,* he looks at the company's documents and provides *negative assurance,* which means the CPA finds no reason to believe the information prepared by company management is not correct. For example, the CPA looks over the company's financial statements, noting whether they are of proper appearance. For example, do the statements contain appropriate explanatory notes and disclosures per the AICPA disclosure checklist? Do they conform with GAAP? Reviews are usually performed for privately owned companies when the users of the financial statements require some sort of assurance about the financial statements' assertions but don't require a full-blown audit.

✔ **Compilations:** If a CPA is hired to do a compilation, he can compile financial statements (using information provided by company management) that omit footnote disclosures required by GAAP or that use another *comprehensive basis of accounting* such as cash or income tax accounting (see Chapter 6). Preparing the statements this way is okay as long as omitting the explanatory notes and disclosures is clearly indicated in the report and there is no intent to mislead users.

When footnote disclosures have been left out, CPAs add a paragraph to the compilation report stating that management has elected to omit disclosures. This paragraph lets the user know that if the financial statements did contain the explanatory notes or disclosures, that information may affect their conclusions.

Here's an example of the language used when a company is omitting compilation disclosures:

> Management has elected to omit substantially all the disclosures required by generally accepted accounting principles. If the omitted disclosures were included in the financial statements, they might influence the users' conclusions about the Company's financial position, results of operations, and its cash flows. Accordingly, these financial statements are not designed for those who are not informed about such matters.

Chapter 16

Studying the Report to the Shareholders

• •

• •

Much of this book is devoted to explaining how financial statements (the income statement, balance sheet, and statement of cash flows) are prepared. But what happens to them after they're done? Do they just get filed away in case anyone asks to see them?

Absolutely not! The financial statements become the heart of a company's annual report to its shareholders. An annual report is a document that the company can share with its current owners, potential investors, creditors, the media . . . it can be an important public relations tool that shows the outside world how the company is doing. For many companies, the report is also a regulatory requirement.

In this chapter, I explain the ins and outs of a corporate annual report, including the three key purposes it serves. I also discuss the Form 10-K, an annual filing that the U.S. Securities and Exchange Commission (SEC) requires from most publicly traded companies.

Why Private and Public Companies Treat Annual Reports Differently

A corporate annual report (which may also be called the *annual report,* the *annual report to shareholders,* or the *annual review*) may look very different depending on whether the company in question is private or public.

The corporate annual report for a *private* company — one whose stock isn't traded on the open market — is usually a bare-bones document that gives users just the mandatory information about how the company performed in the past year. You don't find many bells and whistles in a private company's report. That's because most private companies are *closely held* (they have a small number of owners), so they aren't too concerned about how a larger audience will react to the report. On the other hand, a public company's report is often loaded with bells and whistles, such as marketing material designed to tout the company to potential investors and creditors.

Another key difference between the annual reports of private and public companies is that private companies don't always have their financial statements audited, while public companies do. A private company usually has its financial statements audited only if doing so is required to fulfill a business purpose. (Perhaps auditing is required by a certain creditor, for example, or by an insurer providing *bonding* — compensation to customers in case the company does not fulfill its obligations.)

As I explain later in this chapter, public companies' financial statements must always be audited in order to fulfill regulatory requirements. What does it mean for the statements to be audited? After the company creates the statements, it employs an independent certified public accountant (CPA) to gather sufficient information to express an opinion on whether the statements are materially correct. (In other words, they don't contain any misstatements that could significantly impact the decisions made by the financial statement users.)

Only after a public company's financial statements are audited can they be included in the company's annual report to the shareholders.

In this chapter, I focus on the annual reports that large public companies prepare. That way, you get a picture of what the most elaborate reports look like.

Finding annual reports online

Your financial accounting textbook most likely reproduces an actual corporate annual report. But if it doesn't, or if you want to see other examples of what a report looks like, you can easily access the corporate annual report for just about any publicly traded corporation online.

Go to the home page of any company in which you have an interest. Look for an "Investor" link on the home page, and click it. Voila! Chances are you're looking at the annual report. If you can't easily find the "Investor" link, don't spin your wheels. Just do a Google or Bing search using the key phrase "(Company name) corporate annual report." You'll likely locate it easily.

Fulfilling Three Purposes

In this section, I spell out the three distinct goals of the annual report for a public corporation: to promote the company, to display its financial performance and goals, and to meet regulatory requirements.

Something to keep in mind: Going forward, large public corporations will undoubtedly turn more and more toward electronic media to distribute their annual reports. Doing so is a cost-saver and demonstrates a corporation's commitment to using resources wisely.

PR News' Platinum PR Awards recognize outstanding annual reports showing the ingenious use of social media. The 2010 winner was Aetna, which greened up its annual report by releasing its first-ever online summary, saving trees by eliminating 120,000 printed copies of the report. Plus, Aetna made the report sing and dance by embedding 16 videos within. If you want to see this report for yourself, check out `www.aetna.com/2009annualreport/main Creating.html`.

Serving a marketing and PR function

Who doesn't like to toot their own horn? Not any publicly traded company — that's a fact I'll guarantee. A substantial portion of a corporate annual report is devoted to the company's bragging about what it has accomplished during the preceding year and where it expects to go in the contemporaneous year. The language can be quite full of hyperbole and puffery. The purpose of this marketing and public relations material is to keep existing shareholders pumped up about the wisdom of their investment and to attract new shareholders to the fold.

Stating financial performance and goals

Less flashy but of decidedly more interest to serious investors are the sections addressing the corporation's financial performance in the past year and its financial goals. The information in these sections indicates how closely the company came to hitting projected revenue figures, where the company wants to be in the next 12 months, and how it plans on getting there. Additionally, the company addresses how it intends to measure its success in achieving these goals.

Here are some examples of financial goals:

- ✔ Increasing revenue by expanding into global markets.
- ✔ Becoming regarded as a premier employer.
- ✔ Managing operations for the greatest effectiveness.
- ✔ Increasing brand awareness. This phrase is a fancy way of saying the company wants to make sure consumers know about its products. The purpose of brand awareness is also tied to making the company's products preferred over similar ones marketed by the competition.

Meeting regulatory requirements

Most large companies would produce an annual report even if they weren't required to by the U.S. government. That's because an annual report is such a crucial marketing and PR tool. However, because there are stringent regulatory requirements for publicly traded companies, not issuing an annual report isn't an option.

Companies that issue securities that are traded publicly — as well as companies that meet certain other criteria — have to file annual reports with the U.S. Securities and Exchange Commission (SEC). The specific report required by the SEC is called the *Form 10-K.* In the final section of this chapter, I explain which companies have to file this form and what exactly it entails.

To avoid having to create two separate types of annual reports, some companies include in their reports to shareholders all the information that the SEC requires be included in the Form 10-K.

Reading the Annual Report to Shareholders

In this section, I take you through the sections that you most often find in a corporate annual report. With the exception of the audited financial statements, the sections are put together in an effort to draw the external reader into the inner workings of the business in an attempt to raise the users' comfort with — and confidence level in — the company.

Writing the narrative for a corporate annual report is an art. Many times, the report is contracted out to professionals rather than produced in-house, although the company's chief executive or managing director always has a say in the format of the report.

Keep in mind that this section contains just a brief overview of what you may expect to see in a corporate annual report. Especially if a company is very large, it may include a plethora of additional information.

If you have the time, I recommend picking up *Reading Financial Reports For Dummies* by Lita Epstein MBA (Wiley). While I touch on the fundamentals here, this book walks you through reviewing financial reports from A to Z.

Meeting the chair of the board of directors

Most casual investors in a corporation have absolutely no idea who or what the chairperson of the board of directors is. While the duties of the chairperson are quite similar from company to company, the individual holding the position is unique to the particular company.

The chairman of the board of directors is the head honcho who oversees the board of directors (and is usually elected by the other members of the board). The board of directors consists of individuals elected by the shareholders to guide the overall philosophy of the business.

The day-to-day activities of any business are not handled by the board of directors; they're handled by company management. However, approving the hiring of upper management personnel, such as the chief financial officer (CFO) and chief executive officer (CEO), is a function of the board of directors.

In the corporate annual report, you meet the chairman via a letter whose salutation is something like "Dear Fellow Shareholder." The letter gives the company's top management team a chance to review for the users all the great accomplishments the company achieved during the preceding year.

The letter also summarizes goals for the future. It ends by thanking the shareholders for their support and offering a firm promise to work tirelessly to continue earning the trust of the shareholders and growing their value in the company stock.

Highlighting key financial data

In the beginning of the annual review, the company gives the shareholders a very condensed version of how well the company performed during the preceding year. This condensed information provides the lazier readers with what the company perceives as the main points of interest. At the very least, this section contains a summary of operations, earnings per share data, and balance sheet data:

✔ **Summary of operations:** This summary shows the company's bottom line net income for at least three years (and preferably five to ten years). *Net income* is the excess of revenue and gains over expenses and losses during a financial period.

✔ **Earnings per share (EPS):** This calculation shows the distribution of net income over all shares of the company that are outstanding. Many investors home in on this figure, comparing it to their other investments and to other companies' EPS in the same industry. For example, an investor may compare the EPS of The Coca-Cola Company to the EPS of PepsiCo to gauge the value of one company's stock over the other.

Three calculations you may see in an annual review are basic EPS, diluted EPS, and cash dividends. Here's an example of each:

- *Basic EPS:* To figure basic EPS, take net income for the financial period and divide it by the weighted average number of shares of common stock outstanding. The weighted average factors in the fluctuations of stock outstanding during the entire year instead of just taking stock outstanding at January 1 and stock outstanding at December 31 and dividing it by two.

  Any homework assignments or test questions in your financial accounting class will provide you with the weighted average figure (or enough info so you can figure it out yourself). See the sidebar "Calculating weighted average" to walk through a simple example.

  If ABC Corp. has net income of $100,000, and the weighted average number of shares of common stock outstanding is 21,833, basic EPS is $4.58.

- *Diluted EPS:* If the company has issued stock options or long-term debt or preferred stock that the investor has the option to convert into common stock, the company also has to show diluted EPS, which is a complicated calculation. (*Stock options* are benefits allowing employees to purchase a special number of shares of company stock at a determined date.)

Diluted EPS calculates earnings per share by estimating how many shares could theoretically exist after all stock options and convertible debt have been exercised. So if ABC Corp.'s weighted average of common stock outstanding after adding in these extras is 24,989, its diluted EPS is $4.00 ($100,000 divided by 24,989).

- *Cash dividends:* This calculation is the amount per share paid to investors of record. It usually isn't the same amount as EPS, although EPS is one tool the board of directors can use when deciding the dividend to pay to the shareholders of record. See Chapter 9 for more information about dividends.

✔ **Balance sheet data:** This section shows selected figures from the balance sheet in which the company believes the shareholders have an interest. For example, the company may show *total assets,* which are all assets (current and long-term) that the company owns as of the balance sheet date. The company may also show *long-term debt,* which is any debt the company won't have paid off within 12 months of the balance sheet date.

Figure 16-1 shows an example of this condensed financial data.

Year Ended December 31,	2012	2011	2010
Summary of Operations:			
Net operating revenues	$100,000	$ 98,000	$105,000
Earnings Per Share:			
Basic	$ 4.58	$ 4.75	$ 3.89
Diluted	4.00	4.25	3.97
Cash dividends	1.75	1.62	1.24
Balance Sheet Data:			
Total assets	$ 35,271	$ 33,620	$ 39,587
Long-term debt	5,060	3,782	1,318

Figure 16-1: Select financial information.

Even though these figures are very compressed (check out Chapter 10 to see a full-blown income statement and Part III to see a fully developed balance sheet), the figures are based upon — and must reconcile with — the audited financial statements.

Calculating weighted average

In your financial accounting class, your homework assignments or test questions will likely provide you with a weighted average figure. If not, you'll receive enough info so you can figure it out yourself. Here's how:

Say that on January 1, ABC Corp. has 20,000 shares of common stock outstanding. On July 1, it issues another 5,000 shares of common stock. On September 1, it buys back 2,000 shares of common stock (which become *treasury stock,* meaning they're no longer outstanding). What's the weighted average calculation?

Date	Number of Months	Number of Shares Outstanding	Months times Shares
1/1 through 7/1	6	20,000	120,000
7/1 through 9/1	2	25,000	50,000
9/1 through 12/31	4	23,000	92,000
			262,000

You divide 262,000 by 12 months to get 21,833, which is the weighted average number of shares outstanding for the year.

Touting company achievements

In this section, which has a distinct public relations purpose, the company expands upon any facts the chairman of the board discusses in his letter to the shareholders. For example, this section may break out how the company has increased growth *per capita,* which is the average per person living in an area the company serves. Per capita growth could mean that the company sold more products to existing consumers or expanded its sales base into new markets or countries. Companies want to emphasize that they are attracting new customers while still maintaining a bond with existing customers.

Looking into the future

In its annual report, a company also addresses where it sees itself in the short- and long-term future. Doing so addresses any concerns that an investor may have that the business is a *going concern:* that it will be able to stay in business for at least 12 months beyond the balance sheet date, generating or raising enough cash to pay its operating expenses and make appropriate payments on debt.

Obviously, investors aren't going to get all fired up about their ownership in the company stock if they believe the company will be around for only a couple more years. Therefore, annual reviews normally give at least a ten-year plan on growth methodology. A lot of times, companies associate their growth predictions with social and economic transitions — for example, changes in population demographics such as aging and income.

Getting to know key management and board members

This section of the annual report introduces other members of the board of directors, the management team for each division of the company, and committee members (such as members of the audit committee). Most likely, the report includes pictures of all of them posed at the company headquarters.

Walking through the Form 10-K

The U.S. Securities and Exchange Commission (SEC) requires that all companies registered with it annually file the Form 10-K within as little as 60 days after the end of the company's fiscal year. Which companies have to register with the SEC (and are therefore subject to this requirement)? Companies that have a certain class of securities, a certain level of assets or number of holders, and/or which are publicly traded:

- ✔ **Class of securities:** Any company issuing securities traded publicly on a stock exchange or in the *over-the-counter market* (where dealers buy from and sell to interested investors for their own accounts via the phone or computer) must register with the SEC.

- ✔ **Assets or holders:** Any company with more than $10 million in assets and 500 or more holders of any class of equity, such as common or preferred stock, must register as well.

- ✔ **Publicly traded:** Any company whose equity (stock) or debt (bonds) is publicly sold pursuant to a registration statement must register with the SEC.

A *registration statement* is filed with the SEC when a company wants to issue securities to the public. It includes a full and fair disclosure of the securities being issued, info about the company and what it does, the company's financial position, and what the company plans on doing with the proceeds from the issuance.

Registration with the SEC doesn't mean the SEC is giving the company a stamp of approval. It merely means the company has provided all documents required for registration.

The Form 10-K consists of a facing page and four additional parts: business, market/financial, management/corporate governance, and exhibits/financial statement schedules. I explain each part in turn.

Facing page: Identifying the affected company

The facing page of the Form 10-K gives basic info about the company (the SEC registrant), including its name, address, telephone number, and the fiscal year in question. It also lists the title and class of securities (equity and debt) that are registered with the SEC and the number of shares outstanding.

Some more advanced information appears on the facing page as well, such as whether the company is required to file certain reports or has done so voluntarily. For your financial accounting class, you don't need to know that level of detail.

Part 1: Learning more about the registrant

Part I contains information about the company, including an overview of what the company does and any risk factors surrounding it. An example of a *risk factor* may be heightened competition hurting the core business or a significant depletion of the raw materials needed to make its products.

Here is additional required info for this section:

- ✔ The year the company organized
- ✔ Its form of organization
- ✔ Any bankruptcy proceedings, business combinations, or changes in the method of conducting its business

For example, the registrant may state, "We were incorporated in February 1945 under the laws of the State of Delaware and succeeded to the business of a New York corporation."

The Part I information can be incorporated by reference from the annual report to the stockholders if that report contains the required disclosures. If the company opts to do this, it must cross-reference the Form 10-K to the annual report showing what was incorporated and from which pages in the annual report. For example, the company could write, "See page 10 of the 2012 annual report for this information."

Part II: Revealing the company's financial performance

Part II is really the meat of the Form 10-K because it reveals a company's financial performance in the past year. This part features information about where the company's stock is traded, analysis and discussion from company management, and the audited financial statements.

Market information and financial highlights

In Part II, the company tells the SEC in which market the company's common stock lists and trades. Two U.S. examples are the New York Stock Exchange and NASDAQ.

The company also lists the high and low common stock market prices and dividends declared for the year in question. More than likely, the company will also include its key financial data from the annual report to stockholders. (See the earlier section "Highlighting key financial data.")

Management discussion and analysis

Part II also includes a management discussion and analysis section. Normally, management recaps business operations and discusses significant financial trends within the company during the past couple years. For example, for a fast-food restaurant, management would probably discuss how obesity trends are expected to affect the business.

Audited financial statements

The audited financial statements, critical accounting policies, estimates, and explanatory notes and disclosures also appear in Part II. *Accounting policies* include how a company recognizes revenue and expenses and where these figures show up on the financial statements. An example of an *estimate* is the *allowance for uncollectible accounts,* which is what the company anticipates it won't be able to collect from customers who have purchased on account; see Chapter 7. I detail explanatory notes and disclosures in Chapter 15.

While auditing and financial accounting go hand in hand, auditing is a complicated accounting subject taught in a series of auditing classes that are part of the accounting curriculum. So the information in this section is rudimentary, giving you just the basics on the topic.

Auditing is the process of systemically gathering enough evidence to support the facts a company is showing on any company-generated report, including the financial statements. The results of an audit are communicated to all interested users in a format that they can both understand and use for their intended purposes.

The goal of a financial statement audit is for the auditor to form an opinion regarding whether the financial statements are or aren't free from error. Auditors aren't responsible for preparing the financial statements they're auditing. In fact, they *can't* prepare them; to do so would violate the concept of independence (see Chapter 1).

Therefore, the items under audit are company management's responsibility. In other words, the financial statements contain *management assertions* — management's assurance that the information provided is materially correct. A financial accountant uses these assertions to produce the financial statements.

While the company's management assertions must be presented on the financial statements using generally accepted accounting principles (GAAP), auditors conduct their audits using generally accepted auditing standards (GAAS). Breathe a sigh of relief — you won't be tested on GAAS for your financial accounting class. However, if you decide to continue on with your accounting classes, you'll definitely encounter GAAS.

After conducting the audit of the financial statements, the auditor can express one of four basic options:

- ✔ **Unqualified:** An *unqualified* opinion is the best the client can get! It means the audit has been conducted in accordance with generally accepted auditing standards (GAAS) *and* that the financial statements conform with generally accepted accounting principles (GAAP) in all material aspects.

- ✔ **Qualified:** An auditor may have to issue a qualified opinion when the company doesn't use GAAP consistently, or circumstances may have prevented the auditor from getting enough evidence to be able to issue an unqualified opinion. When the end user (a potential investor, for example) sees this opinion, she knows she can't rely on the information in the financial report as much as she could if the auditor offered an unqualified opinion.

- ✔ **Adverse:** As you can probably guess, an adverse opinion is not good! The auditor issues an *adverse* opinion if the financial statements don't present the client's financial position, results of operations, and cash flows in conformity with GAAP. This type of opinion is issued only when the financial statements contain material departures from GAAP. (In

Chapter 4, I explain what constitutes an accounting fact being material. For now, just realize that what is material for one business may not be material for another.)

✔ **Disclaimer of opinion:** This happens when the auditor can't form an opinion on a client's financial statements. For example, a disclaimer may be issued in cases when the auditor is not independent.

I provide examples of properly prepared financial statements in Part III (balance sheet), Chapter 10 (income statement), and Chapter 11 (statement of cash flows). And if you're wondering what this opinion the auditor expresses looks like, wonder no more! Figure 16-2 shows an example of an unqualified opinion that is appropriate to include in Part II of the Form 10-K. The right-hand side shows the opinion letter; the left-hand side is merely a guide for you to see what auditors call each section. The left-hand side is *not* included in the actual opinion letter.

Title:	Independent Auditor's Report
Addressee:	To the Stockholders of Village Shipping, Inc.
Introductory paragraph:	We have audited the accompanying balance sheets of Village Shipping, Inc. as of December 31, 2012 and 2013, and the related statements of income, retained earnings and cash flows for the years then ended. These finanacial statements are the responsibility of the Company's management. Our responsibility is to express an opinion on these finanacial statements based on our audits.
Scope paragraph:	We conducted our audits in accordance with auditing standards generally accepted in the United States of America. Those standards require that we plan and perform the audit to obtain reasonable assurance about whether the financial statements are free of material misstatement. An audit includes examining on a test basis, evidence supporting the amounts and disclosures in the financial statements. An audit also includes assessing the accounting principles used and significant estimates made by management, as well as evaluating the overall finanacial statement presentation. We believe that our audits provide a reasonable basis of our opinion.
Opinion paragraph:	In our opinion, the financial statements referred to above represent fairly, in all material respects, the financial position of Village Shipping, Inc. as of December 31, 2012 and 2013, and the results of its operations and its cash flows for the years then ended in conformity with accounting principles generally accepted in the United States of America.
Name of auditor:	Lexee & Brandon Coppell, TX
Date of report:	February 19, 2014

Figure 16-2: An unqualified independent auditor's report for Village Shipping, Inc.

Part III: Identifying management and corporate governance

Yippee! You've successfully navigated the more detailed parts of the Form 10-K. Heading toward the finish line, next up is a discussion of management and governance. In this very short section, the company lists its directors and executive officers — most likely with a reference back to Part I of the Form 10-K (if that section has already provided sufficient information).

For example, Part III may read as follows: "See Item X in Part I of this report for information regarding executive officers of the corporation." Otherwise, the company lists here each individual's name, title/office, and any other relevant information (such as whether the individual is associated with another unrelated organization).

Now, what about corporate governance? Some of the issues corporate governance addresses are ethical business behavior, responsibility for the community in which the company operates, and equitable treatment of the shareholders. For example, corporate governance demands full and fair disclosure associated with the financial statements so investors can make informed decisions. For a manufacturing company, this section may note that it takes care not to pollute the drinking water of adjacent cities with illegal dumping of factory runoff.

Most companies state that they have a Code of Business Conduct for both employee and nonemployee directors. If the code is not included in the Form 10-K, the form will at least provide information as to where on the company Web site this information resides. See Chapter 15 for more information about corporate governance.

Part IV: Exhibits, financial statement schedules, and signature

I saved the easiest for last! This section merely lists the documents that are part of the Form 10-K and gives the exhibit number where each document can be found. This section can go on interminably, listing such exhibits as "Exhibit No. 6.8.5: 2005 Stock Option Plan of the Company: amended and restated through December 31, 2012." Pretty exciting stuff!

Finally, the last page contains the signature of the chairman of the board of directors, the chief executive officer, the chief financial officer, the principal accounting officer, all directors, and the *attorney-in-fact* (the individual holding power of attorney) attesting to the fact the report does not contain any untrue statement of a material fact or omit any necessary material facts.

Part VI

Feeling Brave? Tackling More Advanced Financial Accounting Topics

The 5th Wave   By Rich Tennant

They're moving on to Chapter 2. That should daze and confuse them enough for us to finish changing the tire and get the heck out of here.

Accounting Text Book Publishers

In this part . . .

The topics I discuss here are most likely covered just briefly in your financial accounting course and textbook. If you decide to continue your accounting education, these are subjects you'll definitely encounter.

First up are business combinations, such as mergers and acquisitions; in Chapter 17, I show you how financial accountants record them. Next is everyone's favorite topic: accounting for income taxes! (Try to stay calm — I know it's tough.) The financial statements you prepare as a financial accountant will probably differ from the financial information you calculate for income tax returns. In Chapter 18, I explain the differences.

Chapter 19 shows you how to account for two types of leases: capital and operating. I discuss this topic from the standpoint of both the *lessee* (the party doing the leasing) and the *lessor* (the property owner). Finally, in Chapter 20 you find out how to fix inadvertent mistakes in the financial statements. I also cover how to account for a change from one accounting method to another and what to do when you find out an accounting estimate is incorrect.

Chapter 17

Accounting for Business Combinations

This chapter discusses an advanced financial accounting topic: business combinations. Although your introductory financial accounting class may not touch on this subject, outside of the classroom, most financial accountants specialize in this area because the rules are quite detailed. So if you're debating whether a career in financial accounting is for you, you may want to learn a bit about this topic now. (You'll certainly encounter it in a more advanced financial accounting course.)

Financial accountants must get information related to business combinations right because people using the information (such as potential investors) depend on it to get the straight scoop on the effect of a combination on financial reports and operations.

In this chapter, you learn about two older methods used to report a business combination: the pooling of interests method and the purchase method. New business combinations can't use either method, but companies that reported business combinations in the past aren't required to restate financial information using the new acquisition method. For this reason, a financial accountant needs to have at least a cursory understanding of the old methods.

Obviously, I also show you the current method used to report a business combination: the acquisition method. This method is the one a financial accountant is going to use for any new business combinations, so I go into a bit more detail about it.

I also explain how to account for investments in equities and briefly touch on the two ways to set up a tax-free business combination — something investors in a business find extremely interesting. After all, who wants to pay taxes if they don't have to?

Explaining What Constitutes a Merger or Acquisition

Before I tackle accounting for business combinations, I want you to have a basic understanding of the lingo surrounding them. Here, I run through a list of key terms you need to know. (Mind you, these are just *key* terms. The list of all terms associating with business combinations is quite long. If you're really interested, you can augment this list with information from your generally accepted accounting principles [GAAP] guide.)

- ✔ **Acquisition:** What occurs when one company acquires another business. The business doing the acquiring (the *acquirer*) takes over, and in essence the target company (the *acquiree*) ceases to exist. Obviously, if the target company doesn't want to be acquired, this can be quite the hostile situation.

- ✔ **Acquisition date:** The date control of a business passes from the acquiree to the acquirer.

- ✔ **Business:** Seems like a no-brainer, but the parties in a business combination actually have to be businesses. To qualify as a business, an entity must have assets and perform activities capable of providing a return to its investors. (The investors are either shareholders for a corporation, partners for a partnership, or the owner for a sole proprietorship.) Determining that all entities involved in a combination are actual businesses is really important because if the acquirer is not actually taking control of a business, this transaction must be handled as an asset acquisition rather than a stock acquisition. (I explain these two types of acquisitions later in this section.)

- ✔ **Closing date:** The date the acquirer legally takes possession of the assets and assumes the liabilities of the acquiree.

- ✔ **Consolidation:** What occurs when many smaller companies are acquired by or merged into a larger one. The companies' financial statements must be aggregated so they appear as a consolidated whole. I talk more about this subject in the upcoming section "Consolidating financial statements."

- ✔ **Goodwill:** An intangible asset (see Chapter 7) that exists when the amount paid by the acquiring company during the business combination transaction exceeds the fair value of the net assets of the business being acquired. *Fair value* is what an unpressured person would pay in an open market to purchase an asset or transfer a liability.

✔ **Identifiable asset:** This is an asset in control of the acquiree to which a fair value can be assigned or an asset that can legally be separated from the acquiree. For example, there are no weird legal circumstances preventing the acquiree from disposing of this asset.

✔ **Merger:** This business combination takes place when two or more companies combine into a single entity. Mergers are usually regarded as friendly — not hostile or unwanted takeovers.

✔ **Parties to the business combination:** The two sides of a business combination are the acquirer and the acquiree. The *acquirer* is the business taking control and is also the party transferring the cash and/or assets — or assuming the debt — to obtain control in the combination. The *acquiree* is the business the acquirer is taking control of. Usually the larger business in the deal is the acquirer, and it's also the company initiating the deal.

Just to confuse things, here's a language note to keep in mind: Even though each of these words means something specific, financial accountants often use the words *mergers, consolidations,* and *acquisitions* interchangeably. In this chapter, I use the phrase *mergers and acquisitions* (or *M&A*) to refer to the process of combining two or more businesses.

As I allude to earlier in this section, M&As come in two different forms:

✔ **Asset acquisition:** One company acquires the net assets of another company, and at the end of the day only the acquiring company survives. For example, if X acquires Y's net assets, Y's books are closed out and X is the surviving company.

✔ **Stock acquisition:** The acquiring company purchases an investment in another company, which is now a subsidiary. The net assets of the subsidiary do not transfer to the purchaser. So if X purchases the investment in Y, Y is now a subsidiary of X. The value of Y reflects in X's financial statement in an account called "investment in subsidiary Y." In this case, you also have to prepare a *consolidated financial statement,* which shows the financial statements of the various businesses brought together by the M&A.

Now that you have the basic terminology in mind, I discuss some of the many issues facing a financial accountant while guiding a business through the combining process. These issues are the biggies, which an advanced financial accounting textbook would cover. And the financial accountant's friend, your GAAP guide, has the skinny on many other issues.

Recognizing the Business Combination

At the end of 2008, the rules regarding how to account for business combinations changed. The accounting method used when dealing with any new business combination is called the *acquisition method*.

Before I show you that method, I give you a basic understanding of two older methods that were previously used to account for business combinations. Am I just stuck in the past? Unwilling to embrace change? No, I'm covering all bases. That's because GAAP do not require companies to retroactively restate their financial statements to conform with the new accounting method. So if you ever serve as a financial accountant for a business involved in a past merger or acquisition, you may need to use a mixed bag of methods.

Before July 2001: The pooling of interest method

Ah, pooling! There is something so neat and organized about this method. Too bad the method really didn't show the economic reality of business combinations. (Hence the reason it's no longer in use.)

To use the pooling of interest method, the business combination had to meet certain criteria:

- ✔ The business combination had to be a single transaction taking place within one year from start to finish.
- ✔ The acquirer had to exchange its common stock for the outstanding common stock of the acquiree.
- ✔ The voting rights of the exchanged stock were immediately exercisable.
- ✔ The acquirer exchanged common stock only — no cash. (The exchange of cash disallowed the business combination from using the pooling method.)
- ✔ The acquirer had to agree not to dispose of the acquired assets within a two-year period.
- ✔ The acquirer couldn't make side deals to benefit certain classes of stockholders.

Using the pooling method, the balance sheet accounts of both entities got thrown together with no accounting for goodwill. In other words, assets, liabilities, and stockholder accounts remained intact but combined. The bad thing about pooling of interests was that assets weren't restated at their fair market value as part of the business combination, which could cause future income to be overstated.

Through 2008: The purchase method

Before June 30, 2001, if a business combination didn't meet the criteria for pooling of interest, the purchase method had to be used. When the pooling of interest method was prohibited for business combinations initiating after June 30, 2001, the purchase method marched on as the only method in town — until (as I explain in the next section) it got exiled on December 15, 2008.

Here's how the purchase method was used in a business combination: The acquiring company recorded net assets (all assets minus all liabilities) at *fair market value:* their value in an unbiased and free trading situation. Then the excess of purchase price over net assets was taken to *goodwill,* an intangible asset (see Chapter 7).

So, if the purchase price was $1.5 million and net assets were $1.25 million, goodwill was booked at the difference between the two amounts: $250,000.

Post 2008: The acquisition method

To better serve the external users of the financial statements, such as potential investors, the Financial Accounting Standards Board (FASB) and the International Accounting Standards Board (IASB) worked together to form a new standard. (I introduce the FASB in Chapter 4 and the IASB in Chapter 6.)

The final result of the partnership between these two boards is FASB Accounting Standards Codification (ASC) 805 *Business Combinations* [Statement of Financial Accounting Standard (SFAS) No.141(R)]. What a mouthful! Its objective is to improve the relevance and comparability of information that businesses provide in their financial statements about business combinations and their effect. (See Chapter 1 for a discussion of how relevance and reliability relate to financial accounting.)

SFAS No. 141(R) accomplishes this goal in these ways:

- ✔ Giving investors a clearer picture of the accounting behind mergers and acquisitions and their effects on the financial statement results

- ✔ Improving the comparability of U.S. financial statements with those worldwide

- ✔ Extending the use of *fair value measurements,* which are purchase price amounts allocating to the assets acquired or the liabilities assumed pursuant to the business combination

The acquisition method is mandatory for any business combination whose acquisition date falls on or after December 15, 2008.

Following are the steps to account for business combinations using the acquisition method. As you walk through them, remember that while each step may seem straightforward, a multitude of factors make a business combination a very complicated accounting extravaganza. A specialty within most accounting firms, properly accounting for business combinations takes in-depth training and on-the-job experience.

Taking you through all the nooks and crannies of combinations is way beyond the scope of this book. But the information I present here will guide you through any basic financial accounting class and serve as a jump-start for the discussion in any advanced financial accounting course you decide to take.

Without further ado, here they are! The steps to use the acquisition method to recognize a business combination are as follows:

1. **Evaluate whether the transaction is a business combination.** To use the acquisition method you have to make sure the event is indeed a combining of businesses, which means the acquiree must have assets and activities capable of providing a return to its investors. If the acquiree doesn't have such assets and activities, the combination is not treated as a business combination under SFAS 141(R). Instead, it is treated like an *asset acquisition,* which means one company acquires the net assets of another company and at the end of it all only the acquiring company survives.

2. **Identify the acquirer.** After you determine the transaction is a business combination, you have to identify the *acquirer,* which is the company taking over the *acquiree* (the target business). I explain these terms in the first section of this chapter.

3. **Decide on the acquisition date.** This is the date when control of the business passes from the acquiree to the acquirer. You may assume the acquisition date is also the *closing* date (the date the acquirer legally takes possession of the assets and assumes the liabilities of the acquiree). Not necessarily. Closing is complete only after legal possession. Depending on how complicated the business combination is, the closing date can be some period of time after the passing of control.

4. **Recognize and measure the net assets involved in the business combination.** You need to know what identifiable assets are acquired and what liabilities are being assumed during the transaction. To do so, you follow the guidelines defining what constitutes an asset or liability per FASB Concepts Statement No. 6 *Elements of Financial Statements.* For example, under Statement No. 6, to be considered an identifiable asset, an item must have a future benefit that will contribute to future cash flow (see Chapter 11).

   You ignore goodwill for now, but you have to address any noncontrolling interest in the acquiree. A *noncontrolling interest,* also known as a *minority interest,* comes into play when another company owns part of the acquiree.

The measurement part of this step pertains to how much the assets are worth and what the assumed debt of the liability is at fair value on the date of acquisition.

Exceptions exist to the rules guiding this step. Some assets and liabilities are recognized and measured in a special fashion. For example, assets the acquiree is holding to sell are measured at fair value less cost to sell. For now, just remember the basics and worry about nuances if and when you take a financial accounting job dealing with business combinations.

5. **Recognize and measure goodwill or gain from a bargain purchase.** You ignored goodwill in Step 4, and now it's time to pay attention to it! Goodwill exists when the purchase price the acquirer is willing to pay exceeds the recognized value of the acquiree's net assets.

I show you how to book a business combination transaction involving goodwill later in this chapter in the "Realizing valuation for the business combination" section.

A *bargain purchase* exists in just the opposite circumstance: when the purchase price is less than the fair value of the acquiree's net assets. Newbie financial accounting students usually assume this situation calls for booking negative goodwill as some sort of contra-asset account. You don't. In a bargain purchase, you book the amount of the so-called "negative goodwill" as income from continuing operations (see Chapter 10).

A financial accountant who used the purchase method in the past to account for business combinations would have booked a bargain purchase as extraordinary income. But these days, it's booked as income from continuing operations.

Reviewing Issues Affecting Mergers and Acquisitions

Accounting for business combinations has always been thorny. You have to decide whether to account for the transaction as a stock or asset acquisition, what costs relating to the M&A are expensed on the income statement (see Chapter 10), and which amounts are taken to the balance sheet as assets or liabilities (see Part III).

In this section, I touch on issues affecting M&As that you may see in your advanced financial accounting textbook, such as contingencies, payments made to employees as a condition of their employment, and valuation.

Understanding contingent considerations

A *contingency* exists when an existing circumstance may cause an action to take place in the future depending on other events that have yet to happen and indeed may never happen. (I discuss contingent liabilities in Chapter 15.) In a business combination, a contingency means the *acquirer* — the business taking control — agrees to make payments to the acquiree in the future, depending on the outcome of an event that hasn't happened yet.

For financial accounting, the important aspect of contingent considerations is whether these future payments are accounted for as part of the purchase price or if they should be an expense reflecting after the M&A comes to fruition. One example of an expense is if part of the arrangement calls for key employees continuing employment in the new business. In this case, the payroll cost would be an expense.

An example of a contingency consideration that could be accounted for as part of the business combination is the handling of preacquisition contingencies involving assets and liabilities. For example, the acquiree has a contractual obligation to purchase an asset that was entered into prior to the acquisition. In this case, the asset needs to be recognized on the balance sheet as part of the business combination transaction.

Providing for golden parachute payments

Golden parachute agreements guarantee key executives lucrative severance benefits if control of the company changes hands followed by management shifts. Employees negotiate these terms, which appear in a contract for employment, so they have covered all their bets when accepting new employment. Let's face it: It would be dismaying to leave one good paying job for another only to be let go in a couple years if control of the company changed hands. In essence, a golden parachute agreement is layoff insurance.

How an acquiring company handles these payments depends on the timing of the golden parachute agreement. If the agreement was made prior to the mere whiff of an acquisition, and the employee will totally be let go, the golden parachute payment reflects as an expense on the target's books.

However, if the subject of the golden parachute agreement comes up during the negotiation process between the acquirer and the target, it's an expense reflecting on the acquirer's books during the acquisition process. When might something like this happen? Well, perhaps the key employee is pretty crucial to the operations of the target business and the acquirer wants to make sure this person doesn't jump ship when the company changes hands.

Realizing valuation for the business combination

Under the new rules put forth by SFAS 141(R), the acquirer in a business combination must recognize the assets it acquires plus the liabilities it assumes (which together equal the *net assets*) plus any noncontrolling interest in the acquiree at their fair value as of the date of acquisition. *Fair value* is what an unpressured person would pay in an open market to acquire an asset or transfer a liability.

To breathe a little life into this concept, Figure 17-1 shows an example of an acquiree balance sheet on the date of acquisition reflecting book and fair values for its assets and liabilities.

Figure 17-1: An acquiree balance sheet on the date of acquisition.

Balance Sheet	Book Value	Fair Value
Cash	20,000	20,000
Accounts receivable	10,000	8,000
Inventory	50,000	65,000
Land	125,000	175,000
Buildings	225,000	225,000
Total assets	430,000	493,000
Accounts payable	75,000	75,000
Common stock $5 par value	100,000	
Retained earnings	255,000	
Total liabilities and equity	430,000	

The acquirer gave 30,000 shares (par value of $10 and fair value of $25) of its common stock as consideration in the business combination to the acquiree shareholders. With this fact in mind, take a look at Figure 17-2, which shows the journal entry to record the business combination. Note that goodwill is the residual value between debits and credits.

Journal entry

Cash	20,000	
Accounts receivable	8,000	
Inventory	65,000	
Land	175,000	
Buildings	225,000	
Goodwill	332,000	
Accounts payable		75,000
Common stock 30,000 shares at $10 par		300,000
Other contributed capital 30,000 shares at $15*		450,000

* $15 is the difference between par of $10 and
fair value of $25

Figure 17-2:
The journal
entry to
record the
business
combina-
tion.

Accounting for acquisition-related costs

If you've ever purchased a house or car or signed student loan paperwork, you know that big-ticket transactions usually carry a price. For example, your student loan paperwork or college application more than likely required you to pay a processing fee.

Well, a business combination has a truckload of expenses relating to it. For example, the investment banker setting up the details of the M&A has to get paid. So do all the legal, appraisal, and accounting talent taking care of the details behind the scenes.

Using the acquisition method under SFAS 141(R), all acquisition-related costs are expensed as they are incurred. (Back in the day, using the purchase method, these types of costs were allocated to the identifiable assets and liabilities, thus creating a situation where goodwill increased.)

Identifying other issues

To round out this section of the chapter, I explain two other issues you may have to account for in a business combination: income taxes and settlements when the acquirer and the acquiree have a preexisting relationship.

Recording income taxes

The acquisition method under SFAS 141(R) requires the acquirer to recognize and measure a deferred tax asset or liability that comes about due to factors resulting from the business combination. This means that the acquirer has to account for any potential tax effects of temporary differences, carryforwards, and any income tax uncertainties of an acquiree that exist at the acquisition date or that arise as a result of the acquisition. Here's what each of these issues looks like:

- ✔ **Temporary differences:** Deferred assets and liabilities can arise because there usually is a temporary difference between financial statements prepared using GAAP and those prepared for tax purposes. I cover this topic in much more detail in Chapter 18.

  For now, a quick example of a *temporary difference* is when under GAAP the company uses straight-line depreciation (see Chapter 12) and for tax purposes uses a more accelerated method. Let's say the company is depreciating a desk costing $1,000 that it anticipates using for 5 years. Under the straight-line method, depreciation is $200 per year ($1,000/5). Using an accelerated method, the same desk has a depreciation expense in the first year of $500. (Note that I'm not using any particular accelerated method.)

  So there is a depreciation expense difference in year one of $300, which leads to an income tax difference too. Eventually, the two depreciation methods will even out with the desk being depreciated for $1,000 using either method — and the income taxes will even out as well. But until then, a temporary difference exists between the two.

- ✔ **Carryforward:** A *carryforward* occurs when the acquiree has net operating losses from prior periods that can be used to offset taxable income in subsequent periods. For example, in 2012, the company has taxable net sales (see Chapter 10) of $1 million and tax-deductible expenses of $1.25 million, resulting in a net operating loss of $250,000 ($1 million less $1.25 million). If the company has taxable income of $400,000 in 2013, its actual taxable income is only $150,000 ($400,000 – $250,000).

- ✔ **Income tax uncertainties:** Uncertainties can result from many different events. One example would certainly be if the acquiree is under examination with the Internal Revenue Service and the exam is not complete or the exam results are being appealed as of the acquisition date.

SFAS 141(R) requires the acquirer to recognize changes in the amount of its deferred tax benefits due to the business combination either in income from continuing operations (see Chapter 10) in the period the combination takes place or directly in *contributed capital,* which is equity the shareholders contribute (common stock plus additional paid-in capital — see Chapter 9).

Handling preexisting relationships

In some cases, the acquirer and the acquiree have a business relationship prior to the date of acquisition. If you think about it, having some kind of relationship makes logical sense. Maybe one of the companies sells merchandise to the other, and it makes good business sense to combine the two companies.

If a business combination puts the kibosh on an existing relationship, the acquirer recognizes a gain or loss on the transaction. In other words, a part of the overall consideration the acquirer gives to the acquiree includes an amount (either positive or negative) that is deemed to permanently close out or *settle* the preexisting relationship.

Two types of preexisting relationships exist:

- ✔ **Contractual relationship:** If one of the parties provides inventory or other merchandise to the other, a contractual relationship exists. For example, the acquiree is an electronics manufacturer that has a four-year contract to provide a merchandising company acquirer with laptop computers at a specified price and quantity.

- ✔ **Noncontractual relationship:** This type of relationship lacks the meeting of the minds you see when two parties sign a contract to provide a good or service for an agreed-upon price. A great example of a noncontractual relationship is when the acquirer and acquiree are the defendant or plaintiff in the same lawsuit; in other words, one is suing the other for copyright infringement (see Chapter 7).

How the heck do you handle the subject of preexisting relationships for any advanced financial accounting assignment or test question? Well, if you're looking at a contractual preexisting relationship, you figure gain or loss at the lesser of the following:

- ✔ The amount by which the acquirer finds the contract to be favorable or unfavorable

- ✔ Any settlement provision in the contract

I can hear you saying, "Wow! That makes perfect sense. Next topic, please!" Not. I realize this subject is rather confusing, so I want to work through an example. Let's say the acquirer deems the contract terms to be unfavorable by $1 million, which gives the acquirer a loss of the same amount. But supposing the contract allows the acquirer to settle the contract for $250,000. Well, the loss is reduced to the lesser of the two figures: $250,000.

Mercifully, the gain or loss for a noncontractual relationship is much easier to understand. You figure it at fair value. In the example of the copyright infringement lawsuit, fair value is what an unpressured person would pay in an open market to settle the suit. If you need to brush up on how to handle gains or losses, check out Chapter 10.

If some of the loss was already recognized as a *contingent liability,* which is a noncurrent liability (see Chapter 8), the settlement loss has to be reduced. For example, if the acquirer has already booked a contingent liability in the amount of $200,000 relating to this lawsuit, the settlement loss is only $50,000.

Defining Investments in Equities

Marketable equity securities are investments that one business makes by buying another corporation's stock. The degree to which the buyer invests in the other company determines this transaction's accounting treatment on the buyer's books. Owning less than 20 percent of the stock in another business is figured using the *fair value* method. Owning between 20 and 50 percent calls for using the *equity method.* When one business has over 50 percent ownership in the other, which gives the business controlling interest, you have to prepare consolidated financial statements.

I discuss each method in turn, starting with the fair value method.

Using the fair value method

You use the fair value method to account for an equity investment when a company owns less than 20 percent of another company's stock. This method is very easy to understand; you pretty much just check out what the fair market value of the stock is at the end of the financial period. For example, you can figure fair value by checking out how much the stock is trading for on a securities exchange such as the National Stock Exchange, Inc., that is registered with the U.S. Securities and Exchange Commission (SEC). If the stock primarily trades in a foreign market, you can use the same valuation method as long as the foreign market is comparable to the U.S. market.

Two types of equity securities use the fair value method:

- ✔ **Trading securities:** These are equity securities the company buys to sell in the short term to make a profit. You record them on the balance sheet initially at cost. Then, as their value fluctuates due to market conditions, they are adjusted to fair value with any gain or loss going to the income statement (see Chapter 10).

✔ **Available-for-sale securities:** This category reflects all equity investments other than trading securities. Available-for-sale securities are initially recorded at their cost. Then, as the market fluctuates, you record them at fair value with any gains or losses being reported in shareholders' equity as "accumulated other comprehensive income" (see Chapter 9).

Putting the equity method in play

You use the equity method when the purchaser's stock ownership in the investee is between 20 and 50 percent. The equity method of accounting recognizes that the investor purchasing the stock is able to significantly influence that investee business. Because of this level of influence, the purchaser has to periodically adjust the carrying amount of its investment for the proportionate share of income or loss less any dividends received. So the value of the purchaser's investment increases when reporting its share of the income from the investee. The value decreases when the purchaser pays out some of its investment in dividends.

For example, let's say that ABC Corp. purchases 40 percent of the common stock of JMS Corp. for $100,000 on January 1, 2012. You record the purchase on the balance sheet initially at cost of $100,000. During 2012, JMS pays out $10,000 in dividends to ABC and has total net income of $300,000, $120,000 of which allocates to ABC ($300,000 × 40 percent).

Using the equity method, ABC increases its investment in JMS on the balance sheet by $110,000 ($120,000 – $10,000). At the end of the financial period, ABC's investment in JMS is valued at $210,000 ($100,000 + $110,000).

Consolidating financial statements

If one company owns more than 50 percent of another business, a parent/subsidiary relationship exists. The parent, of course, is the more-than-50-percent owner (acquirer), and the subsidiary is the acquiree. The parent has to use the equity method to account for its investment in the subsidiary. The financial statements of both are combined and shown together on the income statement (see Chapter 10), balance sheet (see Part III), and statement of cash flows (see Chapter 11).

The parent can have more than one subsidiary. And, yikes! To make it even more convoluted, the parent could also be a subsidiary of another business.

Of course, like most things in life, accounting for this situation is easier said than done. This financial accounting subject is so complex that I can't possibly cover it entirely in this chapter. But I want to cover the basics of how to deal with investments and transactions among the companies within the consolidated group.

Basically, you eliminate transactions taking place between parent and subsidiary, an example of which I show in Figure 17-3. In this example, you learn how to eliminate two different occurrences: investment in the subsidiary, and dividends.

Parent and Subsidiary Partial Consolidating Worksheet							
				Eliminating Entries		Consolidated	
	Parent	Sub		Debit	Credit		
Investment in Sub	95,000	-			95,000	-	
Common Stock	500,000	200,000		200,000		500,000	
Retained Earnings	725,000	75,000		75,000		725,000	
Dividend Income	50,000			50,000		-	
Dividends Declared		50,000			50,000	-	

Figure 17-3: A partial consolidating worksheet.

Here are your facts:

- ✔ The parent owns $200,000 of common stock in the subsidiary, representing 100 percent ownership.
- ✔ During the year, the subsidiary had net income of $75,000.
- ✔ The subsidiary declared and paid dividends of $50,000.

The partial consolidating worksheet shows only the accounts affected by the consolidating factors.

I also want to show you how to prepare journal entries (see Chapter 5) to eliminate sales and cost of goods sold transactions taking place between parent and subsidiary. This example deals with an intercompany sale of merchandise. Here are your facts about this transaction:

✔ The parent sells merchandise costing $5,000 to the subsidiary for $7,000 cash.

✔ The parent's gross profit (see Chapter 10) percentage is 57 percent.

✔ The subsidiary subsequently sells $2,000 of the merchandise it purchases from the parent to an unrelated third party for $4,000.

Figure 17-4 shows the three journal entries. The first reflects the sale on the parent's books. The second reflects the purchase on the subsidiary's books and the subsequent resale of some of the merchandise to its customer. The third reflects the eliminating entry, which has a two-fold effect:

✔ To eliminate the intercompany sale from the parent's books.

✔ To remove the overstated value of inventory from the subsidiary's books. This is figured by taking the ending inventory on the subsidiary's books of $5,000 ($7,000 purchase less reduction in inventory of $2,000) and multiplying it by the parent's gross profit percentage of 57 percent.

	Debit	Credit
Cash	7,000	
Sales		7,000
Cost of Goods Sold	5,000	
Inventory		5,000

To record sale of merchandise from parent company to sub on the parent's books.

	Debit	Credit
Inventory	7,000	
Cash		7,000
Cash	4,000	
Sales		4,000
Cost of Goods Sold	2,000	
Inventory		2,000

Figure 17-4: To record purchase and sale of merchandise on the sub's books.

Journal entries reporting any merchandise sales between parent and subsidiary.

And tah-dah! Here are your eliminating entries:

	Debit	Credit
Sales	7,000	
Cost of Goods Sold		7,000
Cost of Goods Sold	2,850	
Inventory		2,850

To eliminate the impact of intercompany sale from parent to sub.

Consolidated financial statements show the financial position of separate legal entities as though they are one economic entity. Who's interested in this sort of information? Any lenders or investors are interested because from their perspective, the separate business entities are one. Consolidated financial statements give the users a better picture of the business combination's overall financial health.

Classifying Types of Reorganization Dispositions

The bulk of this chapter is about reorganizing businesses through the process of business combinations. Before I close out this subject, I want to give you a heads up on two types of tax-free *reorganizational dispositions.* This phrase is used when a company transfers, sells, or otherwise gets rid of a portion of its business. This is a hot topic because the corporate shareholders may not be too keen on the idea of voting in a disposition structured so that it carries behind it a substantial tax effect.

It would be a nice trick to structure such a transaction in order to be tax-free, wouldn't it? Well, the underlying fact is that the Internal Revenue Service looks at form over substance in this instance. When structured properly, such a reorganization doesn't bring with it enough of an economic change to justify making it a taxable transaction.

I cover two tax-free reorganizations in this section: acquisitive and divisive. To make the explanation user-friendly, I use Corp. A and Corp. B to identify the parties in each example.

The purpose of this section is *not* to educate you in tax code and how to properly structure reorganizations. You'll cover that complex tax subject in your taxation classes, should you choose to take them. Rather, I present this information so if you hear one of these terms in your financial accounting class, you'll have an "Aha!" moment as you remember the association with mergers and acquisitions.

- ✔ **Acquisitive reorganization:** An acquisitive tax-free reorganization takes place when one corporation (Corp. A) transfers most or all of its assets to another corporation (Corp. B). After this transfer takes place, Corp. A *liquidates,* which means it sells or otherwise gets rid of any remaining assets. Immediately thereafter, Corp. B is in control of Corp. A.

- ✔ **Divisive reorganization:** With a divisive tax-free reorganization, one corporation (Corp. A) transfers some of its assets to one or more of its controlled corporations, which means Corp. A owns at least 50 percent of the stock of Corp. B. After the transfer takes place, Corp. A transfers Corp. B stock to Corp. A shareholders.

Chapter 18

Accounting for Income Taxes

*N*obody likes paying taxes. As you read this chapter, it may bring back bad memories of the last time you prepared and filed your own individual tax return. I hate to break it to you, but you have many more glorious years of paying taxes ahead of you! Income taxes are a fact of life. Depending on where you live, you may have to pay federal, state, and local income taxes.

Most businesses have to pay taxes too. I say *most* because one type of business entity, a *flow-through* entity, files an information tax return only. An example of a flow-through business entity is a partnership, which is a business with at least two investors (partners). *Informational* means that while the tax return shows items of income and expense, the business itself doesn't pay the income tax — the partners do.

While preparing income tax returns may not be in the job description of a financial accountant, knowing how to account for income taxes is. Because financial information (for financial statements) prepared according to generally accepted accounting principles (GAAP) differs from financial information prepared for income tax returns, revenue and expense differences may exist between the two. In this chapter, you discover why the differences exist and why they're categorized as either *temporary* or *permanent* differences.

In addition, you learn how to account for tax deferrals, which directly relate to temporary differences. I also discuss operating losses, which serve to reduce taxable income in previous or subsequent years. Finally, you see an example of how the same company has different income before taxes using financial versus tax methods to record accounting transactions.

Like your financial accounting textbook, I discuss only accounting for income taxes for a corporation in this chapter. Any further tax discussion is really a topic of conversation for a taxation class. This chapter gives you all you need to know for your financial accounting class with some extra goodies thrown in.

Identifying Financial Income versus Taxable Income

A company's income as figured using financial accounting may differ from its income as calculated for tax purposes. That's because the reporting standards differ for financial statements and tax returns, and because two distinct sets of users need the two types of income information:

- **Reporting standards:** As a financial accountant preparing or reviewing financial statements for a business, you follow the standards set by regulatory bodies such as the Financial Accounting Standards Board (FASB), which I explain in Chapter 4. A tax accountant, on the other hand, follows U.S Code made available by the U.S. Congress as interpreted by the U.S. Tax Court. *Sec. 177*

- **Users:** As I note in many chapters in this book, the users of a company's financial statements (which include its financial income) are usually individuals and businesses. They may be considering whether to invest in or lend money to the company. The users of a tax document, on the other hand, are usually governmental entities: the taxing authorities (federal, state, and local) to which the business has to report.

Figuring out financial income

You report financial income on the company's income statement (see Chapter 10), which has different sections starting with gross revenue and ending with net income. The relevant section of the income statement for this chapter is the part fairly close to the end of the income statement, "income from continuing operations before taxes." This section is also known as "pretax financial income" or simply "income before taxes."

Income from continuing operations before taxes reflects the final result of subtracting all business-related expenses and losses from all business-related revenues and gains. You determine this type of income before taxes by following GAAP. In Figure 18-1, you see a portion of a company's income statement showing that it had income before taxes of $10,000.

operational income
10g x 35%

Figure 18-1:
Financial
income
provision
for income
taxes.

Income from continuing operations before taxes	10,000
Provision for income taxes	3,500
Net income	$6,500

10,000
x .35
50000
30000
= 3500

Before you can figure the final total for the company's net income or loss, you have to reduce income before taxes by subtracting a provision for the income tax the company will pay when it files tax returns. In Figure 18-1, I assume a tax rate of 35 percent, so the company's provision for income taxes line equals $3,500.

Provision = $3,500

Taking a look at taxable income

Tax accountants figure taxable income using a playbook other than GAAP; they use the Internal Revenue Code (IRC). Honestly, I don't know which is more convoluted, GAAP or IRC. In many cases it's a horse race. Compare a printed GAAP guide to a paper copy of the U.S. Tax Code, and you'll see they are pretty close to being equal in thickness.

What is the purpose of all this taxing hilarity? Before you get started worrying about the government purchasing $10,000 toilet seats, stop to consider how you got to work or to class this morning. Did you take public transportation? Or drive on a paved road? Have ever been on an airplane, whether for recreational or business purposes? Do you (or anyone you know) have children attending public schools? Do you know anyone who receives Social Security disability or survivor benefits or unemployment insurance? All these aspects of our lives (and many more) are subsidized by federal, state, and local tax dollars. *local tax dollars : train*

Tax accountants report taxable income on the relevant tax return. For a corporation, the federal form is Form 1120 – U.S. Corporation Income Tax Return. You can check out Form 1120 at the IRS Web site: www.irs.gov/pub/irs-prior/f1120--2009.pdf.

Like individuals, corporations in the United States have a *graduated income tax rate,* which means their tax rate goes up based on taxable income. The amount of tax (as of this writing) based on taxable income is shown in Figure 18-2. For example, if the corporation has taxable income of $92,500, federal income tax is $19,700.

↑ tax rate
taxable income

handwritten: 92,800 | (19,700)

handwritten (left margin): Federal

	Over —	But not over —	Tax is:	Of the amount over —
	$0	$50,000	15%	0%
	50,000	75,000	$7,500 + 25%	50,000
Figure 18-2:	75,000	100,000	13,750 + 34%	75,000
U.S. cor-	100,000	335,000	22,250 + 39%	100,000
poration	335,000	10,000,000	113,900 + 34%	335,000
graduated	10,000,000	15,000,000	3,400,000 + 35%	10,000,000
income tax	15,000,000	18,333,333	5,150,000 + 38%	15,000,000
rate.	18,333,333	-----	35%	0

Here's how you come up with the $19,700: $92,500 falls in between $75,000 and $100,000. Looking at Figure 18-2, you start with $13,750. Then you find the difference between $92,500 and $75,000 ($17,500) and multiply it by 34 percent, which is $5,950. You add $13,750 + $5,950 to arrive at $19,700.

Also, keep in mind that for simplicity, all examples in this chapter use a constant tax rate rather than a graduated rate.

handwritten (left margin): 50,000 .15 / 0 0 0 0 0 0 0 / 25 0 0 0 0 / 50 0 0.0

Explaining why the two incomes differ

Accountants use a bit of code to talk about the two ways in which business income is calculated. The word *book* refers to financial statements prepared using GAAP. The word *tax* (logically enough) refers to calculations prepared for tax purposes. In some cases, the difference between book and tax numbers, such as income numbers, is huge: A business may have a high amount of positive financial income but have negative taxable income.

The gap between book and tax income is generally caused by three categories of differences: temporary differences, permanent differences, and loss carryforwards/carrybacks. I explain each in turn.

Tackling temporary differences

Temporary differences are items that will balance out over time so the book and tax income eventually match. For example, a business reports some of its items of revenue or expense in one period for financial income and in an earlier or later period for tax purposes. For this reason, accounting geeks may refer to temporary differences as *timing differences*.

Quite a few accounting events can lead to a temporary difference between book and tax income. Here are five of the most common events:

✔ **Contingent liabilities:** A contingent liability is a cost the company may have to pay in the future based on events that haven't yet been ironed out — like a lawsuit. (See Chapter 8 for more discussion of contingent liabilities.) Under certain circumstances, a business can deduct a contingent liability for book income. However, a contingent liability can't be expensed for taxable income until it becomes fixed and determinable. For example, when the company finds out it has to pay damages as a result of a lawsuit, that cost is now fixed and determinable.

✔ **Depreciation:** An example of a temporary difference that most accounting books emphasize is this: For book, the company uses a straight-line depreciation method, and for tax it uses a more accelerated method. (See Chapter 12 for a full discussion of depreciation.) For example, specially expensing depreciation allows a business to write off 100 percent of the cost of the asset in the first year of use for tax purposes. At the same time, financial depreciation methods may call for the asset to be expensed over 10 years. So in other words, in some instances, tax code may allow for expensing the full cost of the asset while for book purposes GAAP depreciation (in this case, straight-line over ten years) must be used.

✔ **Donations:** Like individuals, businesses can deduct donations when calculating their income. For tax purposes, they can deduct only up to 10 percent of their total taxable income. Financial accounting, on the other hand, allows an expense for 100 percent of all qualified donations. This is a temporary difference because, for tax purposes, the company can carry any excess donation forward for the next five years.

If you take a federal taxation class, keep in mind that many items can reduce the 10 percent of taxable income limitation for donations.

✔ **Estimates:** Estimates are any expenses the company figures a reasonable amount for. Here are just two examples:

   • *Warranty costs:* The costs to repair items sold to customers

   • *Allowance for bad debts:* How much in accounts receivable the company reckons it won't collect from customers

While estimates can be deducted for book calculations, a company can't deduct estimates as an expense on its tax return until the company actually incurs the cost.

✔ **Net capital loss:** A company can buy and sell investments in other companies. However, if a company sells stock or other investments and has an overall loss on the transactions for the year, for tax purposes the company can't deduct this capital loss. Never fear! The loss can be offset against future capital gain. For financial accounting, the entire loss serves to reduce net income.

Handwritten margin notes: only up to 10% of total taxable income; excess donation carried forward 5 yrs. offset against future capital gain; sells stock w/ investments (loss) can't deduct. all the difference. can't deduct losses

fines/ penalties (handwritten)

Reviewing permanent differences

A *permanent difference* is an accounting transaction the company reports for book but can't — and never will be able to — report for tax. While GAAP permits reporting the transaction, the Internal Revenue Code does not.

Quite a few accounting events lead to a permanent difference. In this section, I discuss five common ones:

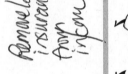

- ✔ **Interest on municipal bonds:** A company may choose to invest in a *municipal bond,* which is a debt instrument (see Chapter 8) that a local government issues to fund a project such as building a new hospital. Under GAAP, you add this income to the company's net income. For federal tax, this investment income is generally never taxed (although this rule may not be true in some states).

- ✔ **Life insurance proceeds:** If a corporation receives life insurance upon the death of an employee, the insurance money is income for financial accounting but never for taxable income.

- ✔ **Meals and entertainment:** For book purposes, companies can expense 100 percent of the cost to provide business-related meals and entertainment incurred in the normal course of business. But for taxes, they can expense at most 50 percent of that same cost.

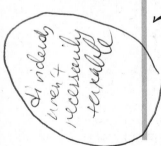

- ✔ **Penalties/fines:** These are expenses a business incurs for breaking civil, criminal, or statutory laws. Say, for example, the president of the company is driving the company car on company business and gets a speeding ticket. You'll be relieved to know that while the company can expense the cost of the ticket on its financial statements, it can't deduct that amount as an expense on its tax return.

- ✔ **Special dividend received deduction:** If a business buys stock in another business, it may receive income in the form of dividends. For financial accounting purposes, you include all dividends a company receives as income. For taxable income, dividends a company receives from other businesses in which it has ownership isn't necessarily taxable income. This subject is not something you'll have to worry about for your financial accounting class, but if you decide to take a corporate taxation class, you'll get the full scoop on how to handle these transactions on the tax return. *stock option expense* (handwritten)

Explaining tax deferrals

REMEMBER

Differences in financial tax expense versus income tax expense due to temporary differences between book and tax income are called *deferred tax assets and liabilities.* Only temporary differences lead to deferred tax assets and liabilities.

Say that a business has one or more temporary differences. For financial reporting under GAAP, the company has a business income tax expense of $25,000, but its tax calculations show the business has income tax payable of $16,000. The difference between the two is $9,000 ($25,000 – $16,000), and that amount is the company's deferred tax dollar amount.

The calculation is fairly easy to understand, but how can you tell if the $9,000 is an asset or a liability? When income tax expense is more than income tax payable, the $9,000 is a deferred tax liability. It's a liability because the $9,000 represents income taxes that will be payable in the future after all the temporary differences even out. Because the amount represents money the business will eventually owe to the government, it is a liability.

If the figures in our example had been reversed, with income tax payable being $25,000 instead of $16,000, the $9,000 difference would be a deferred tax *asset* because income tax payable would be less in the future after all temporary differences are reduced to zero. So sometime in the future, the $9,000 will serve to reduce the amount of tax payable to Uncle Sam, making it an asset right now.

Taking Advantage of Net Operating Losses

A business has a net operating loss (NOL) when deductions on its tax return are more than revenue. This situation isn't always a red-hot fire emergency signaling eminent business disaster. It can happen for many reasons that are relatively benign, such as officers paying themselves a bonus at year end or purchasing an expensive asset for which the company takes one of the allowable special expensing depreciation deductions.

For financial accounting, an NOL is an occurrence that's really noted only by investors and lenders. And depending on the facts and circumstances surrounding the NOL, both sets of users may not be in the least bit dismayed. For example, many drug companies post net operating losses while doing the research to develop new drugs that will eventually be extraordinarily profitable in the future.

For tax accounting, an NOL reduces the amount of tax the company has to pay on earnings in the past or going forward into the future. The Internal Revenue Code rules regarding carrying the net operating loss forward or backward are extensive and won't be covered in your financial accounting class. However, the next two sections provide the basics in case you decide to take taxation or more accounting classes.

Identifying loss carrybacks

Should a business opt to carry the net operating loss back to prior years, it files all relevant amended tax returns showing a reduction in taxable income for the NOL that results in a refund of previously paid income tax. For example, JMS, Inc., has a net operating loss of $20,000 in 2013 and opts to carry back the loss to 2011, a year in which the company had taxable income of $30,000.

Filing an amended return reduces taxable income for 2011 to $10,000 ($30,000 – $20,000), reducing income tax payable. JMS will get a refund when the government processes the amended return. To put this expected refund on the books, you prepare a journal entry (see Chapter 5) debiting an asset account such as "income tax refund receivable" and crediting an income statement account such as "benefit due to loss carryback" for the tax effect of $7,000. Figure 18-3 shows how to figure the tax effect.

Figure 18-3:
Calculating
income
tax refund
receivable
for an NOL
carryback.

Year	Taxable Income	Tax Rate	Tax Paid
2011	30,000	35%	10,500
2012	10,000	30%	3,000
2013	(20,000)	30%	0

NOL of ($20,000) times the tax rate in 2011 of 35% equals $7,000.

Understanding loss carryforwards

A *carryforward* is when the company elects to forgo carrying back the NOL and instead carries it forward to offset taxable income in subsequent years. This decision happens when the company has no taxable income in prior years and has nothing to carry the NOL back to.

For example, in 2012, a company has taxable net sales of $1 million and tax-deductible expenses of $1.25 million, resulting in an NOL of $250,000. If the company has taxable income of $400,000 in 2013, its actual taxable income after carrying the NOL forward is only $150,000 ($400,000 – $250,000).

No amended return is needed in this case because the company reports the NOL as a deduction on the tax return for the year in which it takes it. To get this transaction on the books, you debit the "deferred tax asset" account and credit "benefit due to loss carryforward" for the tax effect of $75,000. Figure 18-4 shows how to figure the tax effect for this NOL carryforward.

Year	Taxable Income	Tax Rate	Tax Paid
2011	(300,000)	35%	0
2012	(250,000)	30%	0

Figure 18-4:
Calculating income tax refund receivable for an NOL carryforward.

NOL carryforward of ($250,000) times the anticipated tax rate in 2013 of 30% equals $75,000.

2013	150,000	30%	45,000

Total tax paid in 2013 after deducting the NOL carryback is $45,000.

Presenting a Side-by-Side Comparison of Book and Tax Calculations

Although I've done my best to keep my explanations simple and clear in this chapter, you may still find the difference between financial accounting and tax accounting confusing unless you can see examples of how both look using the same facts and circumstances. So before I end this chapter, I walk you through a simple comparison between an income tax return and income statement preparation. The comparison is laid out in Figure 18-5.

Comparison of Income Statement to Income Tax Return
For Twelve-Month Period Ending December 31, 2012

	Income Statement	Income Tax Return
Net Revenue	250,000	200,000 (a)
Cost of Goods Sold	75,000	82,000 (b)
Gross Profit	175,000	118,000
Operating Expenses	43,000	30,000 (c)
Fines	25,000	0 (d)
Pretax Income	107,000	88,000
Income Taxes	37,450	30,800
Income After Taxes	69,550	57,200

Figure 18-5: Comparing figures calculated for an income statement to those used for tax purposes.

Here's a list of the temporary differences that exist for the example in Figure 18-5:

✔ Revenue is recorded on the tax return using the *cash method* of accounting, which means revenue is recognized only when cash changes hands. For the financial statements, you use GAAP, which call for the *accrual method* (you record revenue when it is earned and realizable). The difference is $50,000, as shown on line (a).

✔ The company purchases new manufacturing equipment. Using the straight-line method, depreciation for the purpose of financial statements is $8,000. The tax accelerated method results in depreciation of $15,000. Under GAAP, you take depreciation of manufacturing equipment to the "cost of goods sold" account (see Chapters 10 and 12). This temporary difference reflects on line (b) of Figure 18-5.

✔ The allowance for *bad debt,* which is the amount the company estimates it will not be able to collect from customers, is $13,000. The company deducts this amount on the income statement as bad debt expense. It cannot take the deduction on its tax return. See line (c) of Figure 18-5 to spot the difference.

One permanent difference also comes into play. The company was fined $25,000 by the state in which its manufacturing plant is located for dumping without a permit. This permanent difference shows up on line (d).

Look at the final three lines of Figure 18-5 to see how these temporary and permanent differences affect the company's income after taxes. Assume that its tax rate is 35 percent. It's very interesting to see how the same company can have such a wide variance in after-tax income depending on whether the financial accounting or tax accounting rules apply!

Taking Deferred Tax Liabilities or Assets to the Balance Sheet

In the earlier section "Explaining tax deferrals," I note that temporary differences create one of two balance sheet accounts: "deferred tax liability" or "deferred tax asset." How do these two accounts show up on the balance sheet?

You classify a tax deferral as current or long-term depending on the specific asset or liability to which it relates. For example, the estimate for "allowance for bad debt" ties to accounts receivable, which is a current asset. So this portion of the tax deferral will be current.

If the tax deferral doesn't specifically relate to any asset or liability, you classify it as current or long-term based on when you expect it to reverse. For example, the portion of the temporary difference for excess donations that you anticipate carrying forward for more than 12 months is long-term. Chapter 7 shows a complete balance sheet with these accounts.

You may be wondering whether you can net out deferred tax asset and liability accounts. For example, your current deferred tax asset is $7,800 and your current deferred tax liability is $5,400. Can you just show the difference of $2,400 ($7,800 – $5,400) as a deferred tax asset? The answer is no unless the deferred tax assets and liabilities are for the same taxing jurisdiction. So you could net all the deferred tax assets and liabilities that relate to the Internal Revenue Service (IRS). But you couldn't net those relating to the IRS and a specific state Department of Revenue.

If, in your professional judgment, you think reaping the benefit of a deferred tax asset in the future is doubtful, you have to use a valuation allowance to reduce the amount of the asset. An example of this would be if you don't think the company will be able to use up its excess donations before the allowed period of five years expires.

Chapter 19

Accounting for Leases

....

In This Chapter

▶ Laying the groundwork on leases

▶ Learning how the lessee accounts for leased equipment

▶ Making sure the lease is properly classified as operating or capital

▶ Looking at examples of lessor transactions

....

Most businesses need tangible, fixed assets for their day-to-day operations. Rather than laying out the money to purchase all the necessary fixed assets, many companies opt to lease equipment instead. A major advantage to leasing rather than buying fixed assets is that leasing allows for 100 percent financing, which greatly increases a company's cash flow (see Chapter 11).

In this chapter, you look at leasing from the point of view of both the *lessor* (the party owning the leased asset) and the *lessee* (the party acquiring the right to use the asset). You learn the operating and capitalization methods that a lessee uses to record leases, as well as the journal entries a lessee makes to record a lease under both these methods. You also receive a brief introduction to the classification of leases for the lessor. Specifically, I give you a thumbnail sketch of how a lessor handles operating, direct financing, and sales-type leases.

In this chapter, I cover everything you need to know to ace any financial accounting test or quiz on the subject. Along the way, you may pick up some tips to help you negotiate the terms for your own next leased vehicle, apartment, or computer. Nice bonus, huh?

Reviewing Lease Basics

Whether a business is a mom-and-pop lunch counter or a large automobile manufacturer, it needs some basic *fixed assets:* tangible assets the company expects to use for more than a year. Common examples include computers, furniture, and office fixtures, but depending on the type of business, the fixed assets required can be much more extensive. For example, a business making candy bars needs all sorts of mixing, cooking, and wrapping equipment. And a large retail merchandising company needs an awesome amount of store fixtures like display cases and cash registers. (A retailer probably also leases its storefront.) As I explain in Chapter 7, on a company's balance sheet, such fixed, tangible assets are grouped in a category called "property, plant, and equipment" (PP&E).

Businesses won't always buy their PP&E; sometimes they lease these assets. You may have entered into a lease yourself at one time or another. Maybe you're renting an apartment on campus while going to school. Perhaps you're participating in a textbook leasing co-op where you rent your textbooks, returning them after you finish the related class.

Business leases are trickier than most personal leases, so you can't always equate a business lease to a personal one. (However, if you've ever leased a car rather than financing it or purchasing it outright, you probably have some understanding of how convoluted the lease procedure can be.) When you rent an apartment for personal use, you have no claim to that apartment after your lease expires. But depending on how a business lease is set up, the company *could* be the eventual owner of a piece of leased equipment. The terms of the business lease also have an effect on how financial accountants book the lease payments.

Identifying leasing advantages

Why would a business lease instead of buy its necessary equipment? Here are some key motivators:

- ✔ **Cha-ching!** That's the sound of money shaking around in the corporate piggy bank. A major advantage to leasing rather than buying is this: A company usually doesn't have to produce a large outlay of cash at the beginning of the lease the way it would have to with a straight-out purchase.

  In fact, many business leases come with 100 percent financing terms, which means no money changes hands at the inception of the lease. Can you imagine what a boon to cash flow this situation can be? Of course, the business has to make the lease payments each month. But the assumption many times is that the company makes the payments from enhanced revenues it earns as a result of the lease.

- ✔ **Avoiding obsolete equipment:** Another advantage to leasing is working around obsolescence, which means the company anticipates frequently replacing the fixed asset. For example, swapping out computer equipment certainly comes in handy for businesses with the need to stay current with new and faster computer processing technology. The basic purpose of constantly updating computer hardware is to maximize employee productivity.

✔ **Having asset flexibility:** Say that the president of a company grows tired of the company car she is driving. Or say that the employee for whom a company leases a vehicle leaves the company. In either situation, with a leased vehicle the company doesn't have to worry about advertising the car for sale and trying to find a buyer; it just turns the car back into the leasing company.

✔ **Reducing taxes (possibly):** Depending on how the business structures a lease, a major tax advantage may be possible. I discuss this topic later in the chapter in the section "Looking at operating leases." For now, just remember that you treat operating leases like rentals, expensing the entire lease payment when the business makes it.

✔ **Keeping the liability off the books:** Leases may provide *off-the-books financing.* This phrase means that the company's financial obligation (its *liability,* as I explain in Chapter 8) does not reflect on the balance sheet. This fact can affect a financial statement user's evaluation of how solvent the company is because that person will be unaware of the debt.

Some additional economic advantages to leasing can come into play. For example, maybe the equipment the business needs to make its products isn't available for purchase — the company controlling the equipment only wants to lease it. This situation may occur if the piece of equipment is highly technical or the company makes more money through leasing than through selling the item.

Introducing the lessor and lessee

Before I get into the nitty-gritty of accounting for leases, I want to provide a brief lease initiation. Don't worry — it doesn't involve any hazing! Simply knowing who the cast of characters is in a lease and how these characters may interact can go a long way toward making your textbook discussion of the topic more understandable.

A lease always has two parties sitting on either side of the table: a lessor and a lessee. The *lessor* is the party who owns the fixed asset. The *lessee* is the party who wants to acquire the right to use the fixed asset. Think about the example of renting your financial accounting textbook: As the student, you are the lessee; the company that owns and rents out the textbook is the lessor.

One interesting fact about leases is that the lessor doesn't necessarily own the fixed asset just prior to entering into a lease agreement. Sometimes purchasing the fixed asset is contingent upon finalizing the lease agreement. In other words, part of the agreement is that the lessor commits to purchasing the leased asset. This situation may happen if the piece of equipment is expensive or not in high demand. Rather than keeping potentially leasable equipment in inventory that may become obsolete, the lessor advertises that it can lease the asset and then purchases the asset only when it has an interested potential lessee. This approach makes a lot of sense because it cuts down on the expense to store the equipment and increases the lessor's cash flow; the lessor doesn't lay out the cash to purchase the asset until that asset is poised to become a source of revenue.

How a company books leased assets differs depending on whether the company is the lessor or the lessee. Most introductory financial accounting textbooks discuss leases only from the viewpoint of the lessee, so pay close attention to the next section. But to get the complete picture (assuming you're interested in continuing in your financial accounting studies), also check out the last section of this chapter, which gives you the lowdown on accounting for the lessor — a topic that's usually covered in intermediate or advanced accounting courses.

Accounting for the Lessee

The lessee records the lease agreement and lease payments differently depending on whether the lease is written up as a capital or operating transaction. The major differences between the two types of leases involve certain aspects of ownership and immediate versus delayed expensing. Keep reading to find out what I mean.

Looking at operating leases

An *operating lease* has no aspects of ownership and is, therefore, a breeze to account for. Here's an example: Penway Manufacturing leases sewing machines for five years to make men's raincoats. At the end of the five years, Penway has no further obligation to keep or make payments on the sewing machines. Penway returns the machines to the lessor in the condition dictated by the lease agreement.

This type of lease doesn't affect the company's balance sheet as either an asset or a liability. The cost of the lease payments goes on the income statement as "rental expense." For example, if the lease agreement calls for a monthly lease payment of $5,000, each month the accountants at Penway debit "sewing machine rental" (an income statement account; see Chapter 10) and credit cash (a balance sheet account; see Chapter 7) for $5,000.

In other words, this transaction increases expenses by the total amount of the lease payment. Your cash account is reduced when the lease payment check is disbursed. No muss, no fuss — that is the extent of accounting for operating leases.

Operating lease changes are a-comin'

The amount of off–balance sheet lease obligations is estimated by the U.S. Securities and Exchange Commission (SEC) to be in the *trillions* of dollars for publicly traded companies. (Yikes!) For this reason, as I write this chapter, the Financial Accounting Standards Board (FASB) and the International Accounting Standards Board (IASB) have initiated a joint project to develop a new approach to lease accounting to ensure that assets and liabilities arising under leases extending 12 months past the balance sheet date are recognized in a company's statement of financial position. Roundtable discussions started in 2010, and final documents on the topic are expected to be issued in mid-2011. So as you're reading these words, the changes may already have taken place. Be sure to check out the FASB Web site (www.fasb.org) for the latest information on how to treat operating leases.

Walking through capital leases

Capital leases are quite a bit more complicated to account for than operating leases because they have characteristics of ownership. Here's what I mean: The lessee assumes all the responsibilities, benefits, and risks of owning the leased asset. Therefore, the cost of the leased asset goes on the lessee's balance sheet as both an asset (listed as the subject of the lease: the car, equipment, and so on) and a liability ("lease payable").

Many companies operate under the misguided impression that as long as the lease agreement states it is an operating lease, they can treat it as such in their financial statements. Not true. If the lease agreement contains certain characteristics, it is deemed as being a capital lease. Financial accountants always ask to see any lease agreement for which they have to account. Company management could erroneously treat a capital lease as if it's an operating lease. The reason can be as simple as management not being aware that there are important differences in the treatment between the two.

Spotting characteristics of capital leases

To guide you in your lease identification adventure, here are the four characteristics of capital leases — only *one* of which needs to be met in order for the lease to be capital:

> ✔ **The lease transfers ownership of the asset from the lessor to the lessee.** For example, ABC leases a machine from XYZ. After the signing of the lease, the machine is considered the property of ABC. Additionally, because ABC now owns this piece of equipment, it depreciates the equipment for financial statement and tax purposes. (*Depreciation* is the process of spreading the cost of the equipment over its useful life; see Chapter 12.)

✔ **The lessee can purchase the leased asset for a nominal amount at the end of the lease.** Your financial accounting textbook may refer to a bargain purchase. *Nominal amount* and *bargain purchase* mean the same thing: The lease has a clause allowing the lessee to purchase the leased asset for an amount sufficiently lower than its expected *fair market value,* which is what an unpressured party would pay for the same asset in an open marketplace on the date this purchase option comes into play.

You may be wondering how to determine the "sufficiently lower" purchase amount. Unfortunately, generally accepted accounting principles (GAAP) don't give an exact formula for this figure. Luckily, you will not need to make this calculation for your financial accounting class — it will be given to you as part of the example in your textbook or in the narrative of any graded assignments. Financial accountants in practice take into consideration many factors, such as the age and condition of the asset, when setting a figure for the "sufficiently lower" criteria.

✔ **The total lease period is at least 75 percent of the estimated economic life of the asset.** *Economic life* is merely an estimate of how long the lessee company reckons the leased asset will be usable for its intended purpose. So if the estimated economic life of the leased asset is 12 years, you treat a 9-year lease as capital (12 times .75).

✔ **The present value of the lease payments is at least 90 percent of the fair value of the asset.** *Present value* represents the current worth (at the signing of the lease) of the total number of lease payments for the asset. Because this subject is a bit tough to chew, I explain it with an example — keep reading!

Figuring present value

Your financial accounting textbook contains a table for calculating the present value of an annuity of $1. An *annuity* is a series of payments made over time. So let's say your financial accounting professor asks you to figure out if a lease agreement satisfies the fourth characteristic of a capital lease — that of having lease payments with a present value that is at least 90 percent of the fair value of the asset.

Here are the facts and circumstances of this problem:

✔ The fair value of the asset is $205,000.

✔ The lease term is for 5 years.

✔ The lease payments are $50,000 per year.

✔ The borrowing rate on the lease is 10 percent. The *borrowing rate* is the interest rate the company incurs if it finances a purchase rather than leasing the asset.

Go to the table in your textbook that shows the present value of an annuity of $1. Find the 10 percent column, and trace down that column until you get to Period 5. The number at the intersection is 3.7908. Next, multiply $50,000 times 3.7908. This calculation gives you $189,540, which is your present value of the lease payments. Is $189,540 at least 90 percent of the fair value of the asset? Yup, it sure is because 90 percent of the fair value of $205,000 is $184,500.

No textbook handy? You can also find the present value of an annuity of $1 table at this Web site: www.studyfinance.com/common/table4.pdf.

Presenting a capital lease on the financial statements

In this section, I show you how to make journal entries (see Chapter 5) for a capital lease transaction and how to reflect a capital lease on the lessee's balance sheet.

First up: the journal entries, which I show in Figure 19-1. The journal entry is a three-part process involving booking the acquisition of the leased asset, divvying up the lease payment between principal and interest, and recording depreciation for the leased asset. For this example, I use the same facts that I use in the previous section on calculating present value.

1	Equipment	189,540	
	Capital lease liability		189,540

To record acquisition

2	Capital lease liability	31,046	
	Interest expense	18,954	
	Cash		50,000

To record annual lease payment. Interest expense equals $189,540 times 10%.

3	Depreciation expense	37,908	
	Accumulated depreciation		37,908

To record annual straight-line depreciation. No salvage value over the lease term of 5 years (189,540/5).

Figure 19-1: Recording a capital lease transaction.

Capital leases affect both the asset and liability sections of the balance sheet. Referencing the journal entries from Figure 19-1, you record the $189,540 leased asset in the fixed asset section (see Chapter 7) of the balance sheet. You also have to record the obligation to the lessor as a liability (see Chapter 8).

Accounting for the Lessor

Most financial accounting textbooks give only brief attention to how lessees must account for leases. But lessees get more attention than the lessors, who tend to be left out altogether. So, while this subject goes beyond what you need to know for your financial accounting class, I want to give you a brief heads up on how to handle leases from the lessor viewpoint, in case you decide you like accounting so much you sign up for advanced accounting classes.

The lessor decides how much it charges for leasing an asset and structures its lease based on many different criteria. Obviously, the most important criteria to the lessor is profit: how much this lease will increase its bottom line income. The lessor also looks at the credit standing of the lessee and how long a lease term the lessee requires. For example, the lessor will probably charge a potential lessee with bad credit more than it would charge a lessee with a clean credit rating.

Lessors have three major classifications of lease agreements: operating, direct financing, and sales-type. Just as it's easy for the lessee to account for an operating lease (see the earlier section "Looking at operating leases), it's easy for the lessor to account for an operating lease. However, the accounting for both direct financing and sales-type leases is very involved. Due to the complexity of these transactions, even intermediate accounting textbooks usually discuss certain aspects of direct financing and sales-type leases in a section of the accounting for leases chapter that's titled something like "Special Accounting Problems."

Just FYI: A fourth type of lessor classification exists, which is called *leverages leases.* This accounting subject is complex and goes way beyond the scope of this book. This lease involves three parties: a lessor, lessee, and long-term creditor providing financing. It also may involve an investment tax credit allowing companies to deduct a certain percentage of investment costs relating to the transaction from their tax bill. Even if you opt to follow a career path in financial accounting, you may never encounter this event in real-life accounting.

Operating leases

A lessor has to look at the precise criteria surrounding each lease to make sure it can account for a lease as operating. And what are these precise criteria? In a nutshell they are as follows:

✔ First, the lessor has to determine if the lease transfers any of the benefits of ownership to the lessee. (I discuss what has to happen to satisfy this criteria in the "Spotting characteristics of capital leases" section earlier in the chapter.)

✔ If the first criteria is met, the lease has to pass a second test before it can be classified as operating. To pass this test, both the following qualifications have to exist:

• The lessor has to be reasonably sure it will be able to collect the minimum lease payments from the lessee. The bare-bones definition of the *minimum lease payments* is the minimum rental payments called for by the lease over the term. *Reasonably sure* means what a sensible person can expect to happen under normal circumstances. In other words, the lessor doesn't believe the lessee is going to close up shop and disappear into the night during the lease term.

AND

• The lessor has substantially completed all its requirements per the lease agreement. For example, the lessor has delivered the leased equipment according to the terms of the lease. Additionally, any future costs associated with the lease are reasonably predictable. For example, the lease calls for the lessor to pay for up to $500 for repairs taking place during the term of the lease.

Direct financing leases

A *direct financing lease* exists when these two criteria are true:

✔ The lease does not meet the criteria to be classified as operating.

✔ The lessor realizes interest income, but not profit or loss, on the transaction.

The lessor's cost for the asset is the same as the fair market value of the asset, so the lessor's profit on the transaction is limited to the interest income it earns while servicing the lease.

For example, Penway Manufacturing needs a certain type of equipment to make its products but doesn't have the money to purchase the equipment itself. Penway goes to a leasing company that agrees to purchase the asset and enter into a lease agreement with Penway.

Functionally, this type of lease is the equivalent of a straight-out loan. The lessor uses an *amortization schedule,* which shows how much of the lease payment goes to principal versus interest, booking the interest portion as revenue and reducing the amount of "lease receivable" carried on its books by the principal portion.

Sales-type leases

A *sales-type lease* exists when these two criteria are met:

- ✔ The lease does not meet the criteria to be classified as operating.
- ✔ The lessor realizes both interest income and a profit or loss on the transaction.

In order for the second criteria to come into play, the fair market value of the leased asset (what the lessor can lease it for) must be more than or less than the lessor's cost to purchase the asset.

For example, you go into a store to lease a computer. The store pays $1,000 to buy the computer, and it leases the computer to you for $1,500, thus realizing an immediate profit of $500. If your lease term is four months, you may be inclined to think each of your lease payments will be $375 ($1,500/4). However, keep in mind that beyond the immediate profit on the sale, the lessor also usually earns interest income on your use of its money for the four months. Let's say the lessor's interest income on the transaction is $400, making $1,900 the total cost to you for the computer ($1,500 + $400). Each of your lease payments will be $475.

The lessor books $100 each month as interest income ($400/4) with the remainder of your payment ($375) going to reduce its balance sheet asset account called "lease receivable."

Chapter 20

Reporting Changes in Methods and the Correction of Errors

*N*obody is perfect. Regardless of how hard financial accountants try to get everything just right, occasionally mistakes are made or notions about the best way to handle transactions change. Maybe someone simply enters an accounting transaction incorrectly (such as by transposing two numbers — entering $989,000 instead of $899,000). Or maybe a company has been using a particular accounting method for years, but that method no longer provides the most accurate financial statement results.

This chapter explains how to deal with changes in the accounting principles a company follows (and the accounting methods it uses to apply those principles), changes in accounting estimates (a company's best guesses about how future accounting transactions will play out), and flat-out mistakes.

Coping with Accounting Changes

Sometimes the financial accounting staff at a business will be sailing along doing their jobs when the whole transactional process comes to a screeching halt because the old way of doing things is no longer considered to give a fair, full, and complete financial picture. When that happens, the company needs to change the way it accounts for various transactions. Three broad types of accounting changes are possible: changes in accounting principle, changes in accounting estimates, and changes in the reporting entity. Kind of fuzzy about these three types of changes? Well, you're not alone! That's why I cover each in turn in this section.

Correcting an error, which is an inadvertent mistake, does not qualify as an accounting change. To find out how to handle errors (which result in *restatements*), go to the "Dealing with Errors" section at the end of the chapter.

Reporting changes in accounting principles

Financial accountants use generally accepted accounting principles (GAAP; see Chapter 4) to record a company's accounting events, such as earning revenue, paying bills, and purchasing assets. But GAAP don't dictate only one way to handle accounting transactions. Depending on what's going on at the company, the financial accountant may be able to choose among many acceptable ways to handle the same accounting event. At times in the life of the business, it may make sense to choose a different accounting principle than the one that's been used previously.

How does a financial accountant or a company determine which GAAP are preferable to follow? The overriding concept is that whatever GAAP are used must provide a fair, full, and complete accounting for transactions reported on the company's income statement, balance sheet, and statement of cash flows.

The accounting principles a company follows, and the methods a company uses to apply those principles, are referred to collectively as the company's *accounting policies*. For example, in Chapter 12 I discuss *depreciation:* the method a company uses to spread out the cost of a long-lived asset over its expected useful life. One of the accepted methods under GAAP for figuring depreciation is the straight-line method. Any company using this method would disclose that its accounting policy for property and equipment depreciation is the straight-line method. (*Disclosing* means the company includes notes to its financial statements spelling out for the users anything that's not immediately apparent from the figures shown on the financial statements. I discuss explanatory notes and disclosures in Chapter 15.)

Keep in mind that a company cannot simply switch accounting policies in order to improve its bottom line for a given year. A business may switch accounting methods for only three legitimate reasons:

- ✔ Management believes the new accounting method is preferable to the old.
- ✔ Management wants to adopt a recently released accounting principle.
- ✔ The company wants to improve its estimates.

Next, I explain two ways of reporting accounting changes: the cumulative-effect method and reclassification.

Making cumulative-effect accounting changes

Certain circumstances dictate that you use the cumulative-effect method — also known as *retrospective application* — to report accounting changes. Here are three you should know:

- ✔ Changing from the last-in, first-out (LIFO) method for inventory to another method; see Chapter 13 for the full scoop on inventory. (For information about how to handle a change *to* the LIFO method from another method — and for a reminder about what LIFO means — see the upcoming section "Switching to the LIFO inventory valuation method.")

- ✔ Changing accounting policies for long-term construction contracts (contracts that span more than one year).

- ✔ Changing accounting policies as required by a professional pronouncement. (See Chapter 4 for an introduction to accounting regulatory agencies that could issue a professional pronouncement requiring such a change.)

Using the cumulative-effect method, you show the difference between the retained earnings balance at the beginning of the year in which a change is reported and what retained earnings would have been if you applied the accounting change retrospectively in all affected prior periods. This method sounds a lot more confusing than it is in practice.

Here are the steps you follow to use the cumulative-effect reporting method:

1. **Figure out the effect of the accounting change, and adjust the carrying balances of any affected assets or liabilities to reflect the effect.** For example, if the company changes its depreciation method, the book value of the asset and accumulated depreciation balances on the balance sheet will most likely change. See Chapters 7 and 12 for more information about assets and depreciation.

2. **Take an offsetting entry for *net assets* (total assets minus total liabilities) to retained earnings.** So if net assets increase by $1,000 when you adjust the carrying balances of affected accounts, retained earnings also increases by $1,000. Wondering why both increase? I discuss this topic in Chapter 5, but the quick answer is that you increase assets by debiting them and increase retained earnings by crediting it. Every debit must have a corresponding credit, so if your debit increases net assets, a credit will have the same affect on retained earnings.

3. **Reflect the change in accounting method for all prior year financial statements.** In other words, you make a retroactive adjustment. Many financial statements show the prior year financial statements for comparison purposes. For example, if the current year is 2012, the 2008, 2009, 2010, and 2011 financial statements may be included with the current ones.

Say that a company changes depreciation methods. For all years of financial statements shown, you have to reflect the change in depreciation on the income statement and statement of cash flows. You also show the change in the assets' *book value* (their cost plus improvements less accumulated depreciation) on the balance sheet and carry over the change in net income from the income statement to retained earnings.

An *impracticability exception* exists when it comes to adjusting prior periods. This exception applies when the business can't determine the effect of the accounting change as a whole or can't determine the effect on a specific financial period. In that case, the accounting change is reported *prospectively,* which means the changes are spread out over current and future financial statements.

Using reclassification for accounting changes

A *reclassification* occurs when you change a transaction from the way it was originally entered. For example, you reclassify long-term debt as short-term debt, or you consolidate income and expense items so they show up as a single line item instead of two on the financial statement. Reclassification is acceptable if the effect of the change in accounting methods on prior financial periods is deemed immaterial and if company management believes that the reclassification will create a more accurate reflection of the accounting transaction.

When using reclassification, the business can opt merely to include a caption that describes the change either on the financial statement or in the *general ledger:* the list of all the accounts in the chart of accounts and the transactions affecting them. The company should also provide an explanatory note or disclosure on the financial statements (see Chapter 15). For example, an explanatory note may state that $200,000 of long-term debt was reclassified to short-term debt during the financial period because management is opting to pay the debt off early (in the next 12 months) instead of over the projected 60 months.

Figuring out what's immaterial

In my discussion of reclassification in this chapter, I note that this method is acceptable if its impact on prior financial periods is immaterial. But what does *immaterial* mean? Very simply, *immaterial* means the dollar amount in question is not substantive — that is, it doesn't have an effect on the user's decision-making process. What's material for one business may not be material for another.

For example, let's say that a change in accounting method causes a difference in net assets of $50,000. At face value, this amount could be considered a big sum of money. (I certainly wouldn't sniff at winning that much in the lottery!) But what if the net assets for the business are $6 million? In that case, you would most likely consider $50,000 to be immaterial.

Switching to the LIFO inventory valuation method

Chapter 13 is all about inventory, so if you need more than a basic refresher on inventory concepts, check out that chapter before continuing to read this section.

A company can choose how to value its inventory. Two key methods for accounting for inventory are the last-in, first-out (LIFO) method and the first-in, first-out (FIFO) method:

✔ **LIFO:** With this method, the company assumes that its newest items (the ones most recently made or purchased) are the first ones sold. Imagine a big display container of candy bars in a convenience store. If a customer wants to buy one, he takes one off the top. As the supply of candy bars in the container diminishes, the clerk adds more to the top of the old ones instead of redistributing the old bars so they move to the top of the pile. Therefore, the store assumes that the newest purchased items are sold first, which is not always the same as the actual physical movement of the items.

✔ **FIFO:** Using the FIFO method, the company assumes that the oldest items in its inventory are the ones first sold. Consider buying milk in a grocery store. The cartons or bottles with the most current expiration date are pushed ahead of the cartons that have more time before they go bad. The oldest cartons of milk may not always actually be the first ones sold (because some people dig around looking for later expiration dates), but the business is basing its numbers on the oldest cartons being sold first.

Many manufacturing companies use LIFO because the method more closely matches expenses to revenue than FIFO does. That's because the cost of the item being sold has been incurred more closely time-wise to the sale, so there is a better matching of dollar-to-dollar value.

What happens when a company changes its accounting policies to stop using another method and start using LIFO? The company uses the opening inventory balance for figuring all subsequent LIFO calculations. If the company makes the change in 2012, it uses the inventory figure on the balance sheet as of 1/1/2012 as the starting point in figuring cost of goods sold.

The company making this change isn't required to do a full-blown disclosure in the notes to the financial statements (see Chapter 15). All that's required is to show in the notes to the financial statements how much of a change is taking place by using LIFO versus the prior method — both in net income and earnings per share (EPS). (See Chapter 10 for more information about both net income and EPS.) You also have to note that current and prior year financial statements are not comparable because the change was not retrospectively applied.

Changing a company's estimates

Accounting estimates are transactions a company enters into the financial records to reflect its best guesses about how certain transactions will eventually shake out. Sometimes, until a whole transaction comes to fruition, the company isn't 100 percent sure how much revenue or expense to book.

When a company decides on a method to calculate various estimates, the estimates (and the estimation method) are not set in stone. Sometimes unexpected future events affect the validity of the estimate, so changes in estimates are frequently made as new and better evidence is gathered.

Consider a personal example: Say that you're saving to buy a new car. You estimate you'll need to save $5,000 for a down payment on the car of your dreams. Nine months later, when you are ready to buy the car, changing events in the economy and car prices cause your actual down payment to be only $4,000. Did you make a mistake by originally estimating $5,000? No, of course not. With the data available at the time, you made a valid estimate. You could not predict the changing conditions that created the difference in down payment.

Reviewing types of business estimates

Your financial accounting book probably covers at least four major estimates:

✔ **The useful life of tangible assets:** *Assets* are resources a company owns. *Tangible* (or *fixed*) assets include property, plant, and equipment (PP&E) like computers, desks, and manufacturing equipment. When a company purchases *long-term* tangible assets (those that have an expected useful life of more than one year), it has to depreciate them. *Depreciation* spreads the cost of a long-term asset over its expected useful life (see Chapter 12).

How can a company tell for sure how long it will be able to use an asset? It can't. Usually, its estimate is based on past experience or company policy. For example, the company usually trades in vehicles after they hit the four-year mark, so the expected useful life for depreciation purposes is four years. For manufacturing equipment, the expected useful life can be how long the company plans to make the product for which it purchased the machine in the first place.

Suppose the company institutes a cost-savings initiative dictating that its vehicles be traded in after *six* years instead of four. You now have a change in the estimated useful life of the vehicle. Yikes! What to do? Never fear, I discuss how to handle this situation in the upcoming section "Handling changes currently and prospectively."

✔ **The salvage value of a tangible asset:** Some methods of depreciation allowed per GAAP take into consideration the *salvage value* of the tangible asset: how much a company assumes it can get for a long-lived asset when the time comes to dispose of it.

For example, when the company trades in the company vehicle on a new one after four years, it estimates the old vehicle will have a trade-in value of $3,500. This number is merely an estimate; the company won't positively know how much it gets until the transaction actually occurs. (You can read more about this topic in Chapter 12.)

✔ **Collectability of accounts receivable:** *Accounts receivable* (A/R), which I discuss in Chapter 7, is the amount of money customers owe the business for merchandise they purchased or services the company rendered to them. Unfortunately, every business knows that occasionally customers fail to pony up the cash.

In my experience, the prevailing reason that customers fail to pay is *not* because they are unhappy with their purchase, but because they simply don't have the money. Sometimes, the intent is fraudulent from the start — the customer never had any intention of paying. And in some cases, business customers close up shop quietly in the night, never to be heard from again.

Whatever the reason for the uncollectible receivable, GAAP require that businesses extending credit to their customers estimate how much of A/R will eventually prove to be uncollectible. This step involves reducing both net income, by increasing bad debt expense, and the book value of A/R for the amount of the estimate, by increasing the contra-asset account called "allowance for uncollectible accounts."

Contra accounts carry a balance opposite to the normal account balance. Because A/R normally has a debit balance, the contra asset account "allowance for uncollectible accounts" has a credit balance. More about the rules of debits and credit in Chapter 5.

✔ **Warranty costs:** When a company sells a product with a warranty or performance guarantee, it recognizes the estimated cost of servicing the warranty in the same financial period the revenue from the sale is booked. You usually figure the cost of the warranty by using an estimate based on recent experience. For example, in the last two years the actual cost of performing on product warranties was 2 percent of net sales, so the company uses 2 percent of net sales for its current estimate.

Here's how to calculate the estimate: Say that gross sales are $10,000 and *sales discounts* (any discounts the company gives to its best customers) are $2,000, making net sales $8,000 ($10,000 – $2,000). Two percent of $8,000 is $160, which is the company's estimate for warranty expense.

See Chapter 8 for the full story about warranties. Because calculating the estimate for warranties is a frequent midterm or final exam question, in Chapter 8 I also walk you through facts and circumstances surrounding a typical warranty estimate transaction and lay out the appropriate journal entries.

Handling changes currently and prospectively

Changes in accounting estimates have to be recognized currently and also prospectively if appropriate. This means that if the change in accounting estimate affects both the current and future years, the effect is shown in the current and all applicable financial periods.

While the current and future financial statements show the effect of the change in estimate, no change is ever made to prior period financial statements.

Most of my financial accounting students assume that a change in estimate will affect more than one year. To clear up this misconception, consider when a change in accounting estimate may affect only the current year. One example would be if the company originally estimates the useful life of a piece of manufacturing equipment to be ten years. When year eight rolls around, the machine is on its last legs and clearly needs to be junked at year-end. Changing the useful life of the machine to eight years in year eight of its expected useful life does not affect any future periods — only the current period.

Understanding changes in reporting entities

Reporting entities are combinations of businesses that a parent company shows combined on its financial statements, which are also known as *consolidated financial statements.* When a business owns more than 50 percent of another business, the investor business is called a *parent* and the investee is the *subsidiary.* So if something changes in the way the subsidiary shows up on the consolidated financial statements, that constitutes a change in reporting entity.

These changes can occur in three ways:

✔ The parent company creates consolidated financial statements, which is a change from its past practice of preparing individual financial statements for each subsidiary.

✔ The mix of subsidiaries that a parent shows on the consolidated financial statements changes.

✔ The companies included in the combined financial statements change. A *combined* financial statement differs from a consolidated financial statement: It mingles assets, liabilities, equity, and results from operations for two or more affiliated companies. (An *affiliated* company may own less than 50 percent of the voting stock in another company, or it may be one of two or more subsidiaries of another company.)

Business combinations that are reported using the pooling method (see Chapter 17) do not qualify as a change in reporting entity.

A company must use retrospective treatment to show changes to reporting entities. *Retrospective treatment* means you have to restate all prior period financial statements included with the current financial period for comparison purposes. So if the current period is 2012 and the company shows 2011 on its financial statements as well, 2011 has to be restated (but not any prior years).

Dealing with Errors

If you choose to pursue a career path as a financial accountant, you don't have to be perfect. That's quite a relief to see in print, I'm sure! However, you do have to handle any inadvertent mistakes in reporting accounting transactions on the financial statements in complete accordance with GAAP mandates.

In this section, I explain the most common types of errors that occur on the financial statements, and I show you how to go about correcting them.

Reviewing common types of errors

Inadvertent errors fall into three broad categories:

✔ **Math mistakes:** These mistakes occur when the financial accountant just makes a boo-boo. (Please don't ever use that term when talking with your accounting department director!) A good example is when you're totaling a column of figures and you make a mistake adding them up; the mistake affects some aspect of data entry into the accounting software system, flowing through to the financial statements.

You could also make transposition errors, such as entering $959 into the accounting software instead of the correct figure $599.

✔ **GAAP mistakes:** GAAP errors occur in recognition, measurement, presentation, disclosure, or just flat-out using an improper accounting method.

- *Recognition* means determining how an accounting event affects the company's financials, and examples are spread throughout this book. For example, Chapter 10 discusses recognizing revenue and expenses.

- An example of *measurement* is determining an item's fair value. Using assets as an example, the *fair value* is the price a company could receive to sell an asset to an unrelated third party on a certain date (the date of measurement).

- *Presentation* means you show the transaction in the right way on the correct financial statement. For example, assets go on the balance sheet and revenue goes on the income statement, and not vice-versa.

- *Disclosure,* which I discuss in Chapter 15, means you give the users of the financial statements the straight scoop when elaborating on financial transactions.

✔ **Interpretation of facts:** This error happens if the financial accountant misuses or misinterprets available information. For example, consider figuring the salvage value of an asset. Let's say the best information available at the time for salvage value for a particular asset is that its worth at disposal will be $5,000. The financial accountant unilaterally decides not to use this figure but uses $10,000 instead.

Letting counterbalancing errors lie

When an error occurs that is *counterbalancing,* which means that it naturally smoothes itself out over two financial periods, accounting management of a company (with the concurrence of their financial statement auditors) may decide not to take any action.

For example, let's say the financial accountant screwed up recording depreciation in one year. Even though the depreciation entry in the second year was also incorrect, the two errors resulted in a zero net effect. If the books for both financial periods have already been closed, no further action may be necessary — especially if the error is immaterial. The financial accountant just moves on, making sure year three and all subsequent years are done correctly.

Even if the counterbalancing error is immaterial, if the books for year two aren't closed yet, you do have to adjust the beginning retained earnings balance (see Chapter 9) for year two and take action to correct the error in year two prior to closing the books. Any direct corrections of errors to retained earnings are called prior-period *adjustments*.

Companies that are required to register with the U.S. Securities and Exchange Commission (SEC) have strict guidelines to follow in this arena, which are outside the scope of your financial accounting class. See Chapter 16 for information about which companies must register with the SEC, and keep this fact in mind if you continue on with your accounting studies.

Restating the financial statements

A restatement of the company's financial statements may have to be done for many different reasons. For example, the error in question is material, prior period financial statements are shown with the current year for comparison purposes, or the financial statement auditor deems a restatement necessary.

The restatement consists of three steps:

1. **Adjust the balances of any assets or liabilities at the beginning of the first financial period shown in the comparative statements for the cumulative effect of the error.** Say that your first year is 2009, and at 12/31/2008, the cumulative effect of a depreciation error was $100,000. You adjust the book value of the depreciable asset(s) relating to the error by the $100,000.

2. **Take the second half of your Step 1 entry to retained earnings.** You do so because the error would have affected prior years' income or loss, which would have transferred to retained earnings at the end of each year.

3. **Correct the error on each of the financial statements for each comparative year.** So if your contemporaneous year is 2012, you show the effect of the correction on the 2009, 2010, and 2011 financial statements. Your financial accounting textbook may refer to this effect as a *period-specific effect.*

Your last step is to make sure the notes to the financial statements (see Chapter 15) detail the restatement, providing all the information surrounding the event, such as the nature of the error and the effect on net income (both gross and net of income tax).

Part VII
The Part of Tens

"The knots in these figures are too deep for a normal massage."

In this part . . .

This last part, which is featured in every *For Dummies* book, offers some top-ten lists for your consideration. I provide a quick look at ten financial accounting shenanigans companies may try to get away with to inflate earnings, and I share tips on generally accepted accounting principles for ten specialized industries.

Chapter 21

Ten Financial Accounting Shenanigans

- -

In This Chapter

▶ Inflating revenue and misclassifying income

▶ Devaluing liabilities and inflating assets

▶ Staying mum about related-party transactions

▶ Capitalizing costs

▶ Expensing costs

- -

*F*inancial statement shenanigans center around making a company's financial statements look fantastic, even when they aren't. The major areas of concern all artificially inflate the results of operations. The company may report higher net income than it should or manipulate its balance sheet figures, perhaps by underreporting liabilities or showing long-term assets as current. Why do companies mess around with their books and deviate from generally accepted accounting principles? Because they want to attract new investors or creditors by showing them great operating results. In this chapter, I reveal ten such manipulations.

Reporting Revenue in the Wrong Period

In financial accounting, income shenanigans usually result from reporting revenue early. The goal is to appease shareholders and provide justification for bonuses by showing higher-than-actual income. Also, management has a motivation to inflate revenue because high-ranking employees at most publicly traded corporations are rewarded by methods other than their agreed-upon salaries. These reward systems allow for millions of dollars of incentive payments and stock options to be given to those employees as they deliver faster and faster revenues and earnings growth — on paper at least.

With the accrual method of accounting, a company records revenue only when it is earned and realizable. For revenue to be *earned,* the job (whether it involves goods or services) has to be complete based upon the terms of the contract between the company and the customer. For revenue to be *realizable* means there is an expectation the company will be paid. Until both criteria are satisfied, a company can't record a sale to a customer as revenue on the income statement; see Chapter 10.

Reporting Fictitious Income

When a company hires a tax accountant, it wants that accountant to legally apply the tax code to reduce the company's taxable income as much as possible (so it owes the least amount of tax). But when it comes to financial accounting, unscrupulous business owners will seek to increase net income using means not allowed per generally accepted accounting principles (GAAP).

Creating fictitious income involves reporting sales transactions that lack economic substance. Sometimes a sales transaction may occur at face value but lack real intent. Two great examples of this type of shenanigan are channel stuffing and side agreements:

- ✔ **Channel stuffing:** This takes place when customers buy more product than they could possibly need. Channel stuffing normally occurs at year-end. Plain and simple, it's a way for the company to artificially inflate revenue for that year. When this situation occurs, the unspoken agreement between the company and its customer is that the customer can return the unneeded product after the first of the year for a full refund. The net effect is to artificially (and temporarily) inflate gross receipts.

- ✔ **Side agreements:** Another way to artificially (and temporarily) inflate a company's gross receipts involves *side agreements,* which are verbal agreements that change the terms of the sale. For example, a customer places an order buying 5,000 widgets at $100 per widget with the expectation that before the invoice is due to be paid, the price per widget will be reduced to $50. Again, this manipulation tends to occur especially at year-end so the company can inflate its reported revenue.

The first account on the income statement is always *gross sales,* which is the amount of income the company brings in doing whatever it's in the business of doing. Some accountants refer to gross sales as *gross receipts.* Both names mean the same thing: revenue before reporting any deductions from revenue.

Misclassifying Income Items

All money a company receives is not income. And sometimes, a company deliberately misclassifies money it receives in order to manipulate its financial statements.

For example, a business may get a loan from a shareholder or an outside party, such as a bank. The loan amount should be recorded as a liability, but perhaps the business records it as gross receipts. Or the business generates funds by selling shares of the company stock. That amount should be recorded as equity, but again, the company may classify it as gross receipts.

A company may also try to boost its gross receipts by improperly adding to this category any income from the one-time sale of an asset (rather than classifying the amount as *other income*). Another misclassification occurs if the business records interest or dividend income as a reduction of operating expense — for example, a reduction to interest expense — rather than as investment income.

You may be thinking, "What's the big deal?" After all, the effect of these manipulations on the company's net income is probably zero. The big deal (besides the possible fraudulent intent) is that misclassifying income statement items affects ratio analysis: a valuable tool used by potential investors and creditors for decision-making (see Chapter 14).

Failing to Record Liabilities

Liabilities are claims against the company by other businesses or by its employees, such as accounts payable, unearned revenue, and payroll accruals:

- ✔ **Accounts payable** includes money a company owes its vendors for services and products it purchases in the normal course of business and anticipates paying back in the short term. For example, the company purchases inventory from a manufacturer or office supplies from a local supply retail shop.

- ✔ **Unearned revenue** is money received from customers paying the business for goods or services they haven't yet received. An example of this is a deposit. For example, if you place an order for a pair of boots that a shoe store doesn't currently have in stock in your size, the store may ask you to pay a deposit toward the eventual sale before it places a special order for the boots.

✔ **Payroll accruals** are wages and other benefits earned by — but not yet paid to — employees. The accruals should be recorded on both the income statement and the balance sheet (see Chapter 8).

If a company doesn't record its liabilities, the effect is to show the company in a better light by increasing both *net assets* (total assets less total liabilities) and *net income* (all income a company earns in a financial period less all expenses the company incurs while making that income).

Reporting Liabilities in the Wrong Period

Reporting liabilities in the wrong financial period can be just as bad as not reporting them at all. This tactic is often employed at year-end to move items affecting the books in a less than positive way out of the current year and into the next. The ways to accomplish this manipulation are limitless. Here are just a couple examples:

✔ **Holding onto vendor invoices:** For example, the company may collect all vendor invoices it receives during the last 15 days of its financial period in a drawer in the accounts payable clerk's desk and save them until after the beginning of the next financial year. So for a December 31 year-end, all invoices a company receives after December 15 won't be entered into the accounting system until January 2 — which in this case is the next reporting period. This action distorts the financial statements by reducing current liabilities and increasing net income for expensable invoices.

✔ **Booking an inadequate warranty reserve:** If a company provides a warranty for the goods it sells, it also has to book an estimate for how much it will eventually cost to service the warranty. Companies usually figure the cost of the warranty by using an estimate based on recent experience; for example, recent warranty costs have been 2 percent of net sales, so the company figures contemporaneous warranty costs at 2 percent as well.

Suppose during the last month of the financial period the company decides to use 1 percent instead of 2 percent for the warranty reserve. Then, it makes up the underage in the first month of the new financial period. This action serves to artificially reduce liabilities and increase net income — presenting a rosier picture than actual to the users of the financial statements.

Inflating Asset Value

Assets are resources a company owns (like inventory, property, plant, and equipment) or investments (such as stocks and bonds in other companies). Regardless of the assets' *fair market value* — how much the assets would fetch in an open marketplace — most assets go on the balance sheet at their original historic cost. So, if a company owns an office building it paid $500,000 for, and the fair market value (FMV) of the building increases to $700,000, the company can't increase the value of the office building on its books for the additional $200,000.

Continuing with the building example, if an appraisal shows the FMV of the building increases by $200,000 and the company decides to add this increase to the books, there any many ways to hide the inappropriate change. Debiting an asset increases it, and for every debit there must be a credit (see Chapter 5). So if the company increases assets by $200,000, it also needs to credit an account for $200,000. To affect the books in a positive manner, the company could credit gross receipts or owners' equity — both of which serve to artificially make the books look a heck of a lot better.

Here's another trick I see with new clients who don't know any better: A company may decide to ignore all *outstanding checks,* which are checks the company writes and releases that have not yet cleared through its bank. So when the year-end bank statement arrives, let's say ten checks paying bills weren't cashed by the recipient in time to show up on the year-end bank statement. The company temporarily removes these ten checks from the accounting system, adding them back in when they eventually clear the bank. This action artificially increases the year-end cash balance.

That being said, Chapter 9 discusses some investment-type assets that are adjusted to FMV. For example, *trading securities* — debt and equity the business purchases to sell short-term to make a profit — are initially recorded on the balance sheet at cost. Then as their FMV fluctuates, their dollar amount on the balance sheet goes up or down with any gain or loss going to the income statement. The business can't ignore a loss in value or inflate any gain in value.

Improperly Changing Accounting Methods

Accounting methods are the generally accepted accounting principles (GAAP) that financial accountants use to record a company's accounting events. For example, a company uses a specific accounting method to expense depreciation (see Chapter 12) or value inventory (see Chapter 13). GAAP allow the financial accountant more than one acceptable way to handle many accounting events, so the company does have options.

However, there has to be a good reason for any change from one accounting method to another. A company can't just willy-nilly switch back and forth between depreciation or inventory valuation methods (or any other GAAP for that matter) merely to increase the bottom line. For more about this topic, see Chapter 20.

For example, using the declining balance method of depreciation results in depreciation expense of $300,000 and net income of $100,000 for Village Shipping, Inc., in 2012. Village Shipping wants to show its investors a higher net income for the year, so it switches to the straight-line method of depreciation for 2012, which reduces depreciation expense and increases net income by $100,000. Higher net income equals happy investors.

Not Disclosing Related-Party Transactions

A *related party* is a business such as a parent corporation or affiliate that has direct or indirect control over another business. Most business transactions you'll see as a financial accountant are conducted at *arm's length.* That phrase means the company is conducting business with an unrelated third party. For example, if you subscribe to the magazine *Accounting Today,* the subscription order is an arm's length transaction: You don't know the publishers, and they don't know you. The price of the subscription is the same for you or the accountant in the office down the street.

Here's an example of a related-party transaction: A corporation loans money to one of its officers. This situation can be problematic on many levels, and especially if an unspoken understanding exists that the officer never needs to pay the money back. In this case, the loan incorrectly increases liabilities on the balance sheet, affecting investor and credit ratio analyses (see Chapter 14). Depending on the dollar amount of the loan, it may also affect the company's ability to pay dividends to nonrelated investors.

When parties to a transaction are related, the objectivity that naturally occurs in an unrelated third-party purchase or sale may be lost. Financial accountants must adequately disclose related-party transactions (see Chapter 15) so that users of the financial statements are aware these types of transactions exist.

Capitalizing Normal Operating Expenses

Whether a purchase is *capitalized* (recorded on the balance sheet as a capital asset) or *expensed* (recorded on the income statement as an expenditure) depends on both the dollar amount and the type of purchase. Most businesses have a policy covering this decision; see Chapter 7. What a company can't do is decide to capitalize costs instead of expensing them to show a higher net income.

For example, any costs that materially increase the life of an asset are capitalized. Routine repairs and maintenance costs are expensed. So for a car, rebuilding the engine (because it materially increases the car's useful life) is a capital cost. Oil changes and purchasing new tires are expenses that have to reflect on the income statement.

The distinction may not seem like such a big deal until you consider that large publicly traded corporations may have thousands of cars. Misclassifying expenses as capitalized improvements can have a definite impact on the bottom line.

Hiding Reportable Contingencies

A *contingent liability* exists when a current circumstance may cause a loss in the future. For example, the company has litigation pending that's not yet settled. If the loss due to the contingent liability is probable and the amount of loss that could be sustained is reasonably estimated, the company must show this loss on the financial statements.

For example, a company is nearing the end of an Internal Revenue Service examination, and it is probable that the company will agree to exam adjustments increasing its tax owed plus interest and penalties. The amount of the IRS assessment must reflect on the company's books to give investors and creditors an accurate picture of probable future uses of cash. (If the company pays the IRS assessment, the amount of cash available for debt or investor payments will be reduced.) In addition, a note has to be made disclosing this fact in the financial statements; see Chapter 15.

Chapter 22

Ten Industries with Special Accounting Standards

I yak on and on in this book about the generally accepted accounting principles (GAAP) because they are such an integral part of your financial accounting course. While GAAP pertain to most nongovernmental entities, certain types of businesses must follow GAAP that are tailored to their specialized industry. That's because the inherent nature of these industries may require modified accounting principles, financial reporting presentation, and required or recommended disclosures.

Some of these specialized instances of GAAP will probably be mentioned in your introductory financial accounting class. Also, the info in this chapter will serve you well should you select a business in any of these industries for a term paper or graded discussion topic for your class. Keep in mind that in this chapter I simply scratch the surface of this topic. Should you continue with your accounting studies or take a financial accounting job with a business in one of these industries, you'll have to crack open your GAAP guide to get the full scoop.

Airlines

Accounting for the airline industry is complicated because recognition of revenue and expenses can change depending on the type of airline: *legacy* (a major airline such as Delta), *regional* (such as SkyWest), or *cargo* (such as UPS). For example, some regional airlines' expenses are reimbursed by the legacy airlines using their services; therefore, the regional airlines don't record them as expenses. While more than a few accounting issues affect this complicated specialized industry, I want to address two biggies in this section: recognizing revenue and handling airport slots.

✔ **Recognition of revenue:** Under GAAP, airlines have to account for flights paid for in advance as a liability until the subject of the ticket is *uplifted,* which means the customer completes the flight as booked.

If a passenger fails to use a nonrefundable ticket, airlines can consider the flight closed the next day and record the revenue for this unused ticket. Exchangeable tickets not used within a certain time period set by the airlines are similarly booked as gross receipts. To figure a reasonable time period for determining when it is appropriate to book the revenue on an unused exchangeable ticket, the airline looks to historic data reflecting how long in the past it took passengers to re-ticket their exchangeable flights. This time period is normally between 6 and 24 months.

✔ **Landing and take-off slots:** These areas owned by airlines to enter and exit airports can be one of their largest assets on the balance sheet. While they have a physical presence, landing and take-off slots are accounted for as intangible assets (see Chapter 7). This treatment means their cost is initially taken to the balance sheet and then *amortized*: The cost is transferred to the income statement using an allowable amortization method (see Chapter 7).

Finance Companies

If you ever secured a loan to purchase a car, you probably worked with a *finance company,* whose purpose is to lend money to both consumers and businesses. Examples of finance companies include banks, credit unions, and mortgage providers. Two specialized accounting issues that finance companies encounter are creating an allowance for loan losses and transferring receivables:

✔ **Allowance for loan losses:** This allowance has to be figured when the finance company considers it probable that the loan is *impaired,* meaning it won't be recouped in its entirety. The allowance is a reduction in the amount the company figures it will collect. Obviously, to determine the size of this allowance, the finance company must be able to reasonably estimate the amount of impairment.

✔ **Transfer of receivables:** When a finance company (perhaps in an effort to increase its cash flow) transfers a receivable to another finance company, it reports the transfer as a sale if it gives up all control over the receivable in question. Otherwise, if it retains some control over the receivable, the finance company keeps the receivable on its balance sheet as an asset. However, the receivable must be stated separately from other nontransferred receivables.

Franchisors

You are probably very familiar with the concept of *franchises.* What often happens is that a business that starts out as a one-location shop grows to be very popular. The original owners then start allowing other individuals to open shops using the same concept in other geographic locations. The parties to a franchise are the *franchisor* (the party granting the business rights) and the *franchisee* (the individual purchasing the right to use the franchisor's business model).

Some special accounting issues for the franchisor include the fact that the franchisor does not recognize revenue until it has substantially performed all material services per the franchise agreement; for example, the franchise agreement may call for the franchisor to provide a certain amount of training to the franchisee. Also, if the initial franchise fee required at the time of signing the franchise agreement is large in comparison to the *continuing fees* (usually a percentage of sales), the franchisor defers a portion of the initial fee, recording it as earned through future services rendered to the franchisee.

Oil and Gas Companies

This industry is all about mineral interests and the production of crude oil. The work flow of this industry is to find properties that may contain the natural resources (including natural gas), conduct some exploration, develop the properties (for example, put in oil wells), and acquire or produce the natural resource.

How do you account for all this hoopla? For the oil and gas trade, GAAP prefer the *successful efforts method,* which capitalizes costs the company incurs for successful projects. Here are some pointers on how to apply the successful efforts method:

- ✔ Let's say a company finds land in Wyoming that it believes contains mineral deposits. The cost of acquiring the land (regardless of whether the drilling ever reaps any rewards) is *capitalized at historic cost,* which means it is shown on the balance sheet as an asset at the amount the company paid for it plus any other costs involved in its acquisition, such as legal fees.

✔ Any other costs that directly tie back to the successful discovery of any mineral/oil or gas reserves — for example, oil well drilling — are also capitalized.

✔ Any other costs are expensed as they are incurred.

Government Contractors

Another specialized industry specifically mentioned in GAAP guides is government contractors that provide goods or services to the U.S. government. I bet you never would've guessed that! The main accounting issue with this specialized industry is whether the contract between parties is structured as a fixed-price or cost-plus-fixed-fee contract:

✔ With a *fixed-price contract,* the price the government pays for completion of the contract is agreed on at the signing of the contract. So, if the contractor incurs more costs than expected while fulfilling the contract, the contractor eats the extra costs.

✔ In contrast, a *cost-plus-fixed-fee contract* allows the contractor both to receive an agreed-on price and to be reimbursed for allowable expenses. The contract dictates which expenses fall into the allowable category. This way, both the government and the contractor acknowledge there may be unforeseen expenses or cost overruns that are crucial to the successful completion of the project.

Healthcare Entities

Examples of healthcare entities are hospitals, nursing homes, surgery centers, and doctors' offices. A major accounting issue with this type of entity is the significant amounts of money healthcare entities may invest in drugs, linens, and other ancillary services. Because the amount of money is so large, proper treatment under GAAP is key to making sure financial results are accurate and understandable to the users of the financial statements.

Here are some specialized accounting tasks in the healthcare field:

✔ Accounting for and reporting contingencies (see Chapter 8) surrounding medical malpractice claims

✔ Accounting for revenue and cost recognition methods related to setting rates for services provided, working with third-party payers (insurance companies and Medicare/Medicaid), and contracting out certain services (such as x-rays and MRIs) to third-party providers

An issue unique to the healthcare industry is compliance with the Health Insurance Portability and Accountability Act of 1996 (HIPAA). Many accounting firms specializing in accounting for healthcare entities also provide advisory services relating to the security of patient data and Medicare and Medicaid fraud and abuse.

Motion Picture Companies

Motion picture accounting issues include how to account for the production, sale, licensing, and distribution of the films, associated DVDs, and product-related merchandise. The DVD and product-related merchandise aspects are pretty self-explanatory. (All accountants know how to handle the transaction for Lucas Arts when you buy a *Star Wars* T-shirt.) But the other issues are more complex:

- **Production:** Motion picture production involves every step of making the film, from deciding on an initial concept to securing a script to releasing the finished product.

- **Sale:** The sale of a film takes place only when the master copy of the film and all its associated rights are transferred from the original owner to the interested buyer. After the sale takes place, the original owner has no right to any future profits.

- **Licensing:** Licensing means the owner allows others to show the film for a fee.

Accounting for the motion picture industry can be quite harum-scarum because it is very difficult to estimate earned revenue and related costs over the life of a film. To handle this problem, the motion picture industry figures an appropriate estimation method that as accurately as possible matches revenue and expenses to show the film's financial performance.

Not-for-Profit Organizations

These organizations do not have a profit motive when providing their goods or services; see Chapter 6. Accounting issues tailored to this type of entity include recognizing contributions, which must be recorded at *fair value* (their value in an open marketplace). This step is easy for cash — after all, cash is cash! But it can get sticky when a donor contributes assets such as real property or artwork. Many times an appraisal is secured to properly value the contribution.

Another issue is the standard for financial statement presentation. Net assets and income statement accounts have to be broken out to distinguish those that have restrictions and those that don't. For example, a donor may specifically earmark money to be used only to support a specific program the not-for-profit provides.

Real Estate Developers

Specialized GAAP pertain to the costs a company incurs when purchasing and developing real estate for sale or rental — for example, developers who plow over trees and vegetation and level the land to build residential or commercial properties. Most costs a developer incurs are originally capitalized rather than expensed. Here are two examples of capitalized real estate development costs:

- **Preacquisition costs:** These costs take place prior to purchasing the land and may include fees for checking on proper zoning or surveying the land to see where the boundaries of the property start and end.

- **Indirect project costs:** These costs, such as administrative and office expenses, are incurred after the land is purchased and directly tie back to the project.

Computer Software

Here, I'm not focusing on a specific industry but on a tool that is employed in just about every industry: software. Accounting issues regarding software vary depending on whether a company buys software off the shelf to use in its business, purchases software from a developer for resale to others, or develops software in-house that is tailored to its specific business needs. (An example of developing in-house software is a manufacturer writing its own inventory software to track the numerous raw materials required to make its products.)

The primary issues with software revolve around recognizing income and expense. For your everyday Joe and Jane business entity that purchases software off the shelf, the recognition of the expense is easy: The company follows its capitalization policy, which usually means that if it plans on using the software for more than 12 months, the software cost is depreciated rather than expensed. The same holds true for retail stores purchasing software for resale to customers; they account for the software like any other inventory transaction.

But the accounting gets more complicated when the software is developed internally either for *proprietary use* (meaning for use only by the company that writes the computer code) or for sale to others (such as when a software developer sells a computer game to retail stores).

Index

• D •

• J •

Apple & Macs

iPad For Dummies
978-0-470-58027-1

iPhone For Dummies,
4th Edition
978-0-470-87870-5

MacBook For Dummies, 3rd
Edition
978-0-470-76918-8

Mac OS X Snow Leopard For
Dummies
978-0-470-43543-4

Business

Bookkeeping For Dummies
978-0-7645-9848-7

Job Interviews
For Dummies,
3rd Edition
978-0-470-17748-8

Resumes For Dummies,
5th Edition
978-0-470-08037-5

Starting an
Online Business
For Dummies,
6th Edition
978-0-470-60210-2

Stock Investing
For Dummies,
3rd Edition
978-0-470-40114-9

Successful
Time Management
For Dummies
978-0-470-29034-7

Computer Hardware

BlackBerry
For Dummies,
4th Edition
978-0-470-60700-8

Computers For Seniors
For Dummies,
2nd Edition
978-0-470-53483-0

PCs For Dummies,
Windows
7 Edition
978-0-470-46542-4

Laptops For Dummies,
4th Edition
978-0-470-57829-2

Cooking & Entertaining

Cooking Basics
For Dummies,
3rd Edition
978-0-7645-7206-7

Wine For Dummies,
4th Edition
978-0-470-04579-4

Diet & Nutrition

Dieting For Dummies,
2nd Edition
978-0-7645-4149-0

Nutrition For Dummies,
4th Edition
978-0-471-79868-2

Weight Training
For Dummies,
3rd Edition
978-0-471-76845-6

Digital Photography

Digital SLR Cameras &
Photography For Dummies,
3rd Edition
978-0-470-46606-3

Photoshop Elements 8
For Dummies
978-0-470-52967-6

Gardening

Gardening Basics
For Dummies
978-0-470-03749-2

Organic Gardening
For Dummies,
2nd Edition
978-0-470-43067-5

Green/Sustainable

Raising Chickens
For Dummies
978-0-470-46544-8

Green Cleaning
For Dummies
978-0-470-39106-8

Health

Diabetes For Dummies,
3rd Edition
978-0-470-27086-8

Food Allergies
For Dummies
978-0-470-09584-3

Living Gluten-Free
For Dummies,
2nd Edition
978-0-470-58589-4

Hobbies/General

Chess For Dummies,
2nd Edition
978-0-7645-8404-6

Drawing
Cartoons & Comics
For Dummies
978-0-470-42683-8

Knitting For Dummies,
2nd Edition
978-0-470-28747-7

Organizing
For Dummies
978-0-7645-5300-4

Su Doku For Dummies
978-0-470-01892-7

Home Improvement

Home Maintenance
For Dummies,
2nd Edition
978-0-470-43063-7

Home Theater
For Dummies,
3rd Edition
978-0-470-41189-6

Living the
Country Lifestyle
All-in-One
For Dummies
978-0-470-43061-3

Solar Power Your Home
For Dummies,
2nd Edition
978-0-470-59678-4

Internet

Blogging For Dummies,
3rd Edition
978-0-470-61996-4

eBay For Dummies,
6th Edition
978-0-470-49741-8

Facebook For Dummies,
3rd Edition
978-0-470-87804-0

Web Marketing
For Dummies,
2nd Edition
978-0-470-37181-7

WordPress
For Dummies,
3rd Edition
978-0-470-59274-8

Language & Foreign Language

French For Dummies
978-0-7645-5193-2

Italian Phrases
For Dummies
978-0-7645-7203-6

Spanish For Dummies,
2nd Edition
978-0-470-87855-2

Spanish
For Dummies,
Audio Set
978-0-470-09585-0

Math & Science

Algebra I
For Dummies,
2nd Edition
978-0-470-55964-2

Biology For Dummies,
2nd Edition
978-0-470-59875-7

Calculus For Dummies
978-0-7645-2498-1

Chemistry For Dummies
978-0-7645-5430-8

Microsoft Office

Excel 2010 For Dummies
978-0-470-48953-6

Office 2010 All-in-One
For Dummies
978-0-470-49748-7

Office 2010 For Dummies,
Book + DVD Bundle
978-0-470-62698-6

Word 2010 For Dummies
978-0-470-48772-3

Music

Guitar For Dummies,
2nd Edition
978-0-7645-9904-0

iPod & iTunes For
Dummies, 8th Edition
978-0-470-87871-2

Piano Exercises
For Dummies
978-0-470-38765-8

Parenting & Education

Parenting For Dummies,
2nd Edition
978-0-7645-5418-6

Type 1 Diabetes
For Dummies
978-0-470-17811-9

Pets

Cats For Dummies,
2nd Edition
978-0-7645-5275-5

Dog Training For Dummies,
3rd Edition
978-0-470-60029-0

Puppies For Dummies,
2nd Edition
978-0-470-03717-1

Religion & Inspiration

The Bible For Dummies
978-0-7645-5296-0

Catholicism For Dummies
978-0-7645-5391-2

Women in the Bible
For Dummies
978-0-7645-8475-6

Self-Help & Relationship

Anger Management
For Dummies
978-0-470-03715-7

Overcoming Anxiety
For Dummies,
2nd Edition
978-0-470-57441-6

Sports

Baseball
For Dummies,
3rd Edition
978-0-7645-7537-2

Basketball
For Dummies,
2nd Edition
978-0-7645-5248-9

Golf For Dummies,
3rd Edition
978-0-471-76871-5

Web Development

Web Design
All-in-One
For Dummies
978-0-470-41796-6

Web Sites
Do-It-Yourself
For Dummies,
2nd Edition
978-0-470-56520-9

Windows 7

Windows 7
For Dummies
978-0-470-49743-2

Windows 7
For Dummies,
Book + DVD Bundle
978-0-470-52398-8

Windows 7 All-in-One
For Dummies
978-0-470-48763-1